WILKES

His Life and Crimes

WILKES

His Life and Crimes

WINSTON SCHOONOVER

BALLANTINE BOOKS
NEW YORK

This book's story and characters are fictitious. The setting is New York City, and a number of institutions and historic events in the City's colorful history are mentioned, but only as surroundings in which the fictional characters may play. In fact, the author of this novel is but a figment of his own imagination.

The contents of this work were originally published in *CACJ Forum*.

Library of Congress Catalog Card Number: 88-92231
ISBN: 0-345-35963-1

Cover design by James R. Harris

Cover illustration by Richard Rockwell

Text design by Mary A. Wirth

Manufactured in the United States of America
First Edition: August 1990
10 9 8 7 6 5 4 3 2 1

To my wife, Donna,
and, of course,
my partner, John

ACKNOWLEDGMENT

Grateful acknowledgment—as well as admiration and affection—is given to the two thousand members of the California Attorneys for Criminal Justice (CACJ) who gave first life to Wilkes in their magazine *Forum*. Similar appreciation and gratitude goes to the twenty-five thousand members of the National Association of Criminal Defense Attorneys (NACDL) and their magazine *Champion* for continued support and encouragement. Both magazines published an earlier version of this book serially as it bled from the author's pen.

Introduction

"That devil Wilkes" is how a lot of people still refer to my partner, John Wilkes. Long ago, the same reference was given to his famous English ancestor of the same name. This book is about the living John Wilkes, the character I knew and loved, and the world in which we lived during the twenty-plus years we worked together defending the citizen-accused in the courtrooms of New York City.

I managed to scribble these stories between Wilkes's many jury trials—and the equally numerous contempt hearings, bar discipline proceedings, jailings, fights, hospitalizations, kidnappings, campaigns for public office, television quiz shows, and funerals, to mention only a few of the oddball distractions I faced while trying to keep up with my friend.

Wilkes was an imp and impetuously hotheaded at the most inopportune times. He was of the view that any prosecution of his clients was a personal assault on his very being. This philosophy inevitably led to many confrontations with judges, prosecutors, cops, probation officers, witnesses, court clerks, and anyone he considered part of the machine to destroy his client. Out of these battles grew his legend.

Every case Wilkes defended brought on a fight with "the two-headed Hydra"—what he called the judge and DA—over his insistence that he be given enough time to prepare his cases. Wilkes desired to age his cases like fine wine. He quoted Emerson, who might have written the rationale for the Old Wine Defense which my friend made famous, when he said, "Time turns to shining ether the solid angularity of fact."

Wilkes liked the awful facts of his cases to evaporate before he tried them, and clients on bail loved knowing that Wilkes was doing everything he could to keep the courtroom physically and temporally as far apart from them as possible.

Wilkes would explain to them, "If they can't force you to trial, they can't convict; if they can't convict, they can't sentence; and if they can't sentence, well then, baby, you ain't going to jail."

Few lawyers worked as hard to keep their clients from their destinies. In stark contrast were the "walking violations of the Sixth Amendment." Wilkes called them "V-6s"—the derisive term for the alleged defense attorneys who clustered like bacteria in the attorneys' lounge of the Manhattan Criminal Courts Building when not too busy kissing judicial butt to get an appointed case or in courthouse hallways hawking for retained clients like carnival sideshow men. Once a client was landed, a V-6 could take a perfectly defensible criminal case and, quick as a bank deposit, turn it into a lousy plea of guilty.

Wilkes never pleaded a client guilty unless he got a Godfather offer from the prosecution which could not be refused. Otherwise, the DA and the judge had to pay the price: TRIAL BY JURY. The black-robed butchers loathed TRIAL BY JURY and hated Wilkes because he forced so many of them upon them. The judges retaliated by keeping their butchers' thumbs on one side of the scales of justice to insure that Wilkes never got an edge.

The courts of Wilkes's world functioned like a gigantic whorehouse with defense attorneys and prosecutors playing the role of rival pimps dutifully escorting the trick, the defendant, into the court's salon for a good screwing. What follows are my faithfully recorded recollections of Wilke's many seasons spent pimping for justice.

WILKES

His Life and Crimes

1

Meet the Honorable Joseph Blugeot

I do not like your cold justice; out of the eye of your judges there always glanceth the executioner and his cold steel.

NIETZSCHE

The horrible thing about all legal officials, even the best, about all judges, magistrates, barristers, detectives, and policemen, is not that they are wicked (some of them are good), not that they are stupid (several of them are quite intelligent), it is simply that they have got used to it. Strictly they do not see the prisoner in the dock; all they see is the usual man in the usual place. They do not see the awful court of judgment; they see only their own workshop.

G. K. CHESTERTON

It is true. I have been critical in the portraits I have painted of the federal and state judges before whom Wilkes and I appeared the many years we were in practice together. As I look back, I have erred. But it has been on the side of charity!

How is it that when the occasional decent human being gets to don the judicial black, an awful, inevitable transition takes place—hail fellows, well met, so quickly turn into cunning, snapping vipers? How come it's always two against one in a criminal trial? How come when you finish examining a witness, you instinctively feel like turning to Hizoner and saying, "Your witness"?

How come? I haven't the foggiest. All I know is that judges

sooner or later metamorphose into rigid arch-protectors of the state. Nietzsche said the state is the coldest of all cold monsters. Judges are its frozen essence, each day sitting as living proof of the state's coldest lie:

"I, the State, am the people."

BLUGEOT

The life span of a judge is like the fruit of the lemon tree: sweet blossoms turning to bitter fruit. Some of the blossoms are rotten from the start. So it was with Judge Joseph P. Blugeot.

Blugeot, unlike so many of his colleagues, was neither stupid nor a fool. There were even times in his court when a burst of fairness broke out, typically when the defendant was white, female, and pretty. Other than that, he was a uniformly wicked judge with the temperament of a cultivated mass murderer—like the Butcher of Lyon.

Blugeot fancied himself a cultured man of the world. He was fluent in several of the romance languages and loved to make derisive comments in Latin or an archaic Italian dialect to demonstrate his worldly intelligence. His favorite phrase—always interjected at the conclusion of a hearing to suppress an involuntary confession—was *"Non refert quomodo veritas habeatur, dommodo habeatur."* It was the motto of the Spanish Inquisition: "It matters not how the truth was obtained, so long as it has been obtained."

In any language, Joseph P. Blugeot was a judge to be avoided.

JOHNNY WAD

For the longest time, Wilkes and I were able to keep all of our clients out of the courtroom of Judge Joseph P. Blugeot. Then came Johnny Wadkins, aka Johnny Wad, a nineteen-year-old black kid from Harlem who had been arrested for the high crime and misdemeanor of possessing one marijuana cigarette.

His first lawyer, a V-6 whom Wad hired at Montgomery Ward, being unable to extract a quick guilty plea from his client, waived jury in front of Blugeot, and agreed to a trial with the judge as trier of fact. In Blugeot's court, a nonjury trial was a slow plea of guilty.

As always, Blugeot used the court trial as a forum to vent his antidefense juridical philosophy. After Johnny Wad's lawyer criticized the arresting officer for employing the odious doctrine of guilt by association in arresting Wad for possession of the joint (the marijuana cigarette was found too closely associated with Johnny Wad at the time of his arrest—squashed under the sole of his foot), the judge sighed at the ridiculous defense argument and muttered to no one in particular, *"Optimi consiliarii mortui"* ("The best counselors are dead").

When the lawyer argued that the prosecution had proven the seized substance to be only a green, somewhat scorched leafy vegetable matter and not the prohibited controlled substance, Blugeot blurted, *"Cymini sectore!"* ("Hairsplitter!").

The V-6 continued arguing that the prosecution utterly failed to prove its case beyond a reasonable doubt. He said, "In the words of Chief Justice Warren, reasonable doubt is the law of the land." Blugeot responded, "No, I think Cicero said it best: *'Salus populi suprema lex'* ('The safety of the people is the supreme law')."

By this time, a concerned Johnny Wad, young and completely ignorant in the ways of the law, turned to his V-6 and asked, "Who is this guy?" His attorney shrugged and closed his plea to Blugeot with the comment, "The evidence produced is so insufficient that my client would be acquitted in any courtroom in the western world." To which Blugeot sighed contemptuously and responded in Sicilian, *"Sì, poi vinni assoltu tanti voti e tanti comu in Italia troppo spissu'e d'su"* ("Yes, he was acquitted many times as in Italy is too often done").

After hearing this torrent of untranslated word salad, a disturbed Johnny Wad asked his V-6, "Ain't he supposed to speak to us in English? Don't the dude know English, man? I don't dig the mother's jive!'' The V-6 again shrugged his shoulders as Blugeot pronounced Johnny Wad guilty and set a sentencing date in three weeks.

By this time, Johnny Wad realized he was in deep trouble and that his V-6 was not doing much to extricate him from it. Johnny Wad, being a bright kid, severed himself from his V-6 and pounded on our door.

TO TAKE OR NOT TO TAKE

Why take this petty matter, you ask? It certainly wasn't because Johnny Wad's case had any great legal issues or notoriety—i.e., the potential for lots of ink and free advertising. Wilkes knew that to the public, a lawyer's name in the news, no matter what the context (except in an indictment, or worse yet, a conviction) means you're newsworthy and therefore a great lawyer. That's bad logic, but great for business. Thus, Wilkes's exclamation each time he saw his moniker in the news: ''Ink! Gimme ink!''

But Wad's routine misdemeanor case offered no prospect of ink. There was no fee Wilkes could charge to compensate for the horror of an appearance with a black defendant before Judge Joseph Blugeot. And anyway, we had just pulled in some of our biggest fees in the history of the firm. We did not need the few bucks we might milk from this case.

So if it wasn't money, ink, or issues, what was it that caused my friend to take Johnny Wad's case? Absolutely nothing. There wasn't anything in this case but work, worry, and defeat. We turned down Johnny with a polite and emphatic ''Not on your life.''

A VOICE FROM THE PAST

The next day, Wilkes got a call from our former client, Field Marshal Lyle Diderot, leader of the infamous Whiz Kids, an East Side gang which won its nickname by urinating on its fallen mugging victims. Wilkes had won a particularly disgusting rape case for the Field Marshal years ago, and he now learned the unfortunate fact that Johnny Wad was Diderot's first cousin. Diderot told Wilkes, "You gonna take Johnny's case, man." Wilkes thanked the Field Marshal for the referral, but declined as respectfully as he could, claiming the press of business.

"Some pencil-neck mouthpiece done got Johnny guilty in fronta some cracker judge who don't speak English. Gonna take all your voodoo to keep Johnny Wad outa da Tombs," said Lyle Diderot. "They done violated his rights," he added.

Again Wilkes declined, adding that if Johnny's rights had been violated, any decent lawyer would vindicate them. Wilkes was about to recommend someone when Diderot busted in, "You gonna represent Johnny Wad or we gonna violate all the rights you gots. You know those rights you gots? You gots the right to walk to court with two good legs. You gots the right to read da law with two good eyes. You gots the right to breathe with two good lungs."

So as it turned out, there was an excellent reason to take Johnny Wad's case. It wasn't the kind of retainer you seek out in the business, but it was one Wilkes could live with. We took the case.

JUDGMENT DAY

They came for him as they had come for thousands of others—with a trundle cart. In the name of the People, they judged him a traitor to the revolution. In the name of the State, they came to place him under the cutting edge of the national razor.

The doors flew open to the small place in the dungeon that kept the condemned man. The bright light of day nearly blinded him as he was pushed up the steps and thrown bodily into the cart. A huge laughing man with a pot belly pulled the cart toward the site of the execution. Crowds filled both sides of the streets taunting the man, some mocking him with shouts of "Liberty! Equality! Fraternity!"—the rallying cry that had paved the bloody road from one monarch, King Louis, to one emperor, Bonaparte. In between and in the People's name, the People killed lots of people.

In a short time they reached the execution place; the condemned man looked up and saw the huge glistening blade that would soon take his head. He looked to the bucket below which would soon receive it. Nearby, an old woman was knitting. She cackled.

He struggled when they came for him. Two, then three strong men grabbed his arms and legs and carried the convulsing, weeping man to the stock. On the way, he drooled; he voided; he screamed to God for his life. The crowd laughed and jeered at him. The last words he heard before the shimmering blade fell were those of the executioner: "Are you ready for sentencing?"

SENTENCING DAY

"Are you ready for sentencing?" asked Judge Joseph P. Blugeot. His words interrupted my daydream of French justice.

"Not quite," said Wilkes. "There's the matter of my motion for new trial."

"Oh yes. The motion for new trial. Mr. Clerk, please pass up the file so I might refresh my recollection." Judge Blugeot opened the file and allowed his eyes to pass for the first time over our motion for new trial. Then he said, "The motion for new trial based in part upon previous defense counsel's inability to speak Latin is denied. Now, Mr. Wilkes, are you ready for sentencing?"

A woman laughed. It was a hard, masculine sound which came from Blugeot's old woman court reporter. Whether she was laughing at our creative motion or what was to come, I don't know.

Wilkes began his pitch for probation. He said, "Judge, before you stands a unique young man. He is nineteen years of age. He lives in Harlem. Members of his family are said to be gang leaders. Yet he stands before you without so much as a prior arrest."

Blugeot interrupted Wilkes before he could make his point. "So what you are saying is that this is the first time he has been caught, right? You're not standing there and telling me with a straight face that this is the first time this man ever smoked marijuana?'' Blugeot obviously did not believe in the existence of first offenders.

"There is certainly no evidence to the contrary before the court,'' said Wilkes.

Wilkes quickly added, "Judge, I want to talk straight to you. This youngster comes from an environment where it's antisocial to be law-abiding. To be nineteen and clean of arrests in Harlem is remarkable. *Judicis officium est, ut res, ita tempora rerum* (A judge's duty is to consider the times and circumstances).''

Blugeot's eyebrows rose. A thin smile formed on his face. He said, "Mr. Wilkes, *Decem annos consumpsi in legendo Cicerone* (I have spent ten years reading Cicero). Your client seems to be, as Cicero said, *'video meliora, proboque, deteriora sequor'* ('one of those who not only sees the correct course, but also approves of it, yet follows the worse').''

"I believe that's from Ovid, Your Honor,'' said my friend tentatively. He wanted to play the judge's erudition game without it becoming too obvious that Wilkes was ten times more learned than Hizoner. Wilkes continued, "Ovid also wrote, *'Qui sapit, innumeris moribus aputs erit'* ('A wise man knows how to deal with all sorts of characters'). In other words, consider Johnny as the deserving individual that he is. Give him probation.''

"All defendants get individual treatment in this court. Now, are you ready for sentencing, Mr. Wilkes?''

TOMBS-BOUND

Other than sparring with Blugeot in Latin—which did seem to amuse the judge—Wilkes wasn't getting anywhere. Johnny Wad was still on track to the Tombs. Wilkes decided to try a more aggressive approach.

Wilkes told Judge Blugeot, "Your Honor, you have a reputation for sentencing black youngsters far in excess of what you sentence their white counterparts. And let me say this: I have never had the pleasure of appearing in Your Honor's court to test that assertion. But I have always been of the impression that hearsay is a most unreliable source of information, and I hope today you will give the lie to the things I have heard. This youngster no more deserves to go to jail than any of the white college kids who routinely appear before the court for blowing pot in their dorms.''

Blugeot's face crimsoned as he lied, "I have not heard of this alleged reputation of mine. *Loquendum ut vulgus*, Mr. Wilkes? (Speaking with vulgar people?) All that I know is that I am very careful in these cases.''

"I understand," said Wilkes.

"I am more careful in these cases than any other."

"I think Your Honor has bent over backwards," chimed the prosecutor.

"I can be so impeccably fair."

"I never questioned your fairness. I beg the indulgence of the court." Wilkes could grovel with the best on behalf of a client in trouble.

"This is something you have to be born with, a gift."

"I concede this," said my friend.

"I have that gift. It is a tremendous gift, and not many judges have the tremendous gift of fairness. It is something that I have to admit, and I admit it with a great deal of pride, but with a great deal of humility, I have it. I have an information, so to speak. It is what has made me a good student in constitutional law, I suppose. It is what made it possible for me to pass the bar examination without an error in the entire examination. It is what made it possible for an intelligent politician seeking advice of those investigative agencies at his command to appoint to the bench some little fellow who was prosecutor in the U.S. attorney's office, and make something out of him.

"I have that gift of fairness. I also have a gift of comprehensive thinking. I think all the way around every subject and get its interrelated parts and put them together as I go piece by piece, step by step. I have this, and why, I almost have the gift of reading minds.

"Yes, I have the gift. And any reputation I have is for fairness to all. It is a reputation I cherish and one that will not be sullied by the reckless remarks of a lawyer whose own reputation for deviousness needs no explication.''

THE SENTENCE

''Now, as to the matter of sentencing. Let the record reflect I have reviewed the presentence report provided by the probation office. I have reviewed the so-called alternative presentence report which you have filed, Mr. Wilkes. Let me say that I find that your written remarks completely misunderstand the serious problem of drugs in the ghetto. Today this boy is a pot head. Tomorrow a heroin junkie. Next week a mugger. Next month a murderer. As night follows day, marijuana leads to narcotics addiction and violent crime.''

''The same might be said of mother's milk,'' said Wilkes.

My friend had stood in silence as Blugeot nearly had an orgasm during his self-congratulatory speech. It was rare for a judge to be so candid. Most of them thought the same as Blugeot about themselves, but few had the exquisite obliviousness to make those thoughts public. Now, Wilkes knew what we always knew. There was no moving Judge Joseph P. Blugeot by appeals to such nonsense as evidence or reason or compassion.

Blugeot turned his eyes to a trembling Johnny Wadkins and asked, ''Mr. Wadkins, are you ready to receive the court's sentence?''

Johnny Wad said with a strong voice, ''As God is my judge, I is innocent.'' It was a comment often heard from defendants. So, too, was Blugeot's response.

''He isn't. I am, and you're not.''

Blugeot's eyes fell to the papers he held. He read the sentence he had written in the Wad file the night before. ''Mr. Wadkins, you have been found guilty by the court, and it is the judgment of the court that you are guilty of the crime of possession of marijuana. You are hereby sentenced to a term of one year in jail.''

I heard an audible gasp from Johnny Wad, who doubled over a bit as if he had just been kicked in the genitals. He turned to Wilkes and mumbled something angry. It was loud enough to hear, but not to understand what he said.

Blugeot picked up on the nature of the comment and asked, "What's that? What's that he said?"

Wilkes looked at Blugeot, put his arm around our client's shoulder, and said matter-of-factly, "My client just said something to me." Johnny Wad added to the tease. He smiled at Hizoner.

"That was a comment directed at me, and I demand to know what it was," said Blugeot.

"It was a comment protected by the attorney-client and work product privileges, which I cannot ethically divulge, as you very well know, Judge," said Wilkes.

"I'm ordering you to repeat what he said. I order it! Now!"

"Are you prepared to hold me in contempt and throw me in jail if I do not divulge this privileged matter?" asked Wilkes.

"Yes. I am. Out with it."

"You racist honky motherfucker," said Wilkes.

Blugeot sat motionless, stunned by the profane epithet. It took him three seconds to utter the next word, and his voice rose two octaves in the process. He said, "WHAAAAAAAAAAAAT!"

"I repeat, you racist honky motherfucker."

"Right on!" said Johnny Wad.

Wilkes then added, "You don't like the answer. You shouldn't have asked the question. I move to strike it from the record."

"Mr. Wilkes, you've just shot your wad. You and your client are in contempt of court. I hereby sentence each of you to one year in custody. That's two now for you, Mr. Wadkins. Want to go double or nothing? I've always found it *beatius est dare quam accipere* (better to give than receive). Mr. Marshal, seize both of these men and take them away."

As they hauled Wilkes from the court, he yelled out, *"Impiorum putrescet!"* It means, "The wicked shall rot." Johnny

Wad added the only foreign language word he knew as they dragged him away: *"Chinga! Chinga! Chinga!"*

BAR TALK

It was a bad day. Worse than even Wilkes had imagined when he reluctantly accepted the Wad case. We could expect Johnny Wad to get hammered. That was no surprise. Nor was it greatly unexpected that Wilkes would be held in contempt. Wilkes was often held in contempt in his long and illustrious career. Each contempt was like a war wound bravely suffered in battle with a brutal adversary.

Yes, it was a bad day, and it wasn't over yet. As they dragged Wilkes and Wad from the court, I made my first contribution to the proceedings: "Your Honor, may I make a motion for bail on behalf of Mr. Wilkes?"

In all of my friend's colorful career, a career filled with contempt citations, no judge ever had the patience to properly hold Wilkes in contempt. I think we beat all of his contempts, at least all of the ones he got when I was with him (some twenty-two if memory serves). We could never have done it without the help of the two most beautiful words in the English language: legal technicalities.

For some foolish reason, I felt compelled to make a record of the legal points that would surely save my friend from the outrageous contempt citation. I guess I was angry, because I only spoke about the unlawfulness of the contempt citation and tried to rub Blugeot's nose in the tyranny of his act. It was, I now know, a display of foolish courage. I should have said something about bail. Better yet, I should have said nothing at all.

I told Blugeot that the information which he forcibly elicited from my friend's mouth was privileged. I told him that, coming as it did by way of a court order, there had been no voluntary publication of the profane comment, and obviously no intent by my friend to offend; Wilkes was merely relaying, upon order of the court, the exact information given him by Johnny Wad. Even had none of these errors occurred, Wilkes had been deprived of a jury trial on each of these issues, I said.

There must have been something in the way I put all this to the judge. As I spoke, Blugeot looked at me as if I were a noisy little bug in need of stomping. And stomp he did just after the following angry, ill-chosen words left my lips: "And last, Your Honor, the words which you found so contemptuous, although admittedly strong, are entirely true."

It was my first contempt and my first trip to the Tombs as a resident.

Loose lips sink ships.

2

To the Tombs

The criminal is prevented, by the very witnessing of the legal process, from regarding his deed as intrinsically evil.

NIETZSCHE

This place is a zoo.

J. J. ROOSEVELT

After being roughly ushered into the court's dark holding tank by a smiling bailiff, I spotted my friend chatting away in the corner with our client, Johnny Wad. For having just been held in contempt by Judge Joseph Blugeot, Wilkes seemed in fine spirits.

Until he saw me. "What the hell are you doing here?" he snapped.

I looked at him, embarrassed to admit that "Well, I, er, uh, was asking, uh, for bail, for you, er, and the bastard held me in contempt, too."

"You idiot!" That was all he said. He didn't have to say any more. He knew that I knew that we now were in a fix that was all my fault. Invariably in the past when Wilkes was contempted, I was able to get him out on bail within a short time pending appellate review of the citation. But I had eliminated that possibility by my foolish comments to the judge following Wilkes's citation. Now I was in jail, too.

"I need to make a phone call," said Wilkes to the bailiff, who still wore a broad Cheshire grin on his puss, reflecting his delight in seeing two Enemies of the People captured, in custody, and wholly dependent on the will of the keeper.

"You'll get it in Tombs," said the bailiff. He then ordered us and several other prisoners to begin a short, forced march into the Tombs.

TOMBS

The Tombs is the forbidding and accurate description of the twelve-floor structure officially designated as the Manhattan House of Detention for Men. It is part of a complex that also houses the criminal courts of the City of New York and the Office of District Attorney for the County, thus making it a self-contained factory for the charging, convicting, and confining of defendants. All under one roof.

Wilkes and I had, of course, done plenty of time in the fortress hand-holding clients. But this was different. When you are a visitor, you know you're soon to be leaving the dungeon. When you're just arrested and a prisoner, you know nothing of the kind. I felt helpless and scared.

It was Friday, October 2, 1970. John Wilkes and your humble servant were about to enter the gates of hell.

BULL PEN

As new arrivals to the Tombs, Wilkes and I had to pass a series of checkpoints prior to our assignment to a cell. Our first stop was one of the first-floor bull pens, a large and gloomy screened cell lined with scarred wooden benches fixed to the walls. The guard opened the door, pointed to the inside, and said, "Welcome to the Tombs, boys. Have a pleasant stay."

We entered, and he slammed the sliding metal door so hard that the resulting crashing clang made me jump. None of the several dozen inmates in the bull pen even looked up. They were preoccupied.

Inside, a shocking, tissue-searing stench filled my nostrils. It was the familiar smell of nervous prison sweat which all defense lawyers have smelled on clients in custody—but never so concentrated and overwhelming as this. I gagged and felt ready to vomit.

Wilkes, still furious with me, quickly went over to the nearest bench and sat down next to a shivering inmate whose eyes were fogged and at half-mast. His skin was gray and sweaty, and he softly murmured moans of pain: he was an addict in withdrawal.

I looked at each of the men in the bull pen. Since the Tombs issues no uniforms to its residents, each of the veterans wore the street clothes he came in with, which were by now reduced to rags in various stages of disintegration. From the smell, many of the men hadn't taken them off for laundering since their arrival. At least a third of the men before me looked as sick as the pathetic addict next to Wilkes. A few slept through their misery on the filthy cement floor; others were doubled over in the agony of withdrawals; but most were huddled with the healthy in a corner intensely discussing the news.

BAD NEWS

The Friday morning *Times* had a big spread on Nasser's funeral and a piece on the Charlie Manson trial in Los Angeles. These were not topics of discussion in the Tombs bull pen. No, these men were recounting the prisoner uprising in the Long Island branch of the Queens House of Detention of the day before. Some spoke with bitterness, recalling the Tomb's riot just last August in which five guards had been taken hostage for about eight hours. The cause then was the same as that which prompted the brothers in Queens to rebellion: the unbelievably wretched conditions in the jails, the guard brutality, the inedible food, the overcrowding, the high bail and long, long trial waits.

I listened for two hours as these men talked, each becoming more and more agitated in the process. "Fuggin' judge buried me alive in dis motherfuggin' shithole. Nine months he gives me, and says I'm lucky not to be goin' to Attica," said one.

It was getting dark in the pen, and the men were huddled

so close that I couldn't make out faces that well. They were now just voices talking ominously of their dehumanizing existence.

Another said, "I had a thirty-minute visit yesterday from my ol' lady. I ain't seen her for two fuckin' weeks 'cause of visiting-hour fuck-ups by the shitheads who run this shitter. Went down to the room, but all the phones was taken up. That wait cost me fifteen minutes. Then when I got a phone, the cocksucker didn't work. I could only look at my ol' lady and yell, but nobody could hear nothin' 'cause everyone's yellin' 'cause none of the motherfuckin' phones works, and the guy next to me is so pissed, he starts using the phone like a hammer to break the glass, but that shit's bullet-proof and the pigs grab his ass and close down the whole fuggin' vistin' room. They dragged my ol' lady away crying, and that was my visit. I'm gonna kill somebody, man."

"Nothin' works here," said another. "Phones, toilets, windows, TV, radio."

"Doctors and lawyers sure as shit don't work here," said another. "I ain't seen my legal Band-Aid since I got here."

And so on.

CHECKPOINT CHARLIE

Eventually a guard started calling out names. One by one the prisoners left the bull pen and walked or staggered, depending on their condition, down the hall out of sight. Johnny Wad's name was called, then mine. As I left, Wilkes looked at me forgivingly and spoke his first words since our imprisonment began: "Call the office if you can. Get help."

I asked the guard where he was taking me and if I could use the phone there. He said nothing. I followed him to a small, cramped room with only a chair, and a balding, middle-aged man sitting behind a beat-up gray metal desk. He wore a white smock. The nameplate on the desk said Checkpoint Charlie.

Without looking up from the paper on his desk, the man,

whom I deduced to be Charlie himself, mechanically recited an admonition he uttered with the sincerity of computer-generated voice simulation. He said, "I am not a doctor. I am merely here to complete medical history forms so that you may be classified. There are only two places you will go from here: the hospital floor or your cell. There are only two classifications here: sick enough or well enough. If you are the former, you go to the hospital. If the latter, you go to your cell.

"Now, please answer yes or no to the following question: Do you now suffer from cancer, tuberculosis, diabetes, leprosy, rickets, malaria, gout, cerebral palsy, eczema, syphilis, venereal disease, chicken pox, smallpox, measles, mumps, scarlet fever, trench mouth, typhoid, meningitis, hemophilia, yellow jaundice, leukemia, cretinism, schizophrenia, beriberi, heart disease, hardening of the arteries, anemia, anthrax, bubonic plague, epilepsy, any flu, cold, or other disease, illness, malady, or ailment which you can think of?"

"Might have a little cold coming on," I said. I hoped to go to the hospital, where things might be more lax and I might get at a phone.

Charlie quickly lifted his head from his form for a second and checked a box on the form. "You look well enough." Then he asked his next question. "Are you addicted, dependent, or otherwise habituated to any medicine, balm, stimulant, narcotic—this includes heroin, morphine, cocaine, amphetamine, barbiturate, marijuana, or other form of dope—sedative, analgesic, anesthetic, antiseptic, antibiotic, sulfa drug, laxative, antacid, or any other substance, whether used for medical, recreational, or other purposes?"

Addicted to laxatives! I wondered about the inmate with that problem and prayed he would not be my cell mate as I said: "I take Alka-Seltzer and a vitamin occasionally." Charlie checked a box. Without lifting his eyes from his desk, he said, "You're definitely well enough. Guard! Next!"

As I rose, my eyes caught a prominent, hand-lettered sign on the wall behind the man's head. It said, THERE IS NO PAIN MEDICATION AVAILABLE IN THIS JAIL.

CAVITY INSPECTION

The next checkpoint waiting me was for body cavity inspection. I was ordered to "get nude" and open every body orifice for the probing eye of a tiny, talkative man with a loud voice, a big flashlight, and a barber's manner. This guy seemed to enjoy his work. He worked quickly to carefully inspect my mouth, nostrils, eyelids, ears, hair, armpits, finger- and toe-nails, my keester, and most degradingly, the shaft of Winston, Jr. What people smuggle in that part of the anatomy, I can't imagine.

The Tombs Inspector of Body Cavities was positively chatty compared to the robot at Checkpoint Charlie. As he was scrutinizing my interior workings with his flashlight, he described a fellow—"the Importer"—who had regularly smuggled dope into the Tombs without his detection. From my experience, this would have been quite an accomplishment.

"The Importer was an expert, a real pro," said the Inspector as he motioned for me to spread my cheeks. "He purposely got arrested on minor dope beefs just to come in here for a few days and get the dopers high and make a little money.

"Never did figure out it was him until he OD'd on the ninth floor—that's where we keep the addicts and troublemakers. The Importer always swallowed heroin-filled balloons, which came out of his body naturally for distribution on the tiers. This time he digested them. Must have had some bad acid indigestion to dissolve the rubber. Anyway, that was it. Like a lot of guys around here, he died a happy man."

I left the Body Cavity Inspector after he determined my body passages were not loaded with contraband. He pointed to an elevator and looked to the next guy in line. I knew I was done when he said to the other, "Get nude."

GOING UP

An elevator that was more of a moving jail cell took me up to
the ninth floor, and I was escorted by a guard to my permanent
cell. I kept thinking about that "no pain medication" sign at
Checkpoint Charlie. The Tombs is notorious for the number
of drug addicts it imprisons. I had just seen a dozen in the bull
pen. If there is no pain medication for them here, what happens when the withdrawals set in? And what happens if I
happen to be celled with such an addict?

When the steel elevator door slammed open on the ninth
floor, the guard grabbed my arm and escorted me out the door
and down a lengthy catwalk adjacent to the upper deck of the
cell block. At my feet, a river of water gushed over the dirty
concrete floor, jumped the side of the walkway to form a wa-
terfall, and splashed on the floor of the cells below.

As we passed the irrigated cell from where the water was
flowing out of a running toilet, the two prisoners within, both
Puerto Ricans, made what sounded like pleas for help. The
guard didn't understand their Spanish, said so *("No habla da
Spinich")*, and kept walking.

In the next cell, two addicts, curled in fetal positions, were
moaning. As we passed the third cell, both the residents clanged
metal cups against the bars and complained of the heat and
humidity. "Man, give us air," one asked.

Although it was no more than sixty degrees outside, it was
at least ninety-five and humid as a steam bath in the Tombs.
All of the inmates were stripped down to their briefs to beat
the heat. They looked like sweat-slickened caged animals—
which they were.

By the time I passed the fourth cell, I already had a headache
from the suffocating heat and humidity, and the earsplitting
noise. The floor and walls of the Tombs's ninth floor formed
a perfect sound box of windowless concrete and steel for the
inmate screams—at each other or at the guards—or the moans
and shrieks of the addicts undergoing the pain of withdrawal.

On top of this, TVs and radios blared. Cell doors slammed. Inmates drummed the bars, the floor, the sinks, the toilets. The cacophony was mind-numbing and disorienting.

By the time I reached the fifth cell, I was thankful that the guard had stopped and was keying the sliding steel door open. I went in and met my roomie.

J.J.

Jackson Jefferson Roosevelt was a small, wiry black man with a clean-shaven, smallish, bald head and a moderate-length gray beard. He was lying naked on the bottom bunk staring at a magazine titled *Yachting*. Only his eyes moved in my direction when I entered the cell.

After the door slammed and the guard disappeared, he said, "Well, lookee here. We got us a motherfuckin' professional man. You a counselor?"

I said yes and watched his eyes return to the yachting magazine. The guys in the flooding cell could use that, I thought. I felt my clothes. They were soaked and stinking with sweat. I started taking them off.

"So you're a lawyer," said Roosevelt as I stripped to my briefs. "I got me a lawyer. The Legal Aid. I seen him 'bout three months ago for 'bout a minute when I first got locked up. Ain't seen him since. Round here, ya do your time, then you gits your trial, then you gits your sentence. Somewhere in there you sees your Legal Aid, and he tells you ya done already served all your time before the motherfuckin' trial even starts. Me, I gots my trial tomorrow."

I asked, "Is it always this noisy in here?" With all the yelling and doors slamming and TVs screaming, the place sounded like a thousand dogs barking in a metal barrel.

"Yep. Drives you crazy. Everyone goes crazy in the Tombs. Funny thing, Legal Aids go crazy, too. Mine tells me they goin' on strike soon because the city ain't gonna pay enough of their shrink bills. I hopes he goes on strike tomorrow. I don't

wanna go to no motherfuckin' trial. He ain't got me no witnesses.''

"What about bail?" I asked.

At this, J.J. turned his head to me and spat out, ''Freedom's
Rent! Ain't nobody here got that kind of motherfuckin' rent
money. The Man always raises da rent soes ya can't make it.
But the Man and Legal Aid will tell you ya don't need no
money to get out. Come to find you had the rent all the time.
The Man says, 'You wants motherfuckin' freedom? You gots
the collateral in your mouth. Just give me one precious little
motherfuckin' word: guilty.' That's motherfuckin' coin of the
realm round here. And when you've lived in this motherfuckin' shithole for a while, you give the Man what he wants.
But he gonna wait 'fore he gits anythin' from J. J. Roosevelt.
Say, man, you a lawyer; don't you know motherfuckin' nothin'
about that?''

I was ashamed to admit my ignorance of much of the daily
reality for Tombs residents. It's what happens to you when
you specialize in clients with money.

J.J. laid his head on the little pillow on his bunk and stared
straight up to the steel bottom of my bunk. "Drives you motherfuckin' crazy here,'' he said. ''The motherfuckin' noise busts
your head. Ain't no ventilation. Always too hot and dirty. We
all stink. Too noisy to sleep or think. Food's no good. Motherfuckin' place is fulla vermin. No exercise. Locked in this
motherfuckin' cell sixteen hours a day. Locked out of the cell
the other eight on that plank they call a catwalk.''

"Look here!" He lifted the crumpled yachting magazine.
"This is the motherfuckin' crap they give ya to read.''

J.J. turned his expressionless face to me and asked, ''You
know about Safari?''

SAFARI

I said I didn't. He leaned up in his bed and became more
animated. "It's what we do for recreation up here. Every day
just before we're locked back into our motherfuckin' cells, we

do a count of the game our hunters find on the floor. Those
motherfuckers which catches the big game gets points. Ten for
rats, five for mices, a tenth for a roach. We all vote on the
points for the exotics, you know, like a salamander or a snake.
Safari record is forty-nine set in 1966 by a motherfucker in for
murder named Johnston Washburn. Unbeatable. Motherfucker gots twenty points just for one animal.''

"What was it?'' I asked.

"Motherfuckin' baby alligator come swimming up his
damned crapper. Never seen nothin' like it. This place is a
zoo.''

TURNKEY

I liked J.J. right off despite his scary exterior and limited vocabulary. I relaxed a bit hearing his Tombs stories, but the
sound of keys turning in the cell door caused me to turn my
attention from J.J. and see none other than my friend John
Wilkes hurriedly going through a ring of keys. "What the hell
are you doing out there?'' I asked.

"There's a motherfuckin' riot going on!'' he shouted. Wilkes
had already incorporated the multipurpose and often-used jail
adjective into his vocabulary. I listened through the normal din
on our tier and picked up the distinct and ominous clamoring
above us.

While trying to make one key after another fit and open our
cell, Wilkes said, "The inmates have taken over the twelfth
floor, and they've got eighteen hostages! They got the guard I
was with in the motherfuckin' elevator.''

Finally he got the right key, opened the door, and I was out.
J.J., after putting on his briefs, followed.

"What'll we do?'' I asked. "Surrender ourselves downstairs?'' I was not much interested in rioting.

"Never make it,'' said J.J. "If we've got the motherfuckin'
guards and the elevators, you ain't goin' noplace. Stick with
me and maybe you won't get hurt.''

Not liking the tentative prospects for staying unhurt, I introduced Wilkes to J.J. in hopes that my new black friend could keep us from harm. After giving the keys to another revolutionary to free the tier, we went up to riot headquarters on the twelfth floor.

The scene there was chaos—a parley of hell-raising sociopaths. Over two hundred raging barbarians were running all over the floor, screaming, arguing, and fighting. Those not so engaged were breaking windows and merrily throwing burning rags and paper to the street below.

J.J. took me into a small room that was used during less tumultuous times as a chapel while Wilkes went off in search of Johnny Wad. "You white boys could be in some trouble lessen you be cool. Since you is a lawyer, you maybe can convince the alleged leaders that you can help. Trouble is, between the motherfuckin' Panthers, the Muslims, and the Young Lords—they is the Puerto Ricans—who knows who's gonna be leading this here riot. Last one, in August, petered out in eight hours—eight motherfuckin' hours!—'cause those motherfuckers couldn't get their motherfuckin' act together."

I looked around and saw what J.J. was talking about. Those savages who weren't trashing the place, or raiding the commissary, or shooting up—after a raid on the eleventh-floor medical clinic, they discovered that there was pain medication in the Tombs after all—were arguing or fighting with each other.

I was startled to see the back of a naked white man wearing a PLO turban in the middle of a heated exchange with a group of angry blacks. They were shouting at each other, and the white man was poking his finger into the chest of one of the blacks and yelling the word of the day, "You're motherfuckin' crazy." Then he turned and—unbelievably—it was Wilkes!

He saw me and J.J. and came over to where we stood and said, "That is what must loosely be called the motherfuckin' command of this uprising. One of the leaders happens to be a Whiz Kid who knows me. And Johnny Wad's vouched for us. They may want us to represent them with the Man.''

"What were you guys arguing about then?" I asked.

Wilkes smiled for the first time since we had been in captivity. "What else? Our motherfuckin' fee!"

3

Akbar

You have put me in here [in jail] like a cub, but I will come out roaring like a lion, and I will make all hell howl!

CARRIE NATION

This riot is the fault of criminal defense lawyers who clog the courts with their motions, delay trials, and keep their own clients in the Tombs.

MANHATTAN'S DISTRICT ATTORNEY (1970)

Friday, October 2, 1970, was the unluckiest day of my life. To get thrown into the Tombs for contempt of court was bad enough, but precisely on the date the inmates of that dark dungeon elected to riot was ridiculous! What a predicament: Wilkes and I were now holed up on the Tombs' twelfth floor along with eighteen guards (the hostages) and two hundred raging barbarians.

The inmates were absolutely out of their minds: crazed with anger from the wretched conditions of the Tombs; insane with glee that they were now free of their tiny cells and oppressive guards. It was an explosive mix of emotions. But it was also apparent they were filled with the fright and excitement that comes when the mob forcibly takes over from all-powerful authority which everyone knows will soon regain the upper hand. Just like it did back in August. In eight motherfuckin' hours!

No matter. The barbarians trashed the place: they threw burning debris out the windows, which I am told looked like slender firefalls to the constant crowd of free people who stood at night in the streets below. The brutes on the twelfth floor bellowed riot rhetoric to folks in the streets—"Kill the pigs!" and "We want the mayor." They cussed; they screamed and fought with each other; they scared the hell out of me.

AKBAR

Not that I blamed them. Anger and violence were natural results of stacking men like cordwood in a cesspool. You don't do that to people and expect gratitude and loyalty in return. But Wilkes and I were revulsed at the meanness of the riot. We looked at the captive guards and saw the fear etched deep in their faces. The inmates taunted them with constant threats of castration and death. We knew it was necessary to quickly make known to these uncaged maniacs just which side we were on.

It took Wilkes about thirty seconds to strip off his suit, put on a Yassir Arafat head covering (made from his torn shirt) and sunglasses (taken from a guard), and announce himself as "Akbar, revolutionary lawyer, leader of the oppressed in the everlasting battle against the capitalist avaricious plunderers."

I quickly followed suit. The idea of joining up with these rioting lunatics was no matter of principle; it was a question of survival. Call it hostage syndrome, discretion, or cowardice, since we still seemed to have a choice in the matter of our fate (unlike the guards), it was really just a matter of natural selection. Our chances were much better if we had some voice in the direction of the madness.

Adopting revolutionary identities was a necessary move. Better not let anyone know who we were so we could have deniability in the riot's aftermath. The PLO headgear and sunglasses would help serve that end by changing our ethnicity while simultaneously generating an air of mystery and connectedness with the barbarians.

FIRST NIGHT

As Akbar and Amadan (my moniker for the riot), Wilkes and I tried to look fierce and authoritative. Luckily, Wilkes's client, Johnny Wad, and J. J. Jefferson, my cell mate for all of ten minutes before we were sprung in the first moments of the revolt, threw their fate in with ours and became our public relations men, soft-selling us to anyone who would listen as "motherfuckin' comrades in the common cause of our liberty."

"These boys is da real thing," said J.J. to those few who were not sacking and pillaging. "They is radical motherfuckin' lawyers in here for revolutionary crimes. Just like us. Called their judge a fucking stooge, a capitalist viper, a hanging racist. They is here 'cause they told the motherfuckin' truth!"

This was only a few miles from the truth, but close enough under the circumstances. Johnny Wad added, "Yeah, man, Akbar here done me good. He told the motherfuckin' greasy pig judge to stick his gavel where the sun don't shine."

There was too much madness going on for any of the barbarians to care about two PLO pinko lawyers. Our two front men didn't get us much of a following, but they did keep us from being put under "revolutionary arrest" and thrown in with the guards. We were tolerated as a couple of oddball off-white curiosities amid the black and brown group madness.

ALL NIGHT LONG

By Friday evening, the movie auditorium had become the revolution's command headquarters. Leaders of the three major gang factions, the Panthers, Muslims, and Young Lords, were doing what came naturally—arguing and brawling over who would lead and what to do. There was no one in control and little prospect of any one group or person taking it.

Worse, no one was even coming close to talking realistically about what had to be done. The best that could be done was to reason with the Man, state the case for better conditions, get promises of improvement and amnesty for the rioters, and return the hostages unharmed. In other words, give up.

None of these ideas entered the inmate discussions—which were more like yelling contests—that first night. Instead, they ranted about forcing Commissioner of Corrections George McGrath to personally drive them all to Kennedy International and give them a million bucks, a pilot, a plane, and free passage to Algeria.

One realistic black said he'd settle for a Big Mac for dinner every night instead and was jeered by the Puerto Ricans as an Uncle Tom. That set off a tag team fistfight between the Lords and Panthers.

A Muslim said it would be just fine if out of this riot they got a right to jail-supplied toothpaste and soap and regular showers. Tombs policy was, you buy your own. Curses and hisses were the mob's response to this reasonable goal.

A Puerto Rican Young Lord said they should make it clear that they meant business and kill a guard every day until Mayor Lindsay personally came to the Tombs and gave in to all their demands.

A loud shout of "Right on!" came from the mob.

A Panther screamed that they should demand more dope for the infirmary as supplies had already been depleted during the rush at the outset of the riot.

"Right on!" again.

These were the only areas of agreement that first tumultuous, frightening night. The barbarians argued over everything. Who should talk. Who should represent them with the Man. Who they would negotiate with. For most of the night, there was no single discussion. Instead, multiple screaming harangues and fights made it impossible to follow any single train of thought. Reason took the night off.

On and on the arguing went all night long. Wilkes, J.J., Johnny Wad, and I just sat quietly in a corner and watched. It was far too volatile a crowd even to attempt to influence at this point. "Better to let the loons exhaust themselves in their rhetoric. It won't accomplish a thing. Wait until they are desperate for direction," said Wilkes. "Then it will be time for Akbar."

I had a feeling as my friend spoke these words that the right time for Akbar would be when the barbarians were back in their cells. With this happy thought in mind, I fell asleep. The last words I heard that horrible first night were those of the most vocal Panther: "We gonna spill da blood of them dried-up cracker guards till the pigs runnin' this shithole drowns in it."

SATURDAY, OCTOBER 3, 1970

The next morning I awakened to the roar, "We want the mayor. We want the commissioner." I got up. The auditorium was nearly empty of barbarians, and Wilkes, J.J., and Johnny Wad were nowhere to be seen. I slipped out to the cell block area of the twelfth floor and saw most of the men shouting out the shattered, barred windows for Mayor Lindsay and Commissioner McGrath. I was surprised to hear a retort every bit as loud from the people in the street. "All power to the Tombs Two Hundred," they chanted. I noticed the Tombs was ringed below by a thin blue line of well-armed police listening to the shouting choruses in silence.

After about an hour of shouting, the barbarians grew hoarse. They were also noticeably fatigued from their all-night caucus and irritable because there was nothing left on the floor to burn or break or shoot up. Most sauntered back to the auditorium to listen to more insanity from the stand-up comics who posed as the leaders of these lunatics. When I got there, the barbarians were arguing over the impending police invasion.

"The white devils will be here in no time to rescue the pigs," said one. "We got to do it." He didn't elaborate on what "it" entailed.

"We gotta have a plan. We need our warriors to take sniper positions for the attack," said another.

"And shoot with what?" asked an intelligent one. "Our dicks?"

With that, another fight started. A Muslim bit a Panther. Two Panthers clubbed a Young Lord. Two Lords beaned a Muslim. The whole assembly was on the verge of exploding in cannibal violence.

Wilkes—Akbar to the barbarians—stood in the center of the auditorium's stage atop a chair, his arms folded before him and his head turning slowly from one side to the other. With shades on his unshaven face, his PLO turban, and his long, naked upper torso glistening with sweat, he was an impressive sight.

In a booming voice, he said eight little words which bought him the mob's attention: "IT IS A GOOD MOTHER-FUCKIN' DAY TO DIE!"

J.J., Johnny Wad, and I figured this was the move we had been waiting for and shouted for the crazies to listen to Akbar. "Listen to the dude, man," we said. "He's cool. He can get us motherfuckers together! He's right on!"

Whether out of exhaustion, desperation, or apathy, most of the barbarians shut up. Maybe it was the pure shock of hearing someone welcome death as if it were a long lost friend. Maybe most were just waiting for one of the gangs to kill this audacious Arab. Whatever the reason, they let Wilkes speak. As he began, I thought that this speech had better be good or we were in big trouble.

"Yes," said Akbar, "it is a good day to die if you want to end your motherfuckin' life in this capitalist shithole for absolutely nothing. Right now, out in the so-called free world, the bourgeois vultures are looking forward to your extermination. We are just so many rats to the grandees who run this motherfucking country. Right now you're doing precisely what they want. You're acting like stupid animals instead of revolutionaries. Just what the capitalist gangsters and their lackeys expect of you!"

Wilkes was shouting at the top of his lungs from the top of the chair. He was gesticulating wildly with his arms as if punching imaginary capitalists would impress this jury of his peers.

"Fools!" he continued. "You are giving them a glorious pretext to raid the place and kill us all to save the guards. All in the name of motherfuckin' Western civilization!"

The mob was listening. I heard only a few rumbles of "Who the fuck is this motherfuckin' camel jockey?" and the like, but most seemed to like the radical crap they were hearing.

Akbar continued. "You want to play puppet for the racist motherfucking white devils out there? They're ready to pull your strings. They're drooling to kill us all! And we'll die for what? For the Man! To justify toilets like this! To show the motherfuckin' world that we're subhuman sewage only fit to be stuffed into the garbage can! To give the Man's motherfuckin' lackeys an excuse to make the motherfuckin' conditions here even motherfuckin' worse! Is that why we took over this motherfuckin' shithole? Is it?"

TRUE BELIEVERS

A group of blacks shouted, "No!"

God, I thought. Wilkes was on a roll. He got in more motherfuckin's in one sentence than I'd ever heard before. And the mob was digging it. It was just like when Wilkes gave a great closing jury argument: What charisma! What electricity! What baloney!

The Young Lords closed in around Wilkes. One said, *"Hombre, digame!"*

Wilkes went on with his political harangue for another hour. It was a magnificent performance. Just like closing jury argument—you rant and rave, you ooze sincerity and dedication for your client's cause, and while you may not believe a word of what you're saying, it's unimportant. What counts is that the audience believes. These raging barbarians believed.

When Akbar ended, he had a following sufficiently large to get a few things decided. Akbar made negotiations with the outside the first priority. We would parlay the guards for amnesty and guarantees of better conditions. We would negotiate only with the mayor or the commissioner, with designated representatives of the press present to play honest broker.

Wilkes suggested a troika lead the prisoner negotiating team and be composed of one Panther, one Muslim, and a Young Lord. He and his assistant, Amadan—me—would serve only as counselors to the barbarian triumvirate.

The idea took with the barbarians, and the rest of Saturday was spent with the three gangs splitting off into caucuses and viciously fighting over what lucky stiff would be their representative.

SUNDAY, OCTOBER 4, 1970

By Sunday morning, a meeting was set up with the commissioner and reporters in the Tombs. We learned over the radio of other riots in two jails in Queens and another in Brooklyn. Mayor Lindsay announced no new prisoners were to be sent to jail, but he was almost immediately overruled by—what else?—a motherfucking judge. I wondered if it was Blugeot.

It was good that the mayor was willing to give such a sign of good faith even if some black-robed bastard, without the good sense to refrain from pouring gas on an out-of-control fire, thought it perfectly okay to send more inmates into a rioting jail.

Our first meeting with Commissioner McGrath and the reporters was a disaster. McGrath only offered the expected—not to raid the place if we would immediately give up and turn over the guards. He said he agreed the jail conditions and trial delays were outrageous and promised his and the mayor's good offices to do all they could to improve things. That was all.

In other words, if we gave up, we would be prosecuted for insurrection and end up spending more time in the Tombs under even worse conditions. The old-timers said these same promises had been made to end the August riot. Not one thing had been done to make good on them.

The troika leaders were not happy. They mumbled to the commissioner about the many injustices that occurred every day in the miserable dungeon. As they got worked up, their expressions of disgust turned angry. One of them, the Panther, looked at Wilkes and said, "Akbar will give you our response." The three inmates stared at my friend.

AKBAR SPEAKS

This was what you call a delicate situation. Wilkes had to convince two very different audiences with his words: he had to appease our three barbarian brothers—this would require Akbar at his phony, radical best. On the other hand, he had to make sure he kept his identity from the commissioner and reporters. The WASP fascist lackeys in the bar don't care for jail riot leaders. Neither do prosecutors. So with turban and shades in place, Wilkes stood half-naked, stinking, and sweaty.

"It is a good day to die," he said quietly, and immediately sat down and said nothing. The commissioner's jaw hit his chest. The reporters did a double take. The troika smiled.

After a minute of uneasy silence, Akbar said, "You offer the same words given last August when our brothers last rose in the Tombs. We listened then to your promises and believed. But things got worse here in hell. Your words are worth less than the breath it takes to say them, and we who have no mouth must scream."

Wilkes sounded like a Sioux chief addressing the Long-Knives about their lousy record on treaty commitments. He leaned forward and got eyeball-to-eyeball with the commissioner.

"Give us your solemn word before these reporters that there will be no reprisals and no prosecutions. Give us the mayor's written promise to act on the conditions of this toilet you call a jail. Pressure the courts to give reasonable bail and speedy trials. Give us these requests, and as Allah is my God, we will give you all you want in peace."

The commissioner shook his head negatively.

"Then it is a good day to die," said Wilkes. He got up and walked out of the room, followed by the troika and myself. As

I left, I turned, put my hand to my turban, and said, "We who are about to die salute you." I heard the commissioner ask as I walked away, "When the hell did we get PLO in the Tombs?"

WINS

The rest of Sunday was spent watching TV to learn what the city planned on doing to us. We were pessimistic after the negotiating session, but our spirits rose when we were told that the mayor would personally address us at 9:30 P.M. on the all-news station WINS. Maybe he'd be reasonable. I prayed he'd give in to our modest demands and end the riot without the storm troopers charging in like a panzer division.

When the time came, we were all in the auditorium listening to the loud radios and hoping. The other news that day hadn't been good. On Saturday the entire Wichita State football team was killed in a plane crash. This day, news of Janis Joplin's suicide filled broadcast after broadcast. But what really got us down was the news about the Kent State massacre. A commission revealed the truth about the Ohio National Guard's murderous attack on unarmed college kids. That news hit close to home.

At 9:30 P.M. the mayor came on the air. Here's what he said: "This is Mayor Lindsay speaking to the men in the Tombs. You have thirty minutes to give up and release the guards unharmed or I will be forced to set into motion another course of action. You know what I mean."

That was it. Short and sweet. No giving in. No compromise. No nothing. Give it up or they're coming in. The barbarians looked to Akbar for guidance. Wilkes rose once more to address them. This time—for the only time I can remember during the riot—the whole place was quiet.

"Comrades! Brothers! Allah be with you! It still is a good motherfuckin' day to die!" Wilkes smiled bravely. I did, too. I knew what kind of day it was—a day to get the hell out of there.

Akbar continued, "Our struggle is at hand! To hell with the motherfuckin' mayor! Allah will protect us! Victory is ours! We have only to define it! I have a plan."

THE RAIDS

At 11:30 P.M. the Tombs was retaken peaceably without force and without casualty. All of the hostage guards were released unharmed.

Within hours, however, the city battalions attacked the three other rioting jails using tear gas and billy clubs. Many inmates were savagely beaten. Only the Tombs avoided a violent end to its rebellion, and for that the city and the barbarians owe a great debt to Akbar.

The plan Akbar offered to the barbarians after the Lindsay ultimatum was his "Thermopylae strategy." He said he would send four inmates, like the few Spartans of ancient Greece, to descend the Tombs elevators and meet the cops and National Guard below in a glorious, bloody battle to the end. When the cops eventually killed the chosen four martyrs and reached the twelfth floor, a peaceful surrender would follow. The deaths of the four martyrs—and however many cops they could take with them—would send the message to the city: "We ain't gonna take this motherfucking shit no more!"

With the courage to match his convictions, Akbar said that he would be "one of the lucky four martyrs who would see Allah in heaven that day." The others would be his able public relations men, Amadan, J. J. Jefferson, and Johnny Wad.

The barbarians loved the idea. Somebody else volunteering to be killed sounded great to them. We were carried to the elevators on the shoulders of the screaming savages. They cheered our courage and our sacrifice. Akbar, still turbaned and wearing shades and no shirt, rode above the sea of black and brown arms triumphant. In front of the elevators, the barbarians let us down, and while we waited to descend, they let out a roar, "Akbar! Akbar! Akbar! Akbar!"

As soon as the elevator doors closed, separating the four of us from the bellowing barbarians, Wilkes punched the button for the eleventh floor and revised the heroic Thermopylae strategy: "We'll get back in our cells, lock the doors, and put on our street clothes. When the cops come, we play dumb. We've been on the ninth floor the whole weekend. No riot for us."

And so we did. We stopped at the eleventh and tenth and finally the ninth floor to tell the barbarian lookouts of Akbar's plan to die in glorious martyrdom. They were told to go up to the twelfth floor with the others and wait for the surrender. This done, we went back to our cells on the ninth floor, the lowest one held by the rioters, and put on our suits. I never thought I'd appreciate putting on a tie as much as I did that night.

The scheme worked better than expected. Wilkes and I were not only not suspected, but the warden was apologetic. I thought he was worried about the lawsuit we might file for being put into such a mess. After all, we were just two wacky criminal defense lawyers who stumbled into the Tombs on a fluke and a bad sense of timing. They let us bail out before the police interrogations of rioters on the twelfth floor even began.

In the weeks that followed, the media reported an intense hunt by the police for "a PLO-type terrorist known as Akbar who led the Tombs insurrection from the beginning to end preaching communism and murder, yet who mysteriously disappeared while on a suicide mission to fight the invading police."

4

Cribber Crawley

O that I were as great
As is my grief, or lesser than my name!
Or that I could forget what I have been,
Or not remember what I must be now!

RICHARD II, ACT 3, SCENE 3

There was no longer the slightest doubt in my mind that
intimidation was the key to winning.

ROBERT RINGER

Just one week after our release from the Tombs, the morning mail brought bad news. The Bar Association for the State of New York wrote:

Dear Mr. Wilkes,
We have received a complaint alleging that on October 2, 1970, you were held in contempt by the Honorable Justice Joseph P. Blugeot as a result of your statement to him that he was, to wit, "a racist honky mother-fucker."

We are informed that this profanity was stated on two occasions to the judge during the sentencing proceedings against a criminal named John Wadkins, alias "Johnny Wad."

Whereas these vulgar remarks are clearly contumacious, defamatory in the extreme, and an outrage to human decency, the Bar has determined it appropriate to

> hold a special expedited hearing to determine what dis-
> cipline, if any, is appropriate under these circumstances.
>
> The hearing has been scheduled for November 1, 1970,
> in the Bar offices in New York City. You have a right to
> appear with counsel and present evidence.

Wilkes was in court arguing motions in a particularly nasty
rape case when the letter arrived. I decided there was not a
minute to waste, what with the speed with which the bar hearing was approaching. I marched straight to the criminal courts
building.

Wilkes had been in fine spirits that morning prior to leaving
for court. Fresh out of the Tombs and busy doing what he
loved best, defending the damned, he was as high as I had
seen him in a long time. "Everyone should lead a prison
riot," he had said to me that morning. "It's positively intox-
icating."

OUTLANDISH

I walked into the courtroom and found Wilkes in the middle
of a heated argument with the prosecutor, Miles Landish. The
DA was attempting to convince the court to order the defendant in this rape case to give a sperm sample. If he refused,
Landish wanted the court to get the sample "by any means
necessary."

"We need the sample for several reasons," said the chubby
prosecutor. "First, it will shed light on the inevitable impo-
tency defense which Mr. Wilkes likes to use in these cases.
Second, with the sperm sample, our forensic people can do
wonders in determining whether his blood type matches the
evidence left at the scene of the rape."

Wilkes was amused by Landish's motion. "You have a fer-
tile imagination. And just how do you propose to get this sample, sir?"

"By court order, of course."

"Ridiculous!" said my friend. "The judge just can't point

to my client and say, 'Let there be sperm!' There are still laws about our precious bodily fluids.''

The two attorneys, ignoring the judge, continued talking directly to each other. Miles Landish said to my friend, "All your client has to do is what he does every night in his cell and put the results in a jar for us.''

The judge evidently thought this a great idea and interjected, "Offhand, Mr. Wilkes, that's the way I see it being done.''

HOLY JUICES

My friend's amusement disappeared from his face. This was getting serious. The state had plenty of evidence to prosecute this case, he thought. He was damned if his own client would give them even more while he was defending. The bodily juices were to be protected at all costs.

Wilkes turned to his client. They huddled and whispered rapidly back and forth. After a few minutes, Wilkes turned to the bench and addressed the judge. "My client informs me that he is a devout Catholic and that what you propose is forbidden by canon and biblical law—remember, Your Honor, Genesis, chapter thirty-eight, verse ten, where for spilling his seed on the ground, God slew poor old seed-spilling Onan. Any order compelling a sperm specimen will violate the First Amendment to the United States Constitution. It would be an outrageous violation of this man's freedom of religion.

"If you like, Your Honor, we can get the bishop in here to discuss this with you this afternoon. I am sure the church would be interested in any such order and would intercede amicus curiae.''

Wilkes's eyes caught mine during this excellent speech. "Oh, I see my associate Mr. Schoonover is in the courtroom," he said. "I'll just ask him to call the bishop—"

The judge instantly put up a hand and said, "No, that won't be necessary.''

"I have a solution," piped Miles Landish. "My office will hire a urologist to conduct a rectal prostate massage so that we can get what we need without any action required of the defendant."

A WHAT!

"A what!" said Wilkes's client. "A rectal what?" Wilkes's client didn't understand much of what was being said, but he understood that word, all right.

"A simple, gentle massage of your prostate gland," said Landish. "It'll give us what we want without your assistance."

"Ain't that still gonna spill my seeds all over the place?" asked Wilkes's client to everyone.

There was a moment of silence as all of the principals pondered this weighty question. Then Wilkes spoke up. "Your Honor, this is an improper use of New York's long-arm statute."

Wilkes's worried client looked to him and grabbed his arm. "Ain't nobody sticking his arm up my butt!"

The judge looked to Wilkes. "Do you have any other legal, as opposed to religious, objections to this procedure?"

"Clean-hands doctrine," said my friend. Wilkes detected that the judge was teetering on the brink of granting this grotesque motion to capture our client's bodily juices. He knew there was only one thing to sway the judge our way, and that one thing had nothing to do with law, morality, religion, common sense, or our client's bodily integrity. It had to do with ink—bad ink.

A CALL TO ROME?

Wilkes said, "I must insist, if the court is seriously considering granting this motion, that I be allowed to fully brief the free exercise of religion and right of privacy issues. Further, I do want the opportunity to consult the archdiocese so that I might as forcefully as possible present the religious underpinnings of my client's rights. So if the court would set this down for a hearing date, I will be able to produce not only a brief, but representatives of the church, perhaps from Rome and the Holy Father himself, to address the court on the gravity of this violation of religious principle.''

You could see the wheels spin as the judge pondered the ramifications of such an order. He knew damn well my friend would make good on his threat to drag the church—and worse, the press—into his courtroom to make Hizoner look like an anti-Catholic pervert. The paper boys would have a field day.

The next two words the judge uttered were slow and difficult in coming. They were said softly so as to be almost inaudible, and his milky face crimsoned as he spoke the words that would keep our client's sperm in its rightful place: "Motion denied.''

CONTRADICTION: JUDICIAL NEUTRALITY

Trial attorneys know the feeling when you enter a courtroom to face a judge more biased against your client than your adversary. It's no fun appearing in front of judges who preside like smiling coroners—with toxic sweetness!—over the death of your client's rights. Before such judges, the merits of the case are largely irrelevant to the outcome. If the defense is to win, it will not be because of the righteousness of the case. In the sperm case, Wilkes won, as he often did, through intimidation.

It was such an unbiased and clear-thinking panel Wilkes encountered when he entered the hearing room of the New York City Bar Association to face his disciplinary hearing for calling Judge Blugeot a "racist honky motherfucker." Hearing officers for bar matters are volunteer lawyers who take on these assignments to better position themselves for advancement to the bench or, failing that, to jockey for a well-exposed spot in the hierarchy of the various local, state, or national bar associations.

Typically, bar discipline officials are WASP lawyers from the big downtown firms who have never set foot in a courtroom and are totally oblivious to the pressures of a real law practice which so often gets real lawyers in trouble.

Wilkes knew in advance what kind of hearing panel we would be facing. After all, he had been here before. So he prepared for the hearing as if he were a defendant in a murder trial. In a way, it was a capital case—Wilkes's legal practice was hanging in the balance.

BAR PREPARATION

Here's what we were prepared to present the panel to defend Wilkes's license. We reviewed all the sentencing records of Judge Joseph P. Blugeot and hired a mathematician to analyze the data. Reviewing cases involving similar facts and circumstances, the mathematician, using regression analysis, demonstrated that blacks fared far worse than whites in Blugeot's sentencing and that race was the only variable that explained the difference.

Next, our investigator, Uriah Condo, discovered that Blugeot currently belonged to an exclusive New York City "whites only" club. Condo found a couple of disloyal club members who were willing to testify to the judge's frequent unflattering comments about minority groups.

Best of all, Condo also found a former Mrs. Judge Blugeot! She told him that Blugeot was deeply racist and often castigated her with racial slurs during their brief, stormy marriage.

We also hired an elderly forensic jargonologist, Professor Henry Bluefnozel, a semantics expert from Columbia who spent his career studying ghetto language and who could explain the middle-class meaning of the three little naughty words that triggered this disciplinary hearing. To make his point, the professor prepared large posters with each of the offensive words painted in large letters. Underneath each was the intended meaning of the word translated from ghettoese.

Into the hearing room we marched, a small army of lawyers, mathematicians, investigators, and the old semanticist, Henry Bluefnozel, with his huge signs under each arm.

CRAWLEY III

The presiding hearing officer, Malcolm Crawley, III, a silk-stocking lawyer from a Wall Street firm that specialized in municipal bond law, began the festivities. "We are gathered here to consider the serious charges against one John Wilkes of the New York bar. The charges are in two counts. First, that Mr. Wilkes did, by the foulest vulgarity, impugn the integrity of an honorable member of the bench. Count two stems from his repeating the outrageous insult of the court.

"In this regard, we have received a certified transcript of the sentencing hearing in *State* v. *Johnny Wadkins, alias Johnny Wad*. This evidence appears to this panel irrefutable proof of misconduct warranting discipline, and therefore we ask you, Mr. Wilkes, if you have any comments in this regard before we turn to the matter of the appropriate discipline."

The two flunkies on either side of Crawley nodded in agreement. Before Wilkes rose to address the kangaroo tribunal, he whispered to me, "I think I know this jerk-off. But from where?"

I shrugged my shoulders. "Maybe from your last disciplinary hearing," I suggested.

Wilkes stood and looked at his accusers. They had mentally already passed that familiar evidentiary point of no return where the judicial eyes glaze over—they had sufficient evidence to convict. They had their man.

DEFENSE CASE

"Hopefully, my innocence will be a factor which will be relevant to more than just the sentence in this matter," said my friend. "If the transcript is the extent of the evidence against me, then I wish to begin my case."

Crawley looked puzzled. He turned to his two equally baffled colleagues on either side, but they had no words to guide him. "What could you possibly say in defense of this outrageous comment?"

Wilkes said, "First of all, the transcript reveals that the court ordered me to repeat a statement made in private to me by my client. I was merely the involuntary conduit of my client's communication. How can this be contemptuous if I was ordered to repeat the comment by the court?"

"Is that your defense? Entrapment?" cracked Crawley. He was ready to rule without hearing more. "That being the alleged defense which is reflected in this transcript, we are now prepared to—"

"Not so fast!" said Wilkes. "I also have witnesses. I shall now call the former Mrs. Judge Joseph P. Blugeot to the stand."

As the former Mrs. Blugeot approached the witness stand, Crawley asked Wilkes, "What is your offer of proof? What could she say to shed any light on your statement to the court?"

Wilkes responded: "Let me put it to you this way. We have conclusive evidence that Blugeot is a bigoted judge who discriminates against minority defendants. We have done a mathematical study of his sentencing practices to present the court demonstrating this fact. Mrs. Blugeot will corroborate it through her own close association with the judge."

IRRELEVANT!

Crawley interrupted. "Absolutely irrelevant! You will not be permitted to continue your defamation of Judge Blugeot in this proceeding. If you were sincere about this bigotry matter, you would have made these charges in the appropriate forum. You cannot justify calling the judge a 'honky racist motherfucker' by such alleged evidence."

With these words, Crawley shot down two-thirds of our defense. Only Professor Bluefnozel remained. "Well, if truth is no defense," said Wilkes, "I call to the stand Professor Henry Bluefnozel."

"For what?" snapped Crawley. His concept of rawhide justice did not contemplate confusing pristine issues with the ambiguity of the facts.

"Since the disputed words were not my own, but those of a young ghetto youth, Professor Bluefnozel, a respected forensic jargonologist, will help this court by explaining the meaning of the words which were meant to be transmitted only to me and were relayed to the court at the judge's insistence."

As Wilkes spoke, the tall, shaggy-haired Professor Bluefnozel ambled forward with his huge signs. Crawley looked at the first sign, which said:

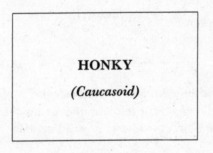

HONKY

(Caucasoid)

"The professor will demonstrate that the words, while perhaps vulgar to a middle-class white, were simply the truth's stark characterization as seen by a nineteen-year-old black ghetto youth who had just been sentenced to a year in jail for possessing one marijuana cigarette."

As Wilkes spoke, the professor revealed the second sign, which said:

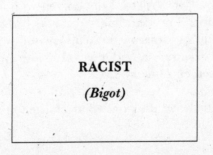

RACIST

(Bigot)

Crawley couldn't help but comment on the visual arts display being given by the professor. "Well, we've seen two of the signs already. I can't wait for the professor to tell us what the word 'motherfucker' means."

At that, Professor Bluefnozel revealed his third sign, which had the nasty twelve-letter word on it and his definition underneath, which read:

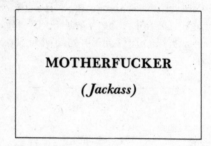

MOTHERFUCKER

(Jackass)

"Actually, the definition of motherfucker," said the kindly professor, "depends entirely on the context in which it is spoken. In rare circumstances, it could actually mean motherfucker."

Crawley huddled briefly with his two toadies and then announced that this evidence, too, was totally irrelevant and did not in any way undermine the offensive nature of the comments uttered at the sentencing hearing. With that, Crawley eliminated our entire defense. There was only one thing Wilkes could do to stop this juggernaut.

"I ask for a recess," he said.

Crawley looked at him sternly. "We have only been going fifteen minutes, Mr. Wilkes. Why do you wish a recess?"

When my friend needed time, he always had a good reason to present. On this occasion, the actual reason was that we had absolutely no defense left, and it was time to regroup and think of one. He then explained:

"Nature calls."

Crawley adjourned the proceedings for ten minutes.

RECESS

Wilkes and I went to the nearest bathroom to confer on what to do.

"Looks like we've had it," I offered, as if to cushion the inevitable. "This is a railroad."

"A bullet train," said Wilkes. "Who is that guy? I know I know him from somewhere."

Wilkes began lifting a toilet lid with his toe and letting it fall and bounce back on the porcelain. He was lost in thought. When Uriah Condo came in to tell us it was time to go back, Wilkes was still within himself.

As we reached the bathroom door, he grabbed my arm and said coldly, "I remember." With that he was out the door.

Wilkes quickly marched back into the hearing room and, with a loud voice, began his summation. He aimed his eyes and words solely on Crawley.

CRIBBER

"You have denied me the right to present evidence. I have only my words left to reason with you now. I am going to tell you a story which may seem strange and out of place, but if you hear me out, its meaning will become clear.

"This is a story about a college student who was a cheat. During his academic career, he devised dozens of ways to dishonestly pass his tests. I will tell you how he did it on one occasion. This person, who was known as 'The Cribber,' came into an economics exam as he did all his tests, totally unprepared. He opened one of his blue books, and instead of answering the exam question in it, he wrote a long, sad letter home to his parents. Into another booklet the Cribber copied the five questions on the exam. When the time was up, he turned in the blue book with the letter home in it, ran out of the class, and made for the library, where he checked out books on economics to help him answer the questions.

"Naturally, with this aid, he was able to answer them magnificently. The Cribber then put the answers in an envelope and mailed them home to Mom 'n' Dad.

"That night he received the expected phone call: "Hello, Cribber? This is Professor Klorowitz. . . . Uh . . . er, I must report something very strange in your exam booklet. . . . It appears to be, of all things, a letter home to your parents."

"With feigned horror, the Cribber cried to the prof that he'd made a horrible error. He mistakenly mailed his folks his exam and turned the letter home in to the professor! The professor, dubious at this, asked for his parents' phone number. He called and instructed the puzzled parents to meet him and 'The Cribber' at the post office, where they could release the as yet undelivered letter to the professor.

"And of course, it worked, because the Cribber had indeed mailed the exam book to his folks after his visit to the library. The Cribber received a great grade in the class, as he did in all his classes.

MORAL

"Today the Cribber is a successful professional man who has undoubtedly made his way in life the same way he did in college. And what is the moral of this story, you ask?"

Actually, no one was asking Wilkes anything at the time. The two flunkies on Crawley's right and left were looking at Wilkes as if he'd lost his marbles. Disbarment was a cinch now for them. Crawley, however, was shaken. His face was beet-red, and he looked like he was about to disappear behind the bench.

Wilkes continued, "The moral is, you never know who you're dealing with. You never know what things a person's done until someone takes the time to investigate and expose a person's crimes. Only mercy met with mercy can wash the sins of the past away."

With that, Wilkes sat down. Everyone was stunned by this odd and apparently irrelevant summation. My friend noted the puzzlement on my face and whispered in my ear, "That son of a bitch is Cribber Crawley! I went to school with the bastard twenty-five years ago!"

DECISION

When Wilkes sat down, Crawley appeared visibly relieved. His tone changed, too. Now he wasn't the contemptuous ass looking to set the land-speed record for the quickest disbarment hearing on record. He brought the kangaroo court to an end: "Thank you for your presentation, Mr. Wilkes. You have given us something to ponder here, and we'll have to think on it long and hard. The issue of the attorney-client privilege is certainly one for us to consider quite seriously. I believe we understand your response to Judge Blugeot was to a court order. Thank you very much."

Crawley's two sidekicks' facial expressions did not change. They still looked like they were listening to a demented person—except now they were looking at Crawley.

He adjourned the hearing, telling us the panel would take the matter under submission and send its decision to us. We walked back to the office and wondered if Crawley's instinct for self-preservation was stronger than the evidence against Wilkes.

We did not have to wait long for the answer. Three days later I came into Wilkes's office, and while looking on my friend's cluttered desk, my eyes snapped to a letter from the Bar Association. I turned the letter around and read it. The crucial part said:

> After thorough investigation and a hearing on the matter, we have found that Mr. Wilkes's statement was the unfortunate relaying to the court of a private communication from his client intended only for his ears. We find no contumacious intent in its accurate transmission upon court order. Complaint dismissed.

I expressed my mild surprise to Wilkes that his not so sub- tle extortionate threat to go public on Crawley's dishonor- able character had worked. "He must have a lot to hide," I said.

"Yes, indeed," said Wilkes. "We all do. And I thank God for it!"

5

*"Take All
You Can Get"*

*One should always play fairly—when one has the winning
cards!*

OSCAR WILDE

*A continuance is absolutely mandatory in order that I per-
sonally be able to interview each of the fornicatrices.*

JOHN WILKES

I'm a good one at daydreaming. I love to daydream. I get
totally lost in my daydreams. Most times I'm reliving a memory just as vividly as if it were an experience happening at this
instant. It's weird what triggers my dreaming. An offbeat remark, something out of place, or even a smell can launch me
into reverie.

Wilkes's comment about hiding things got me to thinking
about the 1950s, about Wilkes and me.

It was 1956, and Wilkes was suffering from another case of
the "I-need-a-continuance blues," better known as phase three
of the Old Wine Defense. He was representing a short, skinny,
sleazy two-bit pimp named Hank "The Lizard" Gidone, a
crook who got his nickname for his reptilian puss, nervous
demeanor, and leathery hide.

The Lizard was scheduled for trial on charges of procuring
the services of seventy-two women of easy virtue for thousands
of New York Johnnies. The indictment looked like a telephone

book. The evidence against him was overwhelming. The Lizard had cheated and abused his women so egregiously that all of them readily agreed to turn state's evidence. Seventy-two Jezebels were soon to wear that most respectable courtroom mantle, that of the wronged fornicatrix.

OLD WINE DEFENSE

Wilkes was none too anxious to see the ladies on the stand. He needed a continuance desperately. So said my friend to the Honorable Henry "Red" Fox: "Your Honor, I have to interview seventy-two tarts, and Mr. Condo, my intrepid investigator, must investigate their rather extensive criminal histories. I need six months."

"That'll be denied," sang the judge.

A week later, Wilkes came back with phase two of the Old Wine Defense. He told Judge Fox, "I'm afraid my client and I have an irreconcilable difference over the handling of this case. I regret that I am unable to reveal the nature of the conflict to you, but you surely understand my dilemma. I ask to be relieved."

"Mr. Wilkes," answered Red Fox, "You can relieve yourself by going to the bathroom." Hizoner chuckled at his scatologic humor. Scatologic was the only kind of logic the judge possessed.

Wilkes screwed himself up and said self-righteously, "I cannot defend this man, Your Honor." This was entirely true, but it was the evidence, and not any conflict, which made it so. Wilkes continued his protest. "I must be allowed to withdraw. That's the law."

"I'll eat the decision that says that!" said Fox loudly.

"It would be far better if you read it," said my friend in equally raised voice.

"No continuance! Trial in two weeks!" So said Judge Fox.

DR. FEELGOOD (PHASE THREE O.W.D.)

Fox's unreasonableness on the trial date question and conflict matter led Wilkes to visit the friendly offices of Dr. Simon Comfort, Wilkes's personal physician and forensic consultant on matters medical and psychiatric. Wilkes called him Dr. Feelgood because the doc dispensed drugs on demand when my friend was feeling low.

Upon learning of the terrible time problems in the Lizard's case, Dr. Feelgood quickly made his diagnosis. "Wilkes, looks to me like you have contracted a case of rapid onset litigious meticulosis, a new disease currently taking a terrible toll of trial lawyers. I must insist that you immediately deliver yourself to the hospital of your choice where I have practice privileges and stay put there for at least, uh, er, hum one . . ."

Wilkes gave the doc a terrible frown.

". . . Uh hum, er, ah two . . ."

Wilkes frowned even harder.

". . . hum, ah, yes, three weeks and not a minute less!"

Within the next hour, Wilkes checked himself into the hospital and sent me on my way to address Judge Fox about the recent turn of events.

HALFADAVIT

With my friend tucked in his hospital bed and eagerly awaiting his first medication, I had the honor of serving the sworn declaration of Dr. Comfort—attesting to my friend's new disease and hospitalization—on Henry Fox. I said, "Judge, due to the exigencies of the unforeseen medical emergency, I must reluctantly request on behalf of my fallen partner an indefinite postponement of Mr. Gidone's trial."

Fox read in deadly silence the motion papers and Dr. Feelgood's affidavit. By the time he finished, he looked at me and reflexively slapped his right hand to his forehead and rubbed to the rear of his balding head. He looked like he had just read a Dear John letter or his tax bill, or even worse—a verdict of not guilty!

Grinning evilly, he held up the motion papers and slowly tore them lengthwise, and then handed one half of the papers to the clerk, who passed them on to me. "Tell your conniving, malingering malpractitioner friend that the shreds of paper you now hold in your little hands are what his bar ticket is gonna look like in ten days if he doesn't show up for trial."

I said nothing. There was no need. We had made our record, and the good judge, his temper once again getting the best of him, had done nothing to sabotage it. Wilkes could not be held in contempt for being ill, and certainly not by the notorious lawyer-hating, Wilkes-despising Judge Henry "Red" Fox.

CONTRETEMPS

Ten days later, Wilkes was still in the hospital when Henry Fox held him in contempt for feigning illness to avoid the Lizard's trial. When I told Wilkes the news, he was thrilled.

"Great break! Appeal! Add another affidavit from the doc attesting to the chronic nature of my litigious meticulosis!"

I pointed out that this would mean extending his recuperation period quite a bit, but Wilkes was not concerned. "Great! We need the time to uncover a defense for the Lizard. And let's not underplay the seriousness of this meticulosis. It's damned debilitating. I need more drugs!"

Wilkes spent two more weeks in the hospital and then was discharged by Dr. Comfort with strict instructions to go home to bed and stay clear of the courtroom or risk relapse and rehospitalization.

After he got home, I visited him every afternoon at his place in Greenwich Village to bring him files and mail and to chat about what was happening in the office and the courts.

I BRING YOU JOY!

As I did most every afternoon during the illness, I opened the front door and walked into Wilkes's place without knocking. My presence I announced with a loud "I bring you joy!" Not that I did actually. All I brought this day were the legal papers on my friend's most recent contempt at the hands of Judge Fox, but Wilkes appreciated the words. They had been the opening salutation of one of Wilkes's famous ancestors.

The setting I viewed that day was no different than those of the past few weeks. Wilkes was lying flat on his back on his sofa dressed only in pajamas and bathrobe. The living room looked like a SWAT team had just been there executing a search warrant—many items of furniture and personal possession were strewn on the floor. Empty codeine bottles, gifts from Dr. Simon Comfort, lay at my friend's bare feet. The television was blaring. My friend was again engrossed in his favorite daytime quiz program.

". . . And now, Mr. Yost, for five hundred dollars, a second refrigerator, and an all-expense-paid weekend in a Catskills resort, answer this question: What was Groucho's description of a manufacturer of padded bras?"

"A man who lives off the flat of the land!" shouted my friend at the boob tube. After the contestant failed to answer the question, the moderator quickly verified Wilkes's answer as correct.

"Jeez," I said, "you always get the answers right. You ought to get on one of those shows."

Wilkes looked up at me as if noticing for the first time my presence. "Huh?" he said. I repeated my suggestion.

"You know, Schoon, I've been sitting around here all day thinking just that. Great opportunity for free national advertising, and who knows? I might win a bundle!"

BIG-GAME HUNTERS

By midyear 1956, TV quiz shows were the hottest entertainment in America. Shows like "The $64,000 Question," "Dotto," and "Twenty-One" were enormously popular, attracting each week audiences of tens of millions. Americans flocked to watch Joe Average win enormous sums of money by answering seemingly impossible questions. On "The $64,000 Question," a marine won the top prize by naming the five dishes and two wines served at the 1939 banquet King George VI held in honor of visiting French President Lebrun. Incredible!

On the same show, a Bronx cobbler won $32,000 by answering questions on Italian opera; a jockey won twice as much for his omniscience in art; Joyce Brothers won the same amount for, of all things, her knowledge of boxing; and a ten-year-old kid outdid them all and won $192,000 in his category, the sciences.

The appeal of the quiz show programs was obvious—the nation's little people demonstrated that they could be as smart as all the eggheads running the world; they were also taking home sums of money most people couldn't earn in twenty years of hard work. No wonder these shows dominated the ratings. They fed two basic instincts: greed and envy.

JACK TWINK

The next morning after my visit, Wilkes drove downtown and entered himself as a contestant on the popular afternoon game show "Take All You Can Get," a program sponsored by the Willard Snap Chewing Gum Company, and hosted by that affable airhead, Jack Twink. It was Wilkes's fondness for Twink that led him to sign up for the "Take" show as opposed to the other popular shows.

Jack Twink was such a handsome fellow on the TV screen that most contestants standing beside him looked like bulldogs. Television's magic hid his one physical flaw—a skin so acne-pitted that only daily belt sander treatments by the show's makeup man could cover them up. Before each show, the makeup man, wielding a small trowel, scooped a moist pile of skin-tone-colored wall spackle and deftly slapped it into the many craters on the Twink's cheeks. After a few minutes of working the slow-drying mix into the holes and light sanding, Twink's cheeks were as smooth as those on a baby's fresh-spanked bottom. Of course, once the stuff dried, his cheeks had a marble hardness, thus raising the danger of fissures during a telecast.

Not even TV could hide the Twink's other flaw. Even with cue cards, it was apparent that the Twink was a bubblehead, one of nature's ironic jokes—blessed with a fine physical temple, but completely lacking in interior design. Jack's pale blue eyes were windows to a great void lying between his ears. Original thought never penetrated that vacuum.

He was perfect for television.

WILLARD SNAP'S SON-IN-LAW

All prospective candidates on the "Take" show were cross-examined by the sponsor's chief executive officer, Joe Magnon, son-in-law of Willard Snap. In screening prospective contestants, Magnon was looking for lively, interesting, and knowledgeable persons capable of exciting the interest of a vast gum-chewing audience.

The interview with Wilkes was short and sweet. Magnon asked my friend for his area of expertise, and Wilkes said, "Pain. I'm a criminal lawyer."

"Pick another area," said Snapp Chewing Gum's CEO.

"Okay. Humor," said Wilkes. "My sanity, or lack thereof, is directly proportionate to my ability to laugh."

Magnon says, "So tell me a joke."

Wilkes said, "When do you know a leper's done playing poker?"

"I dunno," says Magnon.

"When he throws in his hand."

"Hey, not bad," says Magnon. "We could do a couple of shows with you doin' the humor bit and the dummy givin' you the straight lines as questions. Tell me a joke about a dummy."

The dummy was what Magnon called Jack Twink.

"Certainly. A newsman is on the street asking people what they think is the greatest invention of all time. The first person says fire. The second says it's the wheel. Then up comes a man who says it's the thermos bottle. Now, the newsman is very surprised at this answer and asks the man why he picked the thermos. The man says, 'Well, when you pour in the hot stuff, it keeps it hot. When you pour in the cold stuff, it keeps it cold. Hot or cold. How does it know?' "

"Hah!" grunted Magnon. "I know who that man was. It had to be our own Jack Twink! The fence post with cement cheeks and a bouffant hairdo. Say, you'll do, Wilkes. Be here tomorrow at nine in the morning and you're on the show."

FIRST SHOW

The rules of "Take All You Can Get" were similar to all the other game shows: contestant answers questions, wins money, answers more questions, wins more money. Eventually, the contestant either won it all or failed in answering a question and lost it all.

Here's how the exuberant, marble-cheeked Jack Twink introduced the "Take" show on Wilkes's first appearance: "Hey ho, everybody! I'm Jack Twink, the host of 'Take All You Can Get,' Snap Chewing Gum's new and exciting game show. Under our rules, I give contestants a choice of three subjects to choose from. After the selection, I ask a question from that area, which, if answered correctly—hey ho!—wins the contestant money prizes and entitles him to another question. The only catch is that all questions will be related to the first subject selected.

"Sound confusing? Well, hey ho, everybody, it does to me, too, and I'm the master of ceremonies! Ho, hey! Think about that for a while while I introduce our next contestant, a Mr.

John Wilkes. He's a lawyer from here in New York City now on sick leave from work. So let's give him a really big hand in welcome. Hey, ho, hey! Come on out here, John Wilkes, and tell us about yourself.''

WILKES ONSTAGE

Wilkes walked out onto the stage and stood beside the game's host. Jack Twink, a constant toothy smile frozen in concrete on his puss, read from the idiot card. "So you are a criminal attorney here in town, eh, Mr. Wilkes?''

Wilkes nodded in the affirmative. Twink made the mistake of attempting to ad-lib a line. "Does that mean you prosecute people and put them in jail?''

"Not quite," said Wilkes. "I defend the accused, who unfortunately are often threatened with jail based on the lies of the state's witnesses. You see, there's a butcher's thumb on the scales of justice. He wears a black robe and favors the state. It makes my work difficult.''

The "Take" audience was live—which is more than one could say for its announcer—and Wilkes's answer left them silent and uncomfortable. Twink didn't sense this and ad-libbed his next question. "Well, hey ho! How do you know when they're lying, Mr. Wilkes?''

"When they move their lips," replied Wilkes. A few in the audience giggled, but the hapless Twink looked confused for a moment and then started reading the idiot card:

"Well, ho hey!" said the Twink. "Let's not get into that. Let's get into our great game and see if you, John Wilkes, will Take All You Can Get!''

"I'm pretty good at that," said Wilkes.

TAKE YOUR PICK

"You know the rules. I will give you three categories from which to choose. This is a most important selection since all subsequent questions will be related to this area. Your choices are: First, Pope Victor II. Second, literature of the Sudan, or third, the humor of Oscar Wilde. You've got twenty seconds. [PAUSE] Okay, John Wilkes, what'll it be?''

"Well, the only thing I know about Pope Victor II is that he was probably a Catholic, and I haven't kept up on my Sudanese novels, so I'll have to go with the Wilde humor category.''

"Very smart move, Mr. Wilkes. Ho hey! This should be fun! But before I can ask you your first question, let me escort you to the isolation booth so that no distractions will interfere with your answering the questions.''

THE BOOTH

The booth looked like a cross between a jukebox and a rocket ship. It stood about ten feet tall, was adorned with multicolored fluorescent lighting tubes, and had a clear glass front which allowed Twink and the audience to see the contestant. Wilkes entered the booth, put on a set of headphones, and looked prepared to be launched into space.

"Hey ho! Can you hear me, Mr. Wilkes?'' asked Twink, still reading from a cue card. "Okay, here's question number one. Take your time. God bless you and good luck.''

Wilkes stuck his face so close to the glass in front of him that vapor began forming. Twink asked the first question.

"Oscar Wilde once said that he could resist anything in the world except one thing. What was that one thing?''

"Temptation,'' said Wilkes without hesitation.

"That's right! Hey ho, ho hey! Way to go, Mr. Wilkes!'' Twink was the kind of game show host who would express amazement if the contestant knew the name of his own mother. "Good start! Now, will you take the one hundred dollars you've just won or will you try to Take All You Can Get?''

"I'll go for it,'' said Wilkes.

"Okay, great! This one is worth five hundred dollars, so take your time, God bless, and good luck. Hey ho! Here we go. In 1880, Wilde visited the U.S. for a speaking tour. Upon entering the country in New York, a customs agent asked him what items he had to declare. What was Wilde's response?''

WILDE DECLARATION

Wilkes edged a little closer to the glass in front of him. The fog on the glass now covered half of his face. ''I have the answer,'' he said. ''Wilde said, 'I have nothing to declare except my genius!' ''

''Hey ho! That's exactly right! Ladies and gentlemen, let's give our contestant a big hand.''

The small studio audience, prompted by a man holding an audience idiot card that read ''APPLAUSE,'' dutifully clapped loudly.

Twink read from his cue card, ''Now you have the choice again, Mr. Wilkes, but old Jack Twink thinks he knows what you're gonna do. Hey ho! Will you still try to Take All You Can Get?''

''Of course,'' said my friend, his face now totally obscured behind the foggy glass.

''Okay, Mr. Wilkes this is your final question this week. If you answer it correctly—hey ho!—you can come back next week and continue playing for the grand prize of one hundred thousand dollars. Now, for twenty-five hundred dollars—hey ho!—here's the question. Wilde once said that the public has an insatiable curiosity to know everything except . . . what?''

''What is worth knowing,'' answered Wilkes, now just a vapory shadow behind the glass of the rainbow-lit isolation tank.

''Hey ho! Ho hey! Righto, Mr. Wilkes! Come on out here! He sure knows his Oslo Wilde, doesn't he, folks?''

Wilkes climbed out of the rocket ship and shook hands with Twink. After the exchange of a few banalities, Twink informed Wilkes that he could come back the next week or retire with his winnings. The gallery exploded in shouts of ''Come back! Come back!'' as the cue card holders gamely ran in front of them holding high cards which read ''YELL: COME BACK!''

Of course, my friend had no thought of disappointing them. "Mr. Twink," said Wilkes, "I have not yet begun to take all I can get. I shall return!"

RETURN ENGAGEMENT

Wilkes went back to the "Take" show the next week and successfully answered his three questions. Then he went back the following week and did it again. That made nine straight Wilde trivia questions Wilkes got right. Whether it was the topic, Wilkes, the show, or all three, Wilkes became a big attraction, the biggest the show ever had. The TV audiences got so big that the "Take" show moved to prime time, with Wilkes's last question scheduled to be the centerpiece of the first evening show.

As the show gained in popularity, our law office received a few fan letters for Wilkes. I had the honor of opening and reading them. Almost all were requests for loans or gifts of money. There were also several marriage proposals, and fifteen people recently accused of crimes wanted Wilkes to represent them under the most impossible conditions—for free!

The sponsor and the network naturally loved Wilkes because so many people tuned in to the show. Sales of Snap Chewing Gum were never so good. For the first evening show, which would be Wilkes's last, newspaper ads, radio spots, and TV commercials promoted the quiz show with hype more appropriate for a televised speech by Jesus Christ or a demonstration of how to make gold out of fertilizer.

Wilkes loved it all. His name was becoming a household word not only in New York, but all over the country. "It'll be great for business," he kept saying all week before the final show.

FINAL QUESTION

Wilkes was confident going into the studio for the last show. He had memorized everything memorable Oscar Wilde had

ever written or been quoted as saying. He felt he had nothing
to worry about.

As Wilkes won more money each week, the questions about
Wilde got harder and more obscure, and the final question
Jack Twink asked Wilkes that night would be the hardest and
most obscure of them all. I, along with several million fellow
Americans, tuned in to root him on to riches.

It was a somewhat nervous Jack Twink who began the show
that night. This was big-time TV for him, and the first time
he had been in it. "Hey ho! Hey hey! Ho ho! Okay okay. Boy
oh boy, here we go, Mr. John Wilkes. Let's see if you can
Take All You Can Get! Golly, for one hundred thousand dollars, answer this question:

"When Oscar Wilde was sixteen, he attended a ball in Dub-
lin Castle. There, the brash youth approached one of Ireland's
most notable ladies of rank and asked for a dance. The lady
replied contemptuously, 'Do you think I'm going to dance with
a child?' What was Oscar Wilde's response?"

Wilkes put both his hands over his mouth. Despite newly
installed air-conditioning in the booth, sweat poured out of his
face. The camera zoomed in so we could see him ponder. After
a few seconds, Wilkes grabbed the microphone and said carefully, "Wilde told the lady, 'Madame, if I had known you were
in that condition, I would have never asked.' "

HEY HO!

"Hey ho! Mr. Wilkes! You have just won one hundred thousand dollars! Come on out of there! Isn't he great, ladies and
gentlemen? And here he is! Let's give him a big hand. Hey
ho! And let me be the first to shake your very rich hands, Mr.
Wilkes. Congratulations! In just a few days, Snap Chewing
Gum will be presenting you with a certified check for one hundred thousand dollars. God bless you! You're so famous now.
Golly, what would you like to say?"

"How much do I get if I answer that question?" said Wilkes,
to the merriment of the audience. Even the dummy laughed.

"As to the fame," Wilkes added, "I think it's great. As Oscar Wilde said, 'There's only one thing worse than being talked about, and that's not being talked about.' "

"Well, thank you for being one of our greatest-of-all-time contestants, John Wilkes. Good night and God bless."

THE LETTER

It was September 11, 1957, and we were as happy as two guys who just pulled in a hundred thousand smackers could be. Wilkes was singing his chorus of "This'll be great for business" all through a twelve-course dinner at Jack Dempsey's. The future seemed glorious.

The next day, DA Frank Hogan announced that a grand jury would be investigating certain questionable quiz shows. Seems some contestants on "Dotto" and "Twenty-One" were claiming fix. Wilkes and I ignored the announcement. The "Take" show wasn't mentioned, and anyway, Wilkes had received no help in answering the Oscar Wilde questions.

On September 13 we got a letter from the Willard Snap Chewing Gum Company. We expected it. It was the check for the money, of course. Here's what was inside the envelope:

> Dear Mr. Wilkes,
>
> Due to the recent allegations of fraud concerning contestants on certain quiz shows, we are holding up the winnings of certain contestants on "Take All You Can Get." This is not a reflection on you (at this time). We believe that until the air is cleared, we owe it to our viewing audience and consumers of Snap Chewing Gum to hold your purse. Thank you for your patience.
>
> With all due respect,
> Joseph Magnon, CEO
> Son-in-law of Willard Snap

PUNIES

Wilkes's eyes bulged as he read the letter. He looked like Judge
Henry Fox reading one of our motions to continue the Lizard's
case. "Bullshit! Bullshit! Bullshit! I want my money! Now!"
He threw the letter on the floor and began pacing around the
office. A minute later he stopped, pounded his desk, and
howled, "B-U-L-L-S-H-I-T!" for a full minute.

"We're gonna sue those bastards, Schoon," he said, "and
we're gonna get our quiz money, and we're gonna get more
money for libeling my character, and we're gonna get punies!"

By the time he finished, he was smiling. I saw dollar signs
form in his eyes.

"Punies?" I asked.

"Punitive damages. We're suing for a million bucks!"

— 6 —

Wilkes *v.* Willard Snap

Respect for truth is an acquired taste.

MARK VAN DOREN

No self-respecting lawyer does his own legal work!

JOHN WILKES

Charles Van Doren was undoubtedly the most loved and famous TV quiz show contestant in history. Tall, handsome, and urbane, the son of a respected historian, brother of a major poet, a teacher himself at Columbia University, Charlie had everything going for him except for one little thing—a respect for the truth.

Herb Stempel, on the other hand, was everything Van Doren was not. He was not particularly glamorous or attractive; he was an ex-GI graduate of the workingman's college, CCNY. But he had two things in common with Van Doren. He, too, lacked a respect for the truth, for a while anyway, and he, too, was a brilliant contestant on the popular TV quiz show ''Twenty-One.''

''Twenty-One'' first aired in September of 1956. Its format pitted two contestants in a race to win twenty-one points by answering difficult general-knowledge questions worth up to eleven points each. The more points a question was worth, the harder it was.

SHOW BIZ

Herb Stempel was the show's first champion, the first to gather a large TV following, and the first to earn the tag "human encyclopedia." He started on the show in October of 1956 and lasted as champ until his staged encounter with Van Doren on December 5. On that show he lost—if you can call winning almost fifty grand on a phony quiz show a loss.

Since the shows were fixed from the start, it was, as Herb himself later described, "harder to learn the stage directions than the answers to the questions." Shows were fixed for business reasons: Giving selected contestants the answers to the questions enhanced the dramatic quality of the shows. Champions who came back week after week attracted huge followings as unsuspecting audiences tuned in to see if the "champ" would win again or get knocked off and lose the earnings of a lifetime.

Unless the answers were given, producers feared no contestant would ever answer a question correctly unless it was of the Groucho Marx "You Bet Your Life" variety—like who's buried in Grant's Tomb? So they figured they had to create a myth to sustain their shows, and that myth was that the common man is uncommonly smart. To be true to their myth, they fed their champions the answers to the questions. It was no crime. It was entertainment. The only fraud was on the public, and the public loved it. What they didn't know wouldn't hurt them.

DUEL OF THE TITANS

On November 28, 1956, Herb Stempel was challenged on "Twenty-One" by the shy, engaging teacher, Charles Van Doren. Stempel disliked his challenger, perhaps because they were so different, but most likely because he was scripted to lose on the December 5 show to close out an epic, phony battle.

Stempel begged the producer to allow him to contest Van Doren without aids or prompting. Let the best man win, he said. The producer was in partial agreement; the best man should win—that was why he selected Van Doren to come on the show in the first place. But an actual contest of wits? Forget it!

And so Charlie beat Herb Stempel unfair and unsquare, and Charlie went on to win and win and win and win and win and win. And win again. And again. All through December. Win, win, win. All through January. Win, win, win. And February! Win, win, win. And March! Win, win, win.

Charlie answered all the questions according to script and got them right. His main difficulty was learning how to feign looking perplexed while thinking of the answers. He had to learn the timing of dramatic pauses, to give short nervous, puzzled looks as his initial response to a tough question, to make stutteringly insecure verbalizations as answers, and most of all, to look surprised at being right.

BIGGER THAN LUCY

Charlie learned his role very well. He made "Twenty-One" the number one show in the country, bigger than Milton Berle or Ed Sullivan or even, for a short while, "I Love Lucy"—all because Mr. Charm was winning those seemingly incredible battles of wits, which he did, he said, "as a service to the teachers of America."

Charlie became more than a TV idol. He became a symbol of what was best in America: youth, good looks, intelligence, innocence, and character. Making a fortune by his wits, he was a man people believed deserved fame and wealth, and he wore both with a princely grace.

Charlie's picture made the cover of *Time* magazine. He was a news story so great that by the time of his long-postponed scripted defeat, he had an audience so big that the network had the balls to put the show on opposite the ratings-blockbuster "Lucy" show.

Finally on March 11, 1957, to the shock of a nation, Charlie correctly read his scripted wrong answer and lost. The inevitable finally happened; through his popularity and great ratings, Charlie had postponed his date of departure far beyond what anyone expected when he started. With poise and grace, he left the show with $129,000 and a five-year contract to appear as a regular on NBC's "Today" show. He was on top of the world.

TRUTH WILL OUT

The bubble burst for Charlie in the second week of September of 1957, when DA Frank Hogan announced his grand jury investigation of rigged TV quiz shows. Too many contestants like Herb Stempel had been publishing exposés about the phony shows. The story was bound to break open, and when it did, Charlie denied the allegations.

He said, "The truth will out."

And so it did. After testifying before Hogan's grand jury, Charlie and seventeen others got themselves indicted for perjury.

It was the day after Hogan announced his grand jury investigation that Wilkes and I received the letter from Joseph Magnon of the "Take All You Can Get" show informing my friend that his hundred-thousand-dollar purse was being withheld. Wilkes's reaction was immediate and furious. "I want my money! File a suit against the bastards! And file it tomorrow!"

CUT MAN

I was pretty capable of fulfilling Wilkes's insane demands for speedily filing motions and briefs in our criminal cases. In those days, we didn't have word processors to store thousands of pages of form motions and briefs. Today, you just fill in the blanks with the name of your client, weave in a few pertinent factors, push a button, and quick as a flying daisy wheel or laser jet, out pop fifty pages of immaculate, margin-justified legal work. In my day it was different. To comply with Wilkes's unreasonable time demands, I had to use a different kind of computer, the Winston Alfred Schoonover, Series I Gray Matter Limited, and it had numerous limitations: such as limited storage; such as inaccurate recall; such as sluggish processing time.

I had to remember which of our old cases contained motions with similar issues, search the office to locate the desired file, cut and paste the various old pleadings, adding, of course, a smattering of new names and facts from the new case, and voilà! One new, persuasive pleading, and one old, nerve-racked lawyer.

Wilkes said I was the best cut-and-paste man in the business, a pro who worked quickly and deftly to get the job done in the nick of time. Like those cut men in the corner of the ring at the Garden on fight night, standing at the ready to close vicious cuts with the latest quick-acting coagulant, or ice down an eye so swollen from punches that it looks like an immense walnut, or administer a smelling salt to awaken a punch-drunk brain—all in sixty seconds between rounds. Working for Wilkes was like that.

FAKING IT

I did nothing that first day after receiving Wilkes's command. There was nothing to cut and paste. Wilkes and I were criminal lawyers who didn't know the first thing about filing a civil suit. So when Wilkes came into the office the next day, I told him I needed to talk about his civil suit against the "Take" show.

"Got the complaint ready for me to review already, Schoon? Great work. Knew you could do it."

I didn't respond except to suggest we go down to the Guadalajara Café for coffee and doughnuts. He sensed my mood and followed me out the door and down to the street for the short walk to the narrow hole-in-the-wall that was the Guadalajara. We entered and took a seat at the counter. You had two choices at the Guadalajara: the counter or the floor. There were no tables and certainly nothing as elaborate as a booth. There wouldn't have been room for them in the corridor–turned–coffee shop.

The owner, cook, waiter, and bouncer of the place was a dumpy grease-ball we knew as Lunk. Since we were regulars, Lunk didn't ask for payment in advance like he did with the transients and unknowns who staggered into the place for a cup of sobriety or a bowl of sustenance.

"Da usual?" asked Lunk.

"Twice," I replied.

It was time to tell Wilkes I hadn't done anything on the civil suit. I turned to my friend and said, "You know what they say about a lawyer who represents himself?"

"Yeah. He's got a lawyer for a client."

"In this case, he's got two criminal lawyers who don't know a damned thing about civil suits. Makes me feel like a V-6."

AMERICAN TURKEY

"Impossible!" said Wilkes. "A V-6 is too stupid to feel ignorant. A V-6 is like the American turkey—so dumb he's been known to drown by forgetting to lift his head out of the water trough. Do you know that the turkey is too dumb to even propagate? Can't even fornicate! Don't know how. They'd be extinct by now if we didn't grow them as a crop. V-6s are like that. If the judges didn't grow them like a cash crop, they'd all be extinct. As long as judges loathe trial by jury, they'll keep appointing V-6s to cop pleas, and the crop will grow."

Wilkes clearly didn't want to talk about hiring a civil lawyer to handle the suit against the "Take" show. Our coffee and doughnuts arrived as I said, "Look, we need to hire someone else or at least associate someone in with us. We don't know what we're doing."

Wilkes looked at his doughnut as if it were a rare art object. "You know, this isn't even on my diet. Did you know that, Lunk?"

Lunk was drying his hands on his filthy tank top shirt which half-covered his hairy barrel chest. "Sure it is, Wilkie. I made dat one just fer you. Diet doughnut. Wid a hole in the middle."

Wilkes and Lunk chuckled at their old joke, but I would have none of Wilkes's diversion. "What is it? Are you too cheap? Afraid of paying expenses and a one-third contingent fee? What gives?"

"Schoon, don't be such a pessimist. Where's your spirit of adventure? This case is a cinch. And it's a civil case. Therefore, it'll never go to trial, at least not in this century. Look, don't worry about the complaint. We won't need one. Just make a few calls and we'll be fine."

He picked up his greasy plain doughnut, dipped it into the black coffee, and shoved the soggy mess into his mouth. I looked at the oil slick that appeared at the surface of his coffee. Wilkes said, "Um, yum, Lunko, what pastry, what coffee, what servicio!" To me he said, "Lunko's the best grease-and-oil man around, ain't he?"

LETTER TO THE PRESIDENT

As instructed by Wilkes, as soon as I got back to the office, I wrote a letter to Willard Snap, president of the Willard Snap Chewing Gum Company, and the sponsor of the "Take All You Can Get" show, which was then in arrears to my friend Wilkes to the tune of one hundred thousand dollars.

> Dear Mr. Snap,
>   Please be advised that Mr. John Wilkes has retained me as his counsel in the matter of securing his winnings on your quiz program, "Take All You Can Get." My client believes that your withholding of his purse is fraudulent and libelous. He has authorized me to seek the prompt payment of his winnings and, failing that, to sue you and your company for the money he won and for damages for the ugly stain you have placed upon his

name. Hoping that we can resolve this matter quickly
and without resort to the courts, I am sincerely,
  Winston Alfred Schoonover
  Attorney at Law

Within three days of mailing the letter, I received a call from
Jayson Laughlin, a senior partner in a big bluenose downtown
law firm. After introductions, he said coolly, "Say, old boy,
about this little matter of the quiz show winnings, our client,
Mr. Willard Snap, would like to get together for a friendly
chat in the hopes we can work the whole thing out and avoid
a messy court battle. We have an idea that may accomplish
just that. What do you say?"

"Fine," I said. "Just name the time and place."

"Wonderfully agreeable of you," said Laughlin. "How
about tomorrow afternoon, say about three o'clock, in our conference room? And would you mind if we brought a court
reporter? Never can be too careful now, you know?"

"I'd rather you brought the hundred grand," I said. "But
you bring all the court reporters you want. We'll be there."
After I hung up, I had a strange feeling, like I had been frisked
by a pickpocket.

Wilkes told me later I foolishly broke the basic rules of negotiations—make sure you do it on your own turf and that you
bring the agenda. But I was young, and as I had told Wilkes
many times already, I didn't know a damn thing about handling a civil case. And, I thought, neither did he.

INTIMIDATORS

Wilkes did find some pleasure in that my letter drew such a
speedy response. He said he expected it. "These civil guys will
do anything to avoid trial, Schoon. That is our trump card, or
at least one of them."

When I told him that it was Jayson Laughlin who was representing Snap, he was equally pleased. "It figures Snap would
pick him. Wealthy men are always suckers to mistake smooth-

ness for sophistication, and verbal skills for knowledge. Snap's the kind of guy who would always see the ornaments of wealth as a barometer of success. Laughlin's just another silk-stocking potentate waiting in line for a career on the bench.''

I asked why they wanted a court reporter present if we were just going to have a friendly chat to resolve the dispute.

"Intimidation," he said. "Simple as that. But maybe we'll have an intimidator there ourselves."

I hadn't the foggiest idea what Wilkes was talking about save for his own self-confidence.

A WILDE MEETING

When the big oak doors to the conference room at Jayson Laughlin's firm opened for Wilkes and me, I thought I was entering a board meeting of a giant corporation. There were at least a dozen people, all very properly dressed in the latest business fashion—gray flannel—seated around a magnificent rosewood conference table. The table was long, thick, highly polished, and immaculate. It was so beautiful, and I so taken with it, I missed half the introductions of the people around the table.

But I did awaken to hear that a representative of DA Frank Hogan's office was there, two representatives of the TV network, and a curious-looking local college English professor named Phillips. He was seated, smiling, behind a stack of books. Each book bore the name of Oscar Wilde on its spine.

Willard Snap was there, of course, seated at the head of the rosewood table. To his side was Laughlin, busy earning his tremendous fee by keeping three underlings in motion fetching pencils and paper and water for everyone while he himself elegantly puffed on a cigarette.

The court reporter was warming up her fingers as if getting ready to play Chopin at Carnegie Hall. Seated behind her and not at the table were Joseph Magnon and Jack Twink, the two mainstays of the "Take All You Can Get" show. From their nervous, hangdog demeanor, I sensed why we were here. They must have been suspected of cheating on the show, perhaps taking a cut of the winner's take, and we were here to see if Wilkes had been in it with them.

Wilkes surveyed the scene from the foot of the conference table and quickly surmised the purpose of our little get-together. "You want to quiz me on my Oscar Wilde knowledge! You want to do it now! You think you'll catch me cold and thereby show that I got help to win on your show! Right?"

"Say, what?" asked Jayson Laughlin blandly as he took a long drag on his cigarette. He seemed a little uncomfortable with Wilkes's coming so quickly and bluntly to the point. He audibly exhaled a puff of smoke from his lungs and waited for Wilkes to continue.

"So some other contestants on other shows are crooked; maybe even on your own show, I dunno. Therefore I must be, too, eh? Is that your proof, guilt by association? In the great American tradition, eh?"

No one responded to Wilkes. Snap's eyes looked at his son-in-law and then to Twink as if to search for guilt on their faces. The only sounds in the room were Laughlin's loud drags off his cigarette and the court reporter's tapping out her Chopin to Wilkes's lyrics.

Whatever agenda Laughlin had in mind when they opened the door to Wilkes was now out of the window. My friend continued his harangue before Laughlin could assert control.

"I'll do it. Right now! Cold! Without preparation! And with the little lady over there taking it all down for the record!"

Since this is exactly what our unworthy opponents had planned for the day, it was surprising to me how silent they were when Wilkes called them out. Laughlin just puffed on his Parliament and looked at the ceiling. Snap looked at Wilkes like he was the Creature from the Black Lagoon. Jack Twink and Joseph Magnon looked like two guys headed for transportation to Tasmania.

Wilkes filled the void by staring at Willard Snap and saying, "Yes, we'll do it right now, just like you planned it. Right in front of the DA and the TV people and on the record. But there's one little addition to your agenda today. We will do it just like on the quiz show. I win Mr. Snap's money for every correct answer I give. Winner take all. What d'ya say, Snap?''

All eyes turned from Wilkes to the other end of the table, where sat Willard Snap. It was the only time in my life I ever saw the man; to me he looked like William Howard Taft. Massive in size, blockheaded, mustached, and completely expressionless. He stared at Wilkes a minute and finally spoke. ''Mr. Wilkes, I have reason to believe you don't know anything about Oscar Wilde. If I'm wrong, I've done you a disservice. So all right, for every question you answer correctly, you win money, just like on my quiz show. And by the same token, you will, of course, agree that for every question you miss, you forfeit an equal sum from your purse. Seems a fair and practical way to resolve this little controversy quickly and without my having to pay my lawyers here a fortune to defend me in a suit.''

POLICEMAN'S OATH

''Agreed,'' said Wilkes. ''I'll administer the oath to myself.'' Wilkes held up his right hand and said, ''I do solemnly swear that the testimony that I am about to give in this case is the truth, the whole truth, and nothing but the truth, except as to those parts with respect to which I intentionally intend to lie and to which this oath no longer applies, so help me God.''

The court reporter chuckled at Wilkes's impertinence. ''That is the policeman's oath,'' said Wilkes. ''You all should get down to the criminal courts and see what I mean.''

''That will do quite nicely,'' said the silkily voiced Jayson Laughlin while sucking in another drag off his cigarette. He hissed like an irritated rattlesnake, ''Okay, Professor Phillips, why don't you ask Mr. Wilkes a few questions.''

''This is for ten grand, just for starters,'' said the still-standing Wilkes. Although not offered one, I found a seat at the table near Wilkes and took it. The table's rosewood grain was even more beautiful up close than it was from afar.

Willard Snap nodded to the professor, the court reporter tapped out a symbol for an affirmative nod, and the game was on.

PROFESSOR PHILLIPS

Phillips was short, slight, and very serious-looking. The hair on his head looked like a hurricane had just swept over it—tufts of salt-and-pepper hair shot out every which way and gave the professor a slightly crazed look.

Reaching into a worn, tweedy sport jacket, the professor pulled out a sheet of paper, adjusted his horn-rimmed glasses, and asked the first question. "In Wilde's best-known play *The Importance of Being Earnest*, Lady Bracknell conveys in one line Wilde's controversial views on education. What is this famous line?"

Wilkes pulled himself to attention and cleared his throat. He lifted his hands so that his fingers touched his cheeks on both sides, and in a high falsetto he sang out: "I do not approve of anything that tampers with natural ignorance. Ignorance is like a delicate fruit; touch it and the bloom is gone."

The professor piped almost joyously, "Precisely!" Wilkes not only knew the line, he even mimicked the female part correctly! Most impressive! Phillips looked to Willard Snap at the other end of the table, and the big man bellowed, "Another!"

ANOTHER!

"Thirty grand for this one," chirped Wilkes across the length of the table. Willard Snap nodded again, and the court reporter dutifully tapped in his response.

Professor Phillips buried his eyes in his papers and read a second question to Wilkes: "In 1895, Wilde sued the Marquis of Queensbury for defamation of character after the marquess had publicly accused Wilde of engaging in the sexual debauchery of young boys. Wilde ended up being prosecuted for his dalliances with these young men. During cross-examination at the criminal trial, the prosecutor asked Wilde a question aimed at revealing his homosexual history. He asked, 'You talked in *Dorian Gray* about one man adoring another. Did you ever adore a man?' Tell us now, Mr. Wilkes, what was Wilde's reply?"

Without hesitation, Wilkes answered, " 'No, I've never adored anyone but myself.' "

"Right again!" exclaimed the professor. He seemed as excited about Wilkes's mastery of the subject matter as I was. The others, except for Twink and Magnon, were glum. Willard Snap was losing money—quick and effortless, like water down a drain.

Snap adjusted his huge body in his chair. He was noticeably uncomfortable after losing forty grand in less than two minutes. He snapped at the professor, "Give him the hard one."

THE HARD ONE

"Fifty grand for this one," said Wilkes. All eyes went to Snap. He nodded, the court reporter typed, and the professor asked the question. "Wilde received two years hard labor for his homosexual activities. While in custody he developed the idea for his most famous poem. This question has three parts. First, name the poem."

" 'The Ballad of Reading Gaol,' " answered Wilkes.

"Right. When and where was it written?"

"Eighteen ninety-seven, in France," answered Wilkes.

"Correct. Now, one more part," said the professor. He looked at my friend standing confidently at the end of the table and smiled. Embarrassed perhaps by the impossibility of his next question, he covered his mouth with his hand to hide his smile. "For fifty thousand smackers, Mr. Wilkes, please recite the entire poem."

Wilkes looked to Snap. His face no longer bore the confidence of the moment before. He said, "The whole damn thing? Word for word?"

Snap sneered, "Every damned bit of it."

His snickering grin instantly disappeared when Wilkes retorted, "You mean you actually want me to recite all one hundred nine stanzas? It's eighteen pages in my book at home and takes an hour just to read."

"Well," said Snap, "well, well, uh, we'll just have to hear you out. Unless, of course, you'd like to forfeit fifty thousand and we'll just forget about questioning you on the validity of the game show winnings."

ENCIRCLEMENT

"Oh no," said my friend, looking to Snap and then to Jayson Laughlin. "It's my favorite poem, a great one, and I'd love to do it for you and the money. It's about a young soldier Wilde knew at Reading Jail. He was executed for killing his wife. I think you'll like it."

Wilkes started the poem and began circling the long, beautiful red-brown table. He began, as the poem did, talking about a person with blood on his hands:

> "He did not wear his scarlet coat,
> For blood and wine are red,
> And blood and wine were on his hands
> When they found him with the dead."

As Wilkes walked around his captive audience, he kept his eyes on either Snap or Laughlin, as if he could not choose which to torment most with the verse. As he polished off one beautiful stanza after another, their heads sank into their chests while those of the suspects, Magnon and Twink, elevated. Wilkes looked like a lion circling a small herd of antelope, imprisoning all with his stare, but eyeing a choice one—or two—for his supper.

As he circled, he managed to get out about two stanzas per circumference of the long rosewood table. As he did, he gestured, pounded, stamped in all the places where the poem was angry; he was monotone when the poem turned to narration;

and he was quiet and soft in the poem's gentle moments. In ninety minutes, Wilkes circled the table 54½ times, reciting the poem as if he had lived it.

THE MASTER

Wilkes was a master of timing and delivery that afternoon. I don't know how he did it, but each time he got to a particularly biting line, he was in perfect position to deliver it in the face of either Snap or Laughlin. In front of Snap, as if to remind him of the consequences of not paying Wilkes his prize money, he recited:

> "For Man's grim Justice goes its way,
> And will not swerve aside:
> It slays the weak, it slays the strong,
> It has a deadly stride."

Later, in front of the smoke-shrouded head of Laughlin, Wilkes delivered an apt line to the swine who was trying to steal his prize money—" 'They hanged him as a beast is hanged'!"

Wilkes marched on, singing the stanzas out as if they were his own. Twink now wore a toothy grin and let out an occasional "Hey ho!" as Wilkes poured out stanza after beautiful stanza. Despite deadly stares from Willard Snap, Magnon was also vocally cheering Wilkes on.

The next time he got to Laughlin's position, he stopped to recite this refrain in the face of the lawyer:

> "But this I know, that every Law
> That men have made for Man,
> Since first Man took his brother's life,
> And the sad world began,
> But straws the wheat and saves the chaff
> With a most evil fan."

After ninety minutes of glorious recitation and sweat soaking through his suit coat, but still going strong, Wilkes delivered the final lines standing in front of a thoroughly dispirited Willard Snap:

> "And all men kill the thing they love,
> . . . The coward does it with a kiss,
> The brave man with a sword!"

He finished with a quick bow to the table and then marched to a seat and sat down for the first time all afternoon. No one said anything for a few moments until the professor gasped, "By God! He got every goddamned word of it! Beautiful! Bravo, sir! An exquisite rendition!"

SNAP DECISION

Thirty minutes later, we walked out of Jayson Laughlin's conference room, the one with the beautiful rosewood table, with an even more beautiful check for $190,000. "I told you we'd get the money without a suit," said Wilkes.

I congratulated him on his virtuoso performance. It was even better than on the quiz show.

"The irony," said Wilkes, "is that their game show was not fixed as far as I know. It was one helluva lot cleaner than what just went on in there. My hardest part was memorizing the lines."

Wilkes delighted in these little surprises. It was a game. Keeping me in the dark was his way of making my life full of the unexpected. I didn't mind. In fact, I loved it.

"Turns out that Professor Phillips had a daughter in trouble with the law years ago, and I snatched the damsel from distress, to the great relief of Papa. And Papa also loved my performance on the quiz show and knew I would not stoop to such a depraved level as to cheat on TV, seeing as how I was never given the opportunity. So after they contacted him and he discovered who it was they were going to give this afternoon's pop quiz to, he called me up and offered a few areas for me to study.''

''Well, that was extremely nice of him,'' I said. ''Shows you how grateful he was for you helping his daughter.''

''Grateful? The guy wants fifty grand for his kindness. And he is going to get it. Share the wealth, you know.''

We continued our walk to the bank with Wilkes waxing philosophic about the depraved condition of man, the rising crime rate, and our inexhaustible line of future clients—optimism you might expect from a man carrying a check for $190,000.

7

Judge Yulburton Abraham Knott

When the mind is made up, the ear is deaf to even the best arguments. This is the sign of a strange character, in other words, an occasional will to stupidity.

NIETZSCHE

The Lizard doesn't need a lawyer; he needs an exorcist.

JOHN WILKES

After a wonderful interlude lolling around in the money and glory of the big win on the quiz show, Wilkes got an invitation to return to reality when Judge Henry "Red" Fox ordered him to appear for trial setting in the long-postponed case of *State* v. *Hank Gidone, aka "The Lizard,"* wherein our client faced seventy-two counts of pimping and pandering. It was with a good bit of anxiety that my friend and I, with our creepy client in tow, slogged through the rain to the balding judge's court for the first court proceeding in the Lizard's case in over a year. As luck would have it, we were late.

"Sorry we're late, Your Honor," said Wilkes. "But it's pouring outside and traffic's a real mess." Wilkes's words were said with such enthusiasm as to strip the apology of any meaning.

Red Fox started rubbing his balding pink head front to back, as was his habit when angry. He rose from his throne and marched straight to the nearest window and studied the traffic and climatic conditions for several seconds, then turned and marched back to the bench muttering, "So it is. So it is."

Such was my friend's credibility with Judge Henry "Red" Fox.

STROKE OF LUCK

"You are probably wondering why I've summoned you here, Wilkes," said the judge after seating himself. "Well, I'm going to inform you that, with the aid of that quack doctor you have on retainer, who is well paid for his opinions, I'm sure, and those maggots on the appeals court, who are well paid for theirs, you've succeeded in your sick charade. Your malingering to get a continuance worked. My contempt citation was reversed. And you have had plenty of time, between television appearances, to prepare for Mr. Gidone's trial."

The judge's face was now crimson, and he stroked his balding red pate vigorously. It was a scene I had seen a million times. Wilkes in front of a reddening judge who became more furious by the moment, and all without my friend saying a word. But Fox was being unusually candid about his feelings this day, which meant something was afoot. A judge wouldn't mess with the trial record by such reckless truthful comments about how he felt unless . . .

"It's the appellate judges I can't understand," Fox continued. "Maggots! Reversing my order! The fools! They've undermined this case!"

He stroked his nose-to-neck forehead even harder. "In case you haven't heard, Wilkes, I'm now in civil, so I have the great pleasure of informing you that the case of *People* v. *Hank Gidone, aka 'The Lizard,'* will not be tried by this court."

Hooray! I yelled in my thoughts. Wilkes and I usually had more sense than to speak audibly in court about what we really felt. Said Wilkes, "Terribly sorry to hear that, Your Honor. It's always been my pleasure to know I was going to trial in this department."

As long as you were going and not ever arriving.

"Cut the crap, Wilkes. You no more want to be in this court with me than I want to be in it with you. But you ought to love where I'm sending you. Your colleague of the defense bar, Yulburton Abraham Knott, as you know, just got appointed to the bench, and I'm giving him you as his first trial. Ha! It'll probably ruin him! He'll probably regret he ever left the practice of law!"

The judge rose to his feet smiling. "Now the moment I've been waiting for. Mr. Wilkes, it gives me great satisfaction to say to you and the Lizard, get the hell out of my court!"

KNOTT'S LANDING

Years later, in his prime, Judge Knott proved to be one of the cruelest judges ever to have pulled on the black sheet. He was meaner than Red Fox, more unscrupulous than Lester Throckton, and just about in the league of the infamous Judge Joseph Blugeot. Worse, being a former defense attorney, he knew all the tricks of the trade, so there would be no pulling the wool in his court. Wilkes would have some of his biggest courtroom battles with Judge Knott, but at this time we were in happy ignorance. We thought anything was better than Red Fox. We were wrong.

The first time Judge Knott opened his mouth as a judge was at the Lizard's initial appearance for trial setting. Wilkes was feeling quite chipper that morning, so much so that we took the unusual step of driving to work. My friend drove his new De Soto, bought with proceeds of his quiz show winnings, into the court parking lot and into a stall marked reserved for court witnesses.

No sooner had we alighted from the new car than a big black man, the security guard, came rushing up to us, yelling and gesturing with his arms. "Jesus Christ!" he said.

"Yes," said Wilkes as he stepped back from the car and looked it over, "it is a spectacular vehicle, isn't it? And you may call me by the earthly name, John Wilkes. Perhaps you recall me from the 'Take All You—' "

The guard looked Wilkes over in disgust and interrupted him, "What the fuck're you doin' here? This is for witnesses only."

"I'm gonna be a witness, and so is Mr. Schoonover here," said Wilkes.

"You two look like a couple of shysters to me."

"Quite right," said Wilkes. "Lawyers we are, but I'm still going to be a witness. You see, I'm about to start a trial, which means, if history is prologue, that I will be held in contempt, and since I'll be held in contempt, I of course will be the best, if not the only witness in my own defense."

OMEN

The guard was quietly considering this as we seized the moment and began walking toward the courthouse. The guard didn't follow or even call out. It was a good omen for the day to come. And we were going to appear before good old Y. A. Knott, former brother in the trenches of the defense of the citizen-accused. Although Wilkes and Knott were no more than passing acquaintances, we figured we'd at least get the time of day in his court.

Trial settings usual take about thirty seconds, but given that Y. Knott was new to the bench, we figured this one might take as long as a minute. It was thus with some surprise that when court commenced, Judge Yulburton Abraham Knott opened a thick binder and began reading a prepared speech. Here is what he said:

> "I have reviewed the entire file in this case and conversed with Judge Fox about it. It appears to me that one party to this case has stalled these proceedings for almost two years. All court hearings preceding this one have been a complete waste of the taxpayer's money; the motions to continue have been a patent insult to the intelligence of the trial court. I am appalled by the file before me. The artifice, the gimmickry, the outright fraud of one party—

it is incredible that both the defendant's and the State's right to speedy trial have been trampled on by the gamesmanship of one party."

AND SO ON

For thirty-seven minutes, Knott read his diatribe and detailed all the horrible tricks played by *one party* to delay the case. Wilkes and I had an excellent idea that the one party being referred to was one John Wilkes. This was one helluva judicial baptism.

Knott concluded: "There will be no more phony, ritual motions in this court. There will be no more contemptible game playing here. And most of all, there will be no continuances! Trial in ten days."

Without another word, Knott sprang up and race-walked into his chambers, but not disappearing from view before Wilkes could get out his sole contribution to the proceedings: "Have a nice day."

THE LIZARD RANKS LAST

Judge Y. Knott came out of the judicial blocks a Wilkes-hater having taken a crash course in judicial distemper from Red Fox. From the start, he demonstrated his bias against defendants and delay, a readiness to help the prosecution without prompting, and an egomania and pompousness befitting a Louis XIV.

Our client, Hank "The Lizard" Gidone, was to prove as big a problem as the judge. Of all the defendants Wilkes represented in his long, colorful career—and this included mass murderers like Elmo Lead, sex perverts like Senator Hyman Taurus Fabricant, drug fiends like Peter Silkings, hit man mobsters like Vito Di Voccio, professional thieves like Lyle Diderot, thieving professionals like Judge Milton Purver, J. Daniel Conway, Earnie Libido, and the Reverend Bob Smite,

and crazies like Dr. Lorenzo Pound, aka Dinero the Profit—
the Lizard was the most thoroughly loathsome client my friend
ever represented.

Most times, Wilkes got along fine with his clients. Of course,
he clearly had his favorites: fee-paying ones were all alone at
the top of the list. But in terms of crimes, Wilkes liked murderers best. If they were hit men, they knew the rules of the
game and didn't whine and moan. There was simply a quiet
understanding as is common between two professionals.

Passion killers were so frightened by the court proceedings
that they worshipped Wilkes as a modern pathfinder leading
them out of a wood-paneled jungle filled with life-threatening
terrors.

Drug entrepreneurs were next on the most-favored-criminal
list. These clients were well-educated, good-natured, and fi-
nancially well-endowed. To them, indictments and lawyers
were just an occupational hazard, much like a nuisance tax.
They accepted the pain of fee paying quite nicely, and it was
always a pleasure to take their money.

Bank robbers were next on the favorites list only because
Wilkes enjoyed representing lunatics. Only crazies rob banks.
Yes, it is where the money is, but it is also where the armed
security guards are and the marked money and the trained
tellers (trained to push silent alarms and to say in trial, "That's
the man. I'll never forget that face").

They shoot enough pictures of bank robbers from the wall
cameras to satisfy the most finicky fashion photographer. And
the pay is no good robbing banks. You figure that the two or
three grand they give the robber works out to about ten cents
an hour over a twenty-year stretch at Lewisberg.

So you had to be nuts to rob banks, and that is why my
friend enjoyed the bank robbers. He loved exploring the un-
bounded expanse of minds freewheeling toward the blessed in-
finity of Bonkersville. It relieved a lot of the boredom from the
practice of law.

BOTTOM OF THE BARREL

Actually, any client, no matter what the charge, who fit the profile could reach Wilkes's most-favored-client status. If they were deliciously crazy, or just rich, good-natured entrepreneurs, or even stupid, obedient, unquestioning followers, it was fine with Wilkes. As long as they paid their retainers in full and up front, my friend treasured their business like the family jewels.

There was only one class of crook that Wilkes despised taking on as a client even if they paid—the flesh merchants. He could be a kiddie porn peddler, or the creep who makes the flicks, or maybe an alien smuggler who stuffs half a dozen "illegal" humans in the trunk of his Camaro, or maybe a pimp like Hank "The Lizard" Gidone, on the hunt for fresh meat at Grand Central, thirteen-year-old virgin runaways being the prime target.

HOW DO I HATE THEE

When it came to the Most Despised Client, the Lizard was right at the top of the list. Wilkes represented the Lizard for over two years, and all he heard from him were unjustified complaints and incessant demands for attention: "Man," the Lizard would often say, "can't chew get my bail no lower? Murderers gots less bail than me." This comment first came two weeks after we got the ungrateful bastard sprung on fifteen thousand dollars bail.

The Lizard never took responsibility for *anything* he did. He took the art of rationalization to heights Wilkes and I had never seen before in a crook. The Lizard's frequent refrain on innocence went like this: "Hey, dude! The motherfuckin' cop said on the witness stand that he arrested me at nine in the mornin'. The pig lied, man. It was ten. Therefore, I am not guilty."

The Lizard's respect for human life was on a par with that of Adolph Eichmann. He called his whores "rental units" and constantly lied to us that the balance of our retainer would be coming soon: "I got my rental units out tonight working for you, Wilkes. Man, I'll have what I owe in the office in the morning."

His favorite "rental unit"—one he chose to sleep with—was deaf, dumb, and blind. He'd brag to Wilkes about how he instructed her to let him know when she was ready for sex: "I tells the bitch, 'Honey, just grab my thing and pull on it once if you wanna do it. And, baby, if you don't wanna do it, just pull on it seventy-five times.' Hah, hah, hah!"

A STITCH IN TIME

A whining, perverted pathological liar is bad enough, but the Lizard was also the downright meanest man we ever met. No white slaver ever treated his peons as cruelly as the Lizard did his stable of harlots. "When my bitches start holding out on me," he told us, "man, I puts a stop to it. First thing, I make 'em drink a glass of Drano. That usually brings most of 'em around and cleans out their pipes, too, man, but if it don't, well, man, I can gets ugly and I tells 'em, if you hold out on me, bitch, I will put you outta work for good, and I threaten to personally sew up their rental unit vaginas and put 'em out of the screwing business, ya dig? Not one of 'em's ever tried me on that, man. See, that's why I always say, 'A stitch in time.' Ya dig?"

With this statement of personal philosophy, he showed us his big gold pendant hanging from his neck and pointed to the inscription, which said, "A Stitch in Time."

No wonder when they got the chance, every one of the Lizard's whores gladly became witnesses for the prosecution. The same feelings caused Wilkes to say, "The Lizard doesn't need a lawyer; he needs an exorcist."

PRETRIAL PREP

Only the Old Wine Defense had saved the Lizard from prison thus far, but after two years of delay burdened with the Lizard's constant bitching, Wilkes was rather looking forward to trial, or more precisely, the end of the trial.

Given almost two years of delay, we had plenty of time to investigate the case, so during our remaining days until trial we worked on trying to improve the Lizard's appearance. One look at the Lizard by the jury and the presumption of innocence would evaporate quicker than a bead of water on a hot griddle.

Let me describe the Lizard's standard attire. Over a small Afro, he wore a gold-colored beret. On his left earlobe, a large gold ring hung like a tire from a tree limb. Gold mirrored sunglasses covered his beady reptile eyes, and a gold cigarette holder shot out of his mouth holding an always lit brown cigarillo.

His zoot suit was fluorescent gold, with the shoulders padded so heavily, it looked like he had huge breasts there. A black silk shirt, open to the navel, revealed his bare chest and a gold chain from which dangled the large round medallion. A needle and thread were emblazoned on the medal, at the bottom of which were the words "A Stitch in Time."

DRESS FOR SUCCESS

The Lizard looked just like a pimp. Wilkes knew that if he walked into a courtroom looking like that, we'd not need to bother with the trial. The Lizard's attire would be all the prosecutor, Miles Landish, needed. Wilkes ordered the Lizard to dress as straight as possible for trial, and the Lizard said, "Sure, baby. My bitches gives me the best threads, man, the best. I'll dude it up right, man. You'll see. Don't you worry 'bout a thing."

The Lizard kept us in great prolonged suspense on the first day of trial. What would he wear? No one found out. The bastard didn't show up for trial. Judge Yulburton Abraham Knott promptly revoked bail, issued a bench warrant for his arrest, and continued the trial for one day.

The next day the Lizard didn't show up again, and Judge Knott, over my friend's vehement protests, ordered us to start jury selection anyway. The judge noted a waiver-of-presence paragraph in the fine print of the bail release order; it said the defendant consented to trial in absentia if he failed to honor his bond release. Wilkes and I had never heard of this condition, but there it was in the form.

Nevertheless, for this part of the trial we were well prepared. Wilkes had brought in Ruby Fulgioni, a grandmother, part-time tarot card reader, psychic, and most important, our jury selection expert.

RUBY

Wilkes was one of the first attorneys to regularly use professional help in picking juries. Today, lawyers often use psychologists or sociologists, but Wilkes dismissed them as amateurs. "I can guess as well as they can," he'd say. But with Ruby it was different. She was a savvy old lady who could really pick 'em.

I loved watching her and Wilkes work a jury. She would listen intently to the answers each prospective juror gave, check their body language, and when the time came for the defense challenge, signal Wilkes to ax the bad ones and pass on the good ones.

No matter what the weather, Ruby wore a rumpled brown wool suit. Terrible eyesight forced her to wear purple horn-rims with red rhinestones embedded on the sides. The lenses were so thick, they could stop bullets. She spoke a blunt Brooklynese which made her sound like a brain-damaged palooka, but atop that squat, frumpy frame rested a first-rate brain that read minds as easily as Wilkes and I read the newspaper. Just the ticket for jury selection.

RUBY AND THE ROVERS

The first thing Ruby said when she saw the panel from which we were to pick the Lizard's jury was, "Dis looks like an SS convention, Wilkie. Wid deez bums you're in real trouble. Get the rovers woikin'."

Like any good psychic, Ruby insisted on all the information she could get on her subjects before she would perform a jury reading. We used rovers to mill inconspicuously in the halls, the court cafeteria, the bathrooms, and sit in the gallery listening to juror chatter, hoping to pick up clues to their biases. I would debrief the rovers and pass on the information to Ruby in time for her to signal Wilkes to ax or pass. For the Lizard's trial, the signal to ax was Ruby blowing her nose. The signal to pass was Ruby not blowing her nose.

Ruby quickly went through a box of Kleenex. She blew her nose so often and loudly that Judge Knott called Wilkes up to the bench during voir dire to ask, "Don't you think it a bit extreme to have a woman that sick in the courtroom?"

As Knott was suggesting to Wilkes that she be removed, Ruby leaned over to me and whispered her evaluation of our jury panel. "Deez guys is killers, Schoonie. Does goils is woise."

Ruby and the rovers soon left us. Not because of Knott's concern for her health, but because Wilkes quickly used up his challenges. Ruby couldn't help after that. She left, head down, muttering, "Piranhas, barracuda, sharks. Some choices." She paused next to Wilkes as she was leaving and whispered, "May God in heaven have moicy on da Lizard, Wilkie. Deez twelve could star in a horror movie as da monsters."

With Ruby's hand still on my friend's shoulder, the doors to the courtroom flew open and slammed against the walls. Everyone turned to see the source of the commotion. There, standing alone in the doorway, was none other than our tardy client, Hank "The Lizard" Gidone, smiling, wearing his gold beret, the gold earring, mirrored sunglasses, cigarette holder with small cigar blazing, and black shirt open to the navel showing off his bare chest and gold "Stitch in Time" medal-lion.

As he had promised, he did change his attire somewhat for this trial. His zoot suit was made entirely of sparkling white and green sequins. It was something Liberace would find gaudy.

HEY, BABY!

"Hey, man," said the Lizard to everyone. He spotted Wilkes and yelled, "What's happening', baby?"

"Seize that man!" yelled Judge Y. Knott. Two bailiffs obe-diently ran to the Lizard and grabbed him.

Ruby said to Wilkes, "Jeez, dat guy looks like a pimp, Wilkie."

Things were deteriorating rapidly, but Wilkes had a kind of cool under fire few trial lawyers possessed. I always thought that if during the middle of a trial an earthquake struck and swept the court out to the middle of the Atlantic, Wilkes would swim up to the judge and calmly ask for a dismissal.

Wilkes surveyed the scene before him. Seventy-two tarts were ready to kill his client from the stand. He had a jury that looked like the Manson Family. He had a judge who hated him and a client under arrest whom he loathed. Wilkes did the only thing any self-respecting lawyer would do.

"Your Honor," he said, "I move to approach the bench to discuss your most inappropriate and prejudicial comments." Putting a negative cast on the request was sure to get the de-sired response.

"That'll be denied," said Judge Knott.

"Then I must move for a mistrial based upon the court's transcending the bounds of a neutral and detached magistrate and joining ranks with law enforcement by arresting my client as he attempted to enter this hallowed hall of justice seeking his day in court."

WHY NOT?

Wilkes was pouring it on thick. And why not? The case was a loser. If the judge does something stupid and like a common flatfoot arrests your client, well then, sock it to him. And, more important, sock it to the record.

Knott, flustered by the motion and recognizing that my friend might have a point, thought a moment and then said to the jury, "Ladies and gentlemen, it appears that Mr. Gidone was late for court today and that perhaps I overreacted by asking the bailiffs to personally escort him to his seat beside defense counsel. This is not evidence of anything, and you are to disregard the incident entirely in determining the defendant's guilt, uh, and, er, or innocence."

He smiled to the jury and politely asked Wilkes and Miles Landish to approach the bench, where he began a memorable exchange with my friend.

"Despite what I just said, your client's bail is still revoked and the warrant for his arrest is being executed now. I should think the reasons are self-evident. If not, I shall make them so. He did not appear at all yesterday and cost the taxpayer a full day of court time. He shows up late today wearing what can only be described as a carnival sideshow outfit and looking like, well, like a pimp. Now, Wilkes, as for your filibustering motion, that will be denied. And any further accusations about this court joining ranks with the DA will result in a contempt citation."

MOTIONS

Wilkes was fearless in the face of judge-made threats. He had heard them so often, the judges might as well have been singing his praises. It meant nothing to him except as ammunition to be turned back on the black-robed monster. Wilkes said, "Thank you, Your Honor. However, given the court's deep-seated feelings of hostility, if not hatred, toward me, which the jury has undoubtedly picked up, I must request a mistrial in order that my client obtain other counsel who will not trigger such reactions from the bench.''

Knott was not one to fall for the judge baiting of John Wilkes. He said with considerable restraint: ''That'll be denied. Everything you said is absolutely false.''

Wilkes, however, was relentless. He replied, ''Well, the record now reflects that you believe I'm being mendacious about this matter. This is tantamount to a charge of perjury. I ask the court to recuse itself.''

''Denied! All of your motions are denied! Now, get out there and try this lawsuit!''

''Let the record reflect that the court is angry with me and red-faced and speaking angrily, almost in tongues, and loudly, too. The record should also reflect that in remonstrating me so vigorously, spittle is spraying from your mouth in my direction, which is very disagreeable to me. Finally, I am sure the jury has heard every word you said and is prejudiced forever against my client. I ask for a mistrial.''

I was surprised he didn't ask for an umbrella. Knott was spraying the place like a broken hydrant. He spit out, ''Denied! Denied! I'll hear no more. Now, get out there or I'll have the bailiff forcibly seat you!''

WILKES IN MOTION

''I move to have the jury questioned as to whether they will be affected by what they have just seen and heard,'' said Wilkes.

Knott grabbed the gavel and looked like he was going to hit Wilkes on the head with it, but pointed it at him instead and said, ''I refuse to hear any more from you. All motions previously made, just made, or to be made are denied.'' To the bailiffs—who were still attending the Lizard—the judge said, ''Gentlemen, would you come here a second?'' To Wilkes he said, ''Now, are you going to get out there and try this case or are these gentlemen going to have to move you after I cite you for contempt?''

"With all due respect, we've been up here about sixty seconds. All I'm trying to do is defend my client. I have to speak to do that. I have been respectfully urging, and I still urge this court to—"

Knott commanded the bailiffs with his favorite phrase of the morning: "Seize that man! Take him to his seat!"

Wilkes was taken by the arms and dragged to his seat next to the Lizard, who had just been dragged to his. The Lizard, shimmering in the glow of the court lights, smiled toothily to Wilkes and said, "Hey, man, you late for court this mornin', too?"

Judge Yulburton Abraham Knott then swept the air with his left hand and said with great affectation, "Let the trial begin."

8

The Trial of Hank "The Lizard" Gidone

You have the right to remain silent—for as long as you can.
NYPD TO HANK "THE LIZARD" GIDONE

You motherfuckers are wasting your time. Those bitches gave me money 'cause they wanted to. I got a high-priced motherfuckin' attorney whose gonna get me out of this mess 'cause no bitches lives with me unless they give me money, and I got five bitches working for me on the streets right now.
HANK "THE LIZARD" GIDONE TO THE NYPD

One of the loneliest, most helpless feelings a defense lawyer ever has in a hopeless case is while listening to the prosecutor make his opening argument. In the Lizard's case, the DA, Miles Landish, described in minute detail the brutalization of woman after woman. They had served as part of the Lizard's stable of "rental units." Now they were about to turn on their former landlord.

As Landish argued, I could feel the growing hatred of the citizens selected to judge our client. And the jury's hatred was not isolated to our client. They hated us, too.

Landish was a dark-spirited fellow who had an unimposing flabby presence which did not command much in the way of attention. But before a jury, he'd turn into a flabby, screaming demagogue—a mad avenging hulk for the state. Wilkes described him as D. H. Lawrence might have, "Sun extinct, and busy trying to put out the sun in everyone else."

On this day, we listened as Landish described, with regrettable accuracy, the life and times of our lowlife pimping client. He took particular delight in yelling out the Lizard's vulgar and incriminating statements made to the police just after his arrest (quoted at the outset of this chapter).

"Isn't it amazing," said Landish, "that such an alleged man could say such things and then have the audacity to come into this court and utter those two little words, not guilty?"

Wilkes sprang up to object. "It's not amazing when you hear the words were manufactured by police coercion. I object to his using the sacred plea of not guilty as evidence of guilt."

"That'll be overruled, counsel," answered Judge Knott. "Evidence will be introduced that your client pleaded not guilty and made the statements in question to the arresting officers."

MORE MOTIONS

Wilkes did try to suppress the evidence of the Lizard's statements made to the police just after his arrest. The theories of suppression were twofold: First, the officers arrested the Lizard in his own home without a valid arrest warrant. The warrant was issued for one "John Doe, aka The Lizard." The description of the suspect was equally spare, but on target: "Wears wild clothing. Looks like a pimp."

Sensing a problem with the brevity of their warrant, the arresting officers, as is routinely done on such raids, sought a consensual entry to the home and assent to the arrest so that the bust would be defense-attorney-suppression-proof.

The cops approached the Lizard's house in two squads, one half of the team covering the rear while the leader of the raiding party took his half to the front door and loudly announced his identity. From the back of the house he heard an equally loud chorus of his colleagues sing out, "Come on in!" And they went in.

This technique of warrantless house entries is known in the system as a "Mississippi Search Warrant" and has been the cause of many a judge declaring, "The officers say they heard someone say enter the house, and they reasonably entered in response. Motion to suppress denied."

Judge Knott said this, too. He said the entry into the house was legal based upon "apparent consent," and he said the rather cryptic arrest warrant was fine as written. Which prompted Wilkes to say, "Warrants are like sex. When they're good, they're very good. And when they're bad, they're still very good."

MISSISSIPPI MIRANDAS

Judge Knott also upheld the Lizard's subsequent statements to the cops as uncoerced and voluntary. Telling the Lizard he had the right to remain silent for as long as he could (known in the business as giving the defendant his Mississippi Mirandas) was "merely an accurate statement of the obvious," said the learned judge.

Wilkes responded testily that "the police statement was made to intimidate the Lizard by suggesting a physical response to his continuing noncooperation."

To this Judge Knott responded, "That is your speculation, Mr. Wilkes. Who am I to judge?"

At the close of the hearing, Wilkes made his usual eloquent pitch for suppression. Judge Knott responded with what would become his usual contribution to the case, "That'll be denied, counsel."

As we walked back to our office after the motion hearing, Wilkes was silent for the longest time. Then he finally barked out, "Marshall, Taney, Harlan, Holmes, Brandeis, Cardozo, and now Justice Yulburton Abraham Knott!"

"Is this a guess-the-one-who-doesn't-fit question?" I asked.

"No," said my friend. "I was commenting on one of the best arguments against Darwinian evolution I ever thought of."

"Or maybe Knott's a missing link, a throwback in time," I offered.

Wilkes just mumbled something about him being just like all the rest, and we marched in silence back to the office.

CLAPTRAP

After Miles Landish finished his opening statement to the jury, Wilkes was covered with twenty-four contemptuous eyes, all belonging to the twelve good and true citizens of the Big Apple sitting as the jury. As he rose to open to the jury, Wilkes leaned over and whispered to me, "They already believe he's guilty, Schoon. It's in their eyes. That belief is about as easy to eliminate as a bad case of the clap."

In his prime, John Wilkes was a spellbinding orator in court. He was so persuasive that many fellow lawyers joked that given enough time arguing before a jury, Wilkes could deprive them of their free will. Part of his skill, he said, was "the ability to act sincere. You've got to make the jury believe you care about the fate of the knuckle-dragging primate you may be defending. They know you know whether he's guilty, and if you betray even for an instant that he is, you're dead."

Of course, that is all well and good when you've got something to say on behalf of your knuckle-dragger, but the Lizard's case seemed absolutely hopeless. Seventy-two of his tarts were prepared to testify against him. On top of that, he had made a very damaging statement to the cops. Even I wondered what my friend could possibly say to this unfriendly-looking jury.

He stood before them in silence, perhaps only a foot from the rail that separated him from them. For several very noticeable seconds he was motionless except for his eyes, which made contact with each juror. Then he placed the palms of his hands straight out before him as if he were about to lean against an invisible wall and said, "What do you see?" After a moment's pause, he let his hands fall to his sides and began pacing slowly before the jurors.

APPEARANCES

"There is a story I like to tell about a Russian prince who went to military school and became the marksman of his class. After he graduated, he returned home. One day he came upon a village and noticed that one of the walls of the village was filled with bullet holes. Upon closer inspection, the prince saw that all of the bullet holes were grouped within small chalk-marked circles. The prince immediately concluded that this village had the greatest marksman in the kingdom. He summoned the head of the village and ordered him to find the marksman. Within a few hours, the man returned with a frail-looking little boy of twelve. The prince looked down at the boy and said in disbelief, 'You are the greatest marksman of this town?' And the boy said, 'Yes, sire.' With a rifle almost as big as he was, the lad marched fifty yards from the wall and fired three rounds into it. Then he calmly walked to the wall, located the bullet holes, and drew a circle around each of them.

"Ladies and gentlemen, the young prince learned one of life's basic lessons in that village. He learned that assumption is the mother of all screw-ups. Things are not always as they appear. Here, as we shall see, a lie is a lie even if monotonously repeated by seventy-two tarts. And it is still a lie whether Mr. Landish whispers it, states it, or screams it so loud as to be a public nuisance."

Wilkes stopped talking and returned to counsel table. The jury's hatred had diminished a bit. Some even seemed amused. Before Wilkes sat down beside the Lizard and me, he again shoved his palms straight out and said, "When I asked you what these were, many of you thought you saw my hands."

Wilkes then slowly turned each hand so that the jurors saw the back side. "But you were only half-right. You didn't see the other side. Remember that as you listen to the ladies of the evening testify. Remember that none of them is being prosecuted for their crimes. Remember the other side—the truth."

For saying absolutely nothing, my friend's short opening must have been effective, since Landish and Judge Knott were agitated by it. Wilkes's sincerity had at least dissuaded the jurors from taking the law into their hands right then by lynching the Lizard on the spot. Some of the carbon monoxide was out of the air. The only problem now was that we had the rest of the case to go, and Wilkes had set up juror expectations for something to controvert Landish's overwhelming evidence.

PARADE REST

I shall skip over the bad part of the case that followed—the presentation of evidence. For the most part, Landish's parade of rental units told the jury a tale of torture and bondage under the Lizard's grisly reign as their pimp. The picture painted was one Attila the Hun would have envied. Terror was the Lizard's means of keeping his stable of whores in line, and it was a very effective motivator of submission. Terror made the Lizard powerful, cocky, and semiwealthy (until he had his first fee chat with Wilkes).

The testimony of one of the fornicatrices, Coreen North, although more poetic, was so typical of the others, you could multiply it times seventy-two and have the entire prosecution case. In the most telling part, she said, "That there man, he turned mean on me. From my other pimp, I had only nice professional customers. I had a lot of them squeaky clean dentists fill my cavity. I had even big-shot lawyers discovering my loophole, while lovely young pilots nestled in my cockpit. I made a lot of money, honey. Then ol' Lizard come along and ruined my life. First he sweet-talked me real good with his promises and jive talk. Brags he's the man who keeps America moving. Says we all gotta have our ups and our downs. Promises I'm gonna be his number one woman. Shit, his words were just noise, man. All he gave me was rotten customers, a sore back, and a mouth full of Drano."

Wilkes's cross-examination of the ladies was as repetitious as their testimony on direct. Yes, they got immunity from prosecution for their whoring in return for singing in court against their pimp, the Lizard. Yes, they had many, many prior arrests and convictions, and most were on probation to some judge for prior tricks with one of New York's finest (who all too often made their undercover pinch after enjoying the fruits of the crime).

But there was a limit to what Wilkes could do. The ladies were united in their hatred of the Lizard and were keen on burying him. They also had a reasonable fear that if he got off, there would be paybacks galore. When Wilkes gave one an opening, she'd regale the jury with stories of how the Lizard cheated her out of her money, set her up with filthy johns, and beat her up when she complained. The horrific force-guzzled Drano and "stitch in time" stories epitomized my friend's failed attempt at impeaching the tarts.

After hearing all this testimony, Wilkes, hamstrung by the laws preventing subornation of perjury, presented no case himself. He simply noted after the prosecutor announced he rested, "Having heard no credible evidence against my client, we rest, too."

At this, Judge Knott leaned over his bench and said, "Mr. Wilkes, you evidently haven't been listening."

UNDERWATER

The Lizard had been listening; he saw himself buried in an evidentiary avalanche of guilt. The presumption of innocence, which at the outset of the case had stood as an impenetrable protective shroud around the Lizard, had vanished long before the final witness left the stand.

The Lizard sensed his nakedness before the jury; he didn't like the exposure one bit. As each of the tarts testified, he kept elbowing Wilkes, urging him to "kill that bitch." As more rental units testified, the Lizard grew angrier. He swore at Wilkes for not "destroying that lying cunt" on cross-examination.

By the time the last lady left the stand, the Lizard was so mad at Wilkes for not demolishing the fornicatrices, he picked up the water pitcher and poured it over my friend's head. He yelled as he emptied the pitcher on Wilkes, "I coulda made those motherfuckin' sluts look like liars! You in with the judge and his helper, the DA!"

This was the opening Wilkes was praying for. He asked to approach the bench, but Judge Knott, who was smart enough to anticipate trouble, stopped Wilkes in his tracks. He said, "The motion which I believe you are about to make is anticipatorily denied."

"Anticipatorily denied?" asked Wilkes. The words hit my soggy friend like a wet towel across the face, but he recovered from the blow quickly. Dripping wet, but excited by the prospect of now having something to work with, Wilkes said, "No, Your Honor, I wasn't making that motion. I was going to move for a mistrial in light of the assault on my person by my client. It is evident to me that even the fair ladies and gentlemen of this jury would be greatly challenged to wash this act of uncontrollable violence and obscene language from their minds."

Standing in the well of the court, his hair awash, his face dripping water on his yellow notepad which he held in his damp hands, his light-colored suit darkened at the shoulders from the water, Wilkes smiled for the first time since the trial began.

Knott was in a fix. He knew better than to continue to joust with my moistened friend in front of the jury. He said, "Yes, by all means, approach the bench and let us work it out." He turned to mug before the jury and say, "Didn't Isaiah say it best, 'Come let us reason together'?"

As Wilkes and Landish came toward the bench, Knott added, "And let us have the Lizard, or rather the defendant, up here, too." I came, too, as this was my role as cocounsel: to be ever present—seen but not heard. When we reached the bench, Knott's cool exterior came away. He was fit to be tied. He whispered loudly in the direction of Wilkes and the Lizard, "What the hell are you trying to do, lose us this case?"

The Lizard said angrily, "Say, man, my mouthpiece should have killed them lying bitches on cross."

Wilkes added, "And just what do you mean—'lose us this case'? Who's us?"

The Lizard was quick on the uptake. "Yeah, man, whatchu mean by that?"

Seeing his perfect case slipping from his grasp by the ill-chosen words of Hizoner, Miles Landish came to the rescue. "Of course, Your Honor obviously meant that the intentional misconduct we have just seen and heard from the defense team is a clear attempt to manipulate a mistrial and thus lose the case for all of us—the defense, prosecution, the court, the jury, and the People of the State of New York."

Knott appreciated the lead. "Yes, yes, precisely!" he lied. "Precisely! It was a completely nonpartisan remark, and I deeply resent the implication you are making, Mr. Wilkes."

In all my years of practice, I never did figure exactly what motivated judges to lie like that. It was probably a combination of the desire to avoid the embarrassment of being reversed on appeal for such stupid comments in a published opinion—thus daunting one's hopes for advancement to that very august court—and the dread of retrying the case the second time after it came back. Particularly if it meant trial with John Wilkes defending.

Knott continued his tongue-lashing of Wilkes. "How dare you challenge the court's integrity. Your insulting question is sanctionable, to say the least." Knott could have held Wilkes in contempt for his simple question of the judge's revealing comment, but the judge was too new to the bench and did not have the foggiest notion of how to do it.

He would learn.

Wilkes asked, "And my mistrial motion? Given what this jury just saw and heard, my client's right to a fair trial has been lost."

"That'll be denied, counsel," said Knott, using the inevitable line which like a thundering Greek chorus filled his courtroom after every defense motion. "He did it to himself, and we will have no self-help mistrials. We're in recess. Final arguments to the jury tomorrow at nine A.M."

PLEA TO THE JURY

I mentioned that facing a jury in the opening statement of a hopeless case is a time filled with fear and loathing. Only one moment is worse in such cases—final argument, especially when you haven't produced a scintilla of doubt about your client's guilt, and the other side has put on the perfect case.

Landish's final argument was just like his long and loud opening, filled with detailed accounts of damning facts and testimony. He closed with a line that summed up my feelings at the time: "After hearing this evidence, ladies and gentlemen, you almost feel sorry for the attorney who has to argue against it. It's a task comparable to bringing the dead back to life. Let's hear what Mr. Wilkes has to say, shall we?"

With that, Landish plopped his large behind into his wooden chair. All eyes turned to my friend, and as Wilkes rose to address the jury, he whispered to me, "Don't I even get a blindfold or a last wish?"

There was only one cherished issue to argue, one sacred subject which the defense must rely upon when the evidence is so one-sided and the jury looks like a firing squad: the prosecution's burden of proof beyond a reasonable doubt. For this, Wilkes uncovered a chart, the JOHN WILKES REASONABLE DOUBT ACQUITTAL METER.

RAW DEAL

"You didn't hear Miles Landish talk too much about this, did you?" Wilkes began explaining his chart and reasonable doubt. He did it in such a fashion that, if believed, would make the guilty verdict extinct.

"You see the levels of certainty I have labeled here and which ones correlate with a not guilty verdict. And you see on the chart examples of witnesses who usually carry with them a certain level of credibility. Well, the seventy-two tarts in this case are all at the very bottom, aren't they? They're there because their story's so pat—sure, pin it on Mr. Gidone, and

JOHN WILKES REASONABLE DOUBT ACQUITTAL METER

LEVEL OF DOUBT-CERTAINTY	TYPES OF WITNESS (EXAMPLES)
ABSOLUTE CERTAINTY	GOD, FEDERAL JUDGE
BEYOND A REASONABLE DOUBT	PRIEST, CLERIC
CLEAR & CONVINCING	FARMER
HIGHLY PROBABLE	TERMINAL CANCER PATIENT
VERY PROBABLE	GRAMMAR SCHOOL TEACHER
PROBABLE	HIGH SCHOOL TEACHER
MORE LIKELY THAN NOT	COLLEGE PROFESSOR
50–50	50–50
GOOD POSSIBILITY	LAW SCHOOL PROFESSOR
POSSIBLE	UNCORROBORATED EYEWITNESS, HONEST POLITICIAN
INFORMED SUSPICION	BURNED-OUT BUREAUCRATS, NEWSPAPER REPORTER
STRONG HUNCH	CASE-INVOLVED WITNESSES
MERE HUNCH	*NATIONAL ENQUIRER* REPORTER, PRESS AGENT
DISTRUST	ANONYMOUS INFORMANTS, PAID INFORMANTS, KNOWN PERJURERS, PROFESSIONAL SNITCHES, CODEFENDANT-ACCOMPLICES, USED-CAR SALESMEN, LUNATICS
*	

GUILTY (brackets: ABSOLUTE CERTAINTY through CLEAR & CONVINCING)

NOT GUILTY (brackets: HIGHLY PROBABLE through DISTRUST)

*Only his survival instinct prevented my friend from inserting the bottom-of-the-barrel category in its rightful place on the chart:

DISBELIEVE	Y. KNOTT, PROSECUTORS, AND COPS AT SUPPRESSION HEARINGS

no charges or probation revocation or sentences to jail for us. That's the deal they've received, and it's the raw deal they're handing Mr. Gidone. Does Mr. Landish really believe these ladies, who sell their bodies for fifty dollars, would hesitate at selling false testimony for their freedom? Are you prepared to rely on that kind of testimony?"

My friend put his hands to the wooden rail that fronted the two rows of jurors. "You know, ladies and gentlemen, when I was in the army, we had a story about reliance and doubt."

Landish jumped up and objected to Wilkes's reference to his old army days. Wilkes responded, "What on earth is the matter with me merely mentioning I was in the army? I certainly wasn't going to say that I served with distinction at the Battle of the Bulge and was wounded twice in destroying an enemy machine-gun nest, or received two Purple Hearts, the Silver Medal, the French Legion of Merit, the—"

Judge Knott cut off my friend and sustained the prosecutor's objection.

ON AND ON

Wilkes continued. He argued the motivation of each of the tarts to lie. He explained the Lizard's highly incriminating postarrest statements as "ambiguous and police-coerced." He hinted at the acceptability of prostitution—"These ladies belong to a profession older than my own, and I would daresay more respected"—in the hopes that a few jurors would refuse to convict on the ground that merchandising sex wasn't all that bad.

In the middle of Wilkes's argument, he asked the court for a brief recess to "rest his tonsils." I knew there had to be another reason since my friend could, if he had to, bellow for hours without the least strain on his voice.

"I've got an idea," he said. "When court reconvenes, I want you to be outside. After I argue for a few moments, rush in and hand me this note."

He handed me a blank, folded piece of paper. I knew my

friend well enough not to take time asking silly questions about it. I simply obeyed.

When court reconvened and Wilkes recommenced his peroration to the jurors, I bounded into the court and, looking quite serious, rushed to where Wilkes was standing before the jurors. As instructed, I handed him the note with great ceremony and sat down.

EYES TO THE DOOR

Wilkes carefully opened the note so as not to let anyone see there was nothing written on it and said, "Ladies and gentlemen! I have wonderful news! This has never happened to me in my entire career! My associate here, Mr. Schoonover, informs me that the actual pimp of the seventy-two tarts has confessed and is in custody. He will be coming through those doors any second."

Wilkes pointed to the two swinging mahogany doors in the rear of the courtroom. The jurors' eyes fastened on the doors. Knott looked, too. So did Landish. We looked and waited and waited and looked.

After about a minute, Wilkes said, "Ladies and gentlemen, no one will be coming through that door. I apologize for misleading you, but I did it to make a point. The fact that every one of you looked to that door indicates you still have a doubt, a reasonable doubt, as to the truthfulness of the tarts' testimony that my client was their pimp. And, I might add, you were not alone in looking. Even Mr. Landish and the judge looked. Even they have a doubt."

With that, Wilkes sat down. It was an interesting and well-exercised gambit by defense lawyers, first used, if my memory serves me, in France by an innovative lawyer who made the same mistake Wilkes did on this day.

REBUTTAL

Miles Landish got up to rebut Wilkes's argument. He was quite brief. "Yes, I looked to the door, but only to see if anyone would be foolish enough to come into this court to perjure himself. And you, ladies and gentlemen, looked out of curiosity. Anyone would. But there was one person who did not look. One person in this courtroom who knows that no one else could stand in his place as the filthy little guilty pimp!"

Landish moved over to the defense table and stuck his finger in the Lizard's face. "This man, ladies and gentlemen, this man's eyes never moved an inch. His head did not turn because he knows, as only he could, that no one would enter this courtroom because he is a guilty son of a bitch!"

I must say that was the best argument I ever heard Miles Landish make in all the many courtroom battles Wilkes and I had with him. Wilkes had made the mistake of failing to properly choreograph his client's eyes to move in the direction of the doors when he majestically pointed there in hopes that the fantasy pimp would burst through them. It's what occurs when you don't share your brainstorms with your client.

Landish was not quite done for the day. As the jury filed out to deliberate their verdict, he said, "Judge, we're concerned about the possibility of jury tampering during deliberations."

Knott gave a look of feigned concern. No one could believe this jury would be out long enough to be tampered with. Nevertheless, this was a ploy aimed at us, so the judge figured there was no harm in playing it out. "Shall we sequester the jury until they reach a verdict, then?" asked the sanctimonious bastard.

"It might be simpler," said the DA, "if we just sequestered Mr. Wilkes with his client in the lockup."

Wilkes was about to start into it with the two of them when we heard the bailiff yell out, "They have a verdict!"

THE SENTENCE

I shall not lengthen this tale to describe the rendering of the seventy-two guilty verdicts. Wilkes demanded a polling of each juror on each count, which led to the Lizard hearing himself pronounced guilty 864 times over the next two and one-half hours.

The Lizard's reaction was expected. He bolted for the door, as well he should have. At sentencing two weeks later, Judge Knott gave him seventy-two consecutive one-year sentences. An angry Lizard left the court with promises to visit Wilkes someday and give him one of his famous Drano cocktails.

After sentencing, Wilkes, never good at taking defeat even in the most hopeless of cases, was despondent. He sulked all the way back to the office. As we entered the Woolworth Building and waited for an elevator, I remembered Lawrence of Arabia's brave line and said to my friend, "There could be no honor in a sure success, but much might be wrested from a sure defeat."

Wilkes looked at me in disbelief. "Yeah," he said, "like what? All I wrested out of this loser was the experience of having the living crap kicked out of me. Lawrence of Arabia never defended a pimp like Hank 'The Lizard' Gidone in front of the likes of Judge Yulburton Abraham Knott."

He had a point.

9

J. Daniel Conway

America gives us a great opportunity if we only seize it with both hands and make the most of it.

AL CAPONE

Will I defend you? Will I defend you? I'll defend you to your very last cent!''

JOHN WILKES

"**O**ut of great suffering sometimes comes great good,'' I said to my melancholy friend. I was still trying to cheer him up, but he wasn't listening. He was still sulking a full week after the guilty verdicts in the Lizard's case. Wilkes hated losing trials. Even unwinnable slam dunks with clients he loathed. His ego had a hard time dealing with the searing rejection that comes with a jury saying, "Guilty. Guilty.''

But it was more than ego. It was also the despair. You throw yourself into an intense battle and despite your best efforts, lose so thoroughly. It takes time off your life. Most lawyers are trained for such defeat. Not Wilkes. He believed he'd always

win. This attitude helped him win cases, but it also made losing much more difficult to accept. And taking seventy-two
guilty verdicts was extra tough to swallow.

DESPAIR

Perhaps more than anything, however, guilty verdicts brought
Wilkes to the depths because he knew they were bad for business: ''You can produce acquittals out of thin air. You can win
sixteen ax murders in a row and be hailed as a forensic Hou-
dini. But lose one jury and you've lost it, you're a bum.''

As if to confirm Wilkes's worst fears, the first days after the
Lizard's guilty verdicts, our phone didn't ring. Not once.
Wilkes had me call the phone company every afternoon to make
sure our phone was still working, and he sank a little deeper
into depression when I told him the phones were fine. ''God!''
he said. ''You know your business is in trouble when you're
calling Ma Bell to see if the phones are still hooked up!''

On the third day, we finally got a jingle, but it turned out
to be an obscene phone call from one of Wilkes's ex-girlfriends.
''When you get caught for doing this, you'll need help,'' he
told the lady. ''Please give me another call.''

On the morning of the fourth day, Uriah Condo, our investigator, called to see if his bill had been paid for his work on
the Lizard's case. I told him the check was in the mail. In the
afternoon, a just-arrested former client called—collect from St.
Louis—to see if we could loan him a grand for bail money. I
didn't even tell Wilkes about that one.

ONE RING

The fifth day was a Friday. Wilkes was moping about the office
when at 10:30 A.M. the phone rang. The ring started a footrace. Wilkes sprang toward the nearest phone and had the
receiver to his ear before the first ring was complete. I ran to
the extension and had it to my ear just a half second later.

''Hello,'' we said.

"Help! This is J. Daniel Conway, president of Capital Ideas. I need a lawyer right now! I got investors pounding at my doors and some government guy trying to lay paper on me. This place is a madhouse! Can you come right now?"

Wilkes said, "Well, you're in luck. My trial folded this morning, so I've got a free day which I was planning to use catching up on my mail."

"I can pay immediately for your efforts. You won't regret representing J. Daniel Conway, Mr. Wilkes. I've heard you're the kind of lawyer I need. Now, please, if you could just get over here right now and deal with these pests, I'll make it worth your while."

"All right," said Wilkes, "but have your checkbook open. We'll be right over."

"Thanks a million," said our new client.

I took the address—the Chase Manhattan Bank Building near Wall Street—and Wilkes and I jumped into a cab and sped to the offices of our new client. When we arrived, the scene we viewed was pure bedlam. It looked like a food riot had broken out. Except none of these screaming people looked poor or hungry. There were doctors still in their hospital greens jumping up and down so hard that their gold pendants flew high above their blown-dry coifs and then crashed into their chests. Stock brokers were there, too. Their suit pockets, bulging from the mass of morning trading markers, were put to good use as padding as they slammed into one another while trying to work their way forward.

The noise level was unbelievable. It was like the uproar of the Giants' fans after Sunday's last-second loss brought on by a lousy referee's call. Dozens of loud, vicious screams pierced the air like fingernails on the blackboard: "Give me my money, damn you!" "Where's Conway!" "I'll kill the bastard!"

WILDCAT

One woman nearest us was clawing like a wildcat at the men in front of her. She threw her elbows at us as soon as Wilkes and I got close behind her. She probably was a nice-looking woman normally, but her face was disfigured with ugly rage. She spat out, "That asshole's gone and lost my money! That asshole's lost my money! He just threw it away!"

"Mr. Conway, I presume?" asked Wilkes.

"No, not that crook. I mean yes, him, too. But I really mean my ex-husband, the stupid jerk. He put our money, half of *my money*, into this snake oil salesman's scam. I can't believe it!"

She turned from us, looked to the front of the room, and saw something. Yelling an unintelligible primordial cry, she plunged into the crowd, elbowing two or three banker types out of the way, and squeezed through a few padded brokers, while deftly avoiding the flying pendants of the doctors at the front of the mob. Then she disappeared from our view.

My friend took his cue from this and plunged into the thick of it, with me right behind. It was only twenty feet to the front of the room, but we had to traverse a gauntlet of flying elbows, fists, hips, shoulders, Gucci briefcases and purses, and gold pendants. When we reached the front, we found our lady leader on the floor with her teeth firmly clamped on the neck of a writhing, cringing fellow who had to be Mr. Ex.

COUNTERPOINT

Wilkes jumped on top of a counter and started yelling for silence. He got nowhere until he screamed, "I'll get your money if you shut your mouths."

After a relative silence came, he said, "You want your money? Okay. Okay. Calm down. You people ought to be ashamed of yourselves. You're acting like a bunch of prosecutors who just lost a motion to suppress. My name is John Wilkes, and I've been retained to—"

"Retained? That bastard gave you our money!" screamed a broker. "Kill him! Empty his pockets!" I reacted quickly and gave the loudmouth a hard elbow to the gut, which doubled him over. Nobody else yelled at Wilkes, but not because they feared my deadly elbow—they wanted to hear good news about their money, and Wilkes was perfectly prepared to give it.

"You want your money, and you'll get it. But the Chase Manhattan, right here in this building, couldn't pay all its customers if they all went crazy and made a run on it in one day. Now, if you just give your cards to my assistant here, I promise we'll get back to you by phone in twenty-four hours. Nothing in the way of business will be transacted today."

YOO-HOO

Wilkes's powers of oratory carried the moment. J. Daniel Conway's clients all left me their cards—not without a few murmured threats—and filed out the front door. After they split, Wilkes tried all the doors off the reception area. They were locked. Then Wilkes sang out, "Yoo-hoo! They're gone. You can come out now."

We heard the clinking of keys on a chain, and the sound of metal rasping and locks being opened. Then a door opened and a man's head popped out of one of the doors. It was a big head, square in shape, topped with wavy salt-and-pepper hair. The face was flat and nondescript.

"Thanks a million for coming," said the talking head. "My name's J. Daniel Conway, president of Capital Ideas." Conway tentatively moved out of his room and surveyed the reception area to make sure no disgruntled clients were in striking distance.

"They're all gone," said Wilkes.

"God, those people send cold shivers up my spine," said Conway. "I've racked my brain trying to make their money work for them. What gratitude! They come at me like a bunch of wild dogs at the first rumor that their treasure's not safe and sound. Spineless cowards!"

CAPITAL IDEAS

"What's that?" I asked, noting what appeared to be legal process in Conway's hand.

Conway held the papers out before him. "This is a present from the United States of America. An invitation to attend their grand jury next week. And they want me to bring all my books. This'll ruin me."

Wilkes suggested we hear something about Capital Ideas, so we sat down in Conway's cushy office, and for the next few hours Wilkes and I listened as Conway described his unbelievably complicated financial business. From what I deduced, Conway took wealthy people's money, brilliantly invested it in stocks, foreign currency, commodities, and whatever else he felt was good for a buck at the moment, and gave his investors a whopping 30 percent annual return. It had all gone so very well the first year, said Conway, but recently he'd suffered a few reverses.

After completing his description, Conway asked, "Well, what can I do? I haven't enough money to give everyone a refund. Not even close to enough. And now there's this grand jury business. What's gonna happen, Mr. Wilkes?"

I SEE

During Conway's description of his business, Wilkes and I had quietly relaxed in chairs so plush, they felt like they were alive and hugging you. My friend closed his eyes, put his hands together as if to pray, and broke his silence: "I see many wealthy and powerful people becoming angry and wanting to take their vengeance. I see their lawyers swarming all over this place ordering their private investigators and accountants to search every document you've ever touched in their quest for money. I see subpoenas by the bushel and hundreds of civil suits. You'll be summoned to so many depositions, you won't remember what this office looks like. And you'll take the Fifth so many times, you'll not remember having said any other words.

"I see the story of wealthy, powerful, greedy people losing their shirts having great entertainment value. I see the paper-boys doing their usual Pulitzer–prize–winning investigation of you and your stable of investors. They'll follow you to work, photograph you receiving subpoenas, run through your garbage, and call you at all hours of the night for an exclusive—which is their lingo for an opportunity to get you to confess.

"I see the attention you get bringing on more government investigations than you would have thought possible. I see the bankruptcy trustees, the IRS vultures, the SEC and FTC snoops, maybe even some Secret Service types, all competing with the federal and state prosecutors for first dibs on your hide.

"Most chilling, I see a telephone-book-size, multicount indictment charging mail fraud, wire fraud, conspiracy, SEC violations, and tax evasion. It'll charge enough crimes to put each one of a cat's nine lives away for a century."

EYE-OPENER

Wilkes opened his eyes and looked straight at the now ashen-faced J. Daniel Conway. He continued, "the future poses many dangers for you, my friend, and you'll need the best legal advice your investors' money can buy."

Conway slumped in his seat at hearing Wilkes's grim prediction of the future. "Yes, yes, of course, and you're just the man for the job, Mr. Wilkes. I've heard a lot about you. Great lawyer, they say, tough as nails, sharp as a tack, a tiger in the courtroom."

Wilkes listened stone-faced as Conway buttered him in clichés. It would take more than that, much more, to retain the services of John Wilkes. My friend's fee-collecting philosophy—it is morally wrong to allow a client to keep his money—

meant it was empty-your-wallet time. Fee collecting for Wilkes was very much akin to a stickup. But Wilkes had his reasons. First was his wealth. Second was his desire to weed out the undesirables. "The client who pays the least complains the most," he'd say. "I hate whiners. Charge a bundle and you don't have many."

J. Daniel Conway reached into his suit for his wallet—the tenderest part of the human anatomy—and pulled out a check. He handed it to Wilkes. "I thought this might do for starters," he said.

Wilkes looked at the check as if it were a banana peel just pulled from the garbage. He tore it up and stood to leave. "Mr. Conway, I can work for myself for nothing and enjoy it much more than working for you at a loss." Wilkes turned to me. "Let's go, Schoon."

"WAIT! FOR GOD'S SAKE! Can't we even talk about this? Please have a seat. I've got an idea."

We returned to our seats. "Give me a figure," said Conway, handing my friend a pen and paper. Wilkes wrote six figures on the paper. Conway's eyes bulged as he read the paper. "I might as well declare bankruptcy as soon as I retain you."

"That's just the initial retainer," said Wilkes. "I'll probably need more as things heat up."

"You obviously love money, Mr. Wilkes," said a glum Conway (this from a man who had probably stolen hundreds of millions in the last year alone).

"Well, yes," said my friend, "Mr. Green and I are old friends, but it's like the prostitutes say, 'You get me off and I'll get you off.' Anyway, you can pay me now or pay everything to a bankruptcy trustee later and petition for appointed counsel. And let me tell you this. With your problems, you don't go to the free clinic."

Conway wrote a check for a sum I'd never imagined possible as a fee. Wilkes told Conway he'd be his lawyer, and we left. As we descended in the elevator, Wilkes said we were going straight to the bank at the lobby level to see if Conway was good for the money. "I'll be damned if six months from now we're gonna stand in line with the many creditors of J. Daniel Conway."

"Capital idea," I said as we skipped off the elevator into the lobby of the Chase Manhattan Bank.

10

Quito to Guayaquil

The female born criminal, when a complete type, is more terrible than the male.

CAESAR LOMBROSO

I can't be bought. But I can be rented.

JOHN WILKES

"**W**ould I let my own mother and father invest in Capital Ideas if I weren't certain of the security of this investment?"

Wilkes and I were in the swank offices of J. Daniel Conway listening to him sell another fifty-thousand-dollar investment opportunity in Capital Ideas. Conway was a great salesman. The psychological leverage he used to persuade his investors to part with their money was a wonder to behold. It was nothing short of a psychological kidnapping in which Conway coercively persuaded the investor to cough up the dough against the latter's better judgment. Wilkes was taking mental notes in hopes of using Conway's technique in future haggles over his fees.

"By my calculations, just this week you've lost a thousand dollars in interest income by delaying to make the investment. And I'm afraid you haven't much time left to make your decision. I've almost got enough investors to form another investment group, so you had best not wait too long to put your money to work. The train's leaving the station."

The investor looked worried about the train leaving the station without his money on board. He told Conway he'd have his check that afternoon. They shook hands as Conway said, "Thanks a million."

THE LIST

As soon as the investor was out the door, Wilkes asked Conway for the documents that had brought us to his office that afternoon. "Let's have the investors list. Yesterday we promised them we'd call them and set up a date for a status conference about their money."

Conway handed over a pile of papers with the name of just about every powerful politician and judge in the city. And sprinkled liberally among those names were ranking religionists—even our former client and con man, the Reverend Bob Smite—editors, journalists, lawyers, doctors, dentists, psychologists, realtors and stockbrokers, architects, accountants, prosecutors, police administrators, and most menacingly, a few recognizable big names from the Five Families.

Wilkes looked at the names and then looked at me. His eyes said, "Our thieving client's a dead man," but his mouth said, "Conway, are there any powerful people who haven't invested in your company?"

Our client, thinking Wilkes had just complimented him, grinned broadly, then broke into laughter. "Needless to say, all the beautiful people have come here to let me play with their money. Impressive group, eh, Mr. Wilkes?"

"I think you don't get my drift," said Wilkes. "Let me put it this way. I'll reduce my fee by fifty percent if you'll make me the sole beneficiary of your will."

MS. VIGILANTE

Conway flinched, but he didn't have time to respond with words. The doors to his office flew open. Standing in the doorway was the good-looking ex-wife of the doctor-investor we had met yesterday. The last time we saw her, she was on the floor of the reception area with her teeth well embedded in the neck of her former spouse. She had not been happy with his big investment (half her money) in Capital Ideas. She did not look happy now. But there was something different today. She still looked like a fashion plate—she wore a bright red Adolfo suit, black Hermes handbag and matching shoes, and short, dark hair which accented her high-cheekboned, pretty face, giving her that same *Vogue* look I noted yesterday. But today she also wore the hardness of a vigilante with blood revenge on the mind.

"I waited until noon for your call. I knew that was all bull yesterday. Aldo, get in here," she said.

ALDO

She was quickly joined by a giant gorilla of a man carrying the unmistakable outline of an Uzi machine gun in his hands. "This is Aldo," she continued. "He kills people for a living."

Wilkes slowly stood up. "Well, as I was just saying to Mr. Conway, a very serious conflict of interest prevents my representing him. Mr. Schoonover and I were just leaving."

"Sit your ass down," growled Aldo.

"You're both in this, like it or not. You may be useful to us," said the woman.

I now made my contribution to the tense confrontation. "Easy, now. I'm sure we can help you, even represent you for no fee." Wilkes glanced at me. "Let's avoid a tragic waste of lives here."

"Tragic waste?" hee-hawed our lady captor. "You know what a tragic waste is? Using good bullets on you three!"

Aldo gave a low grunt, which I interpreted as hilarious laughter. His boss continued, "Conway only knows me as Mrs. Dr. Donald A. McLean, the mad ex-spouse of one of his stupid loser-investors. You can call me Maude. I represent a few persons who have decided that they've had it with Conway and Capital Ideas. We came for our money."

Conway was sprawled in his thronelike chair as if he'd just

been dropped into it from a thousand feet. He began to mumble and slobber.

"What's that? Quit mumblin', man! Get your tongue together," said Aldo.

WORD SALAD

Conway managed a few intelligible phrases: "Don't kill. Please! I can, no shoot! I pay. What, how much?"

Terror ties the most agile tongue.

Maude responded, "The group of investors I represent are into Capital Ideas for one million bucks. Hand it over." She placed her outstretched hand under Conway's nose.

"Now!" barked Aldo.

"I don't, money like that, not here, what, couple hundred in my wallet, take you it, don't shoot, I get it, time," said (so to speak) J. Daniel Conway.

I could not help thinking that just ten minutes earlier, the now-blubbering president of Capital Ideas was deftly maneuvering a prospective investor into parting with his hard-earned capital with the adroit use of language. But here, our hero was reduced to a goo-gooing infant. Grace under fire.

"Perhaps I can translate, Maude," offered Wilkes. "Mr. Conway would be happy to fully reimburse you and the rest of your investors, except that at this moment he doesn't have a million dollars on him." My friend looked at Conway as he said, "Nevertheless, Mr. Conway would be delighted to take you to the closest bank and withdraw the cash necessary to take care of everyone." Conway nodded up and down vigorously.

STYLE

Wilkes picked up the papers that had the details of all of the investments in Capital Ideas. "If you'd just call out the names of your investors, we can determine the exact amount of the interest to be added to each investment and arrive at an agreeable total figure.''

The woman we knew as Maude smiled. ''I like your style, Mr., uh . . .''

''Wilkes, at your service. I was saying, since a conflict prohibits my representing Mr. Conway, perhaps I can be of service to you in a professional capacity.'' Wilkes rose to hand her the investors list.

''Sit your fucking ass down, Wilkes.'' This was Maude speaking. She was doing an excellent job resisting Wilkes's charm attack. ''You'll do what I want when I want. Aldo here hasn't pulled off a round on his Uzi in over a week, and he's dying to spray this place.'' She looked at the trembling J. Daniel Conway and said, ''Where's my goddamn money!''

QUITO

J. Daniel stammered the best he could, ''Not liquid money into money like francs and marks and yen, but like beef or cattle and commodities, and realty and businesses, and wait! Banco de Quito! Quito! A million for a rainy day!''

Maude frowned at Wilkes. ''Okay, Mr. Interpreter, what's he saying?''

''Mr. Conway says that he's out of currency arbitrage at the moment and heavily committed to the overseas commodity markets, also some industrials and land buys, and very little liquid moolah except, it seems, a rainy-day account in a bank in Quito, Ecuador. The Banco de Quito.''

NIGHT FLIGHT

Four hours later, as evening was about to fall, Maude, the *Vogue* kidnapper-terrorist, was at the wheel of a small Lear jet owned by one of her investors, and flying Conway, Wilkes, and me—all under the evil eye of Aldo and the snout of his ugly Uzi—off to Ecuador. We lifted quickly and sharply off the runway and soon saw the sun, colored an unfortunate bloodred, sinking into the distant horizon. As it disappeared, it left behind an orange-brown hue to backdrop dagger-edged black clouds.

The flight took twenty-six hours. Twenty-six hours in that tiny fuselage hopping from New York to Miami to Caracas to Quito. We never left the tiny plane. It was like being inside a hollowed-out wienie. And we never even got a look at Maude. Just mean Aldo and his Uzi. But at least he let us beat the terror and boredom with drink. Even Wilkes abandoned his usual teetotaling for the flight, hoping the booze would serve as a tranquilizer and put him to sleep. It didn't. For him, the trip lasted twenty-nine whiskey sours, and instead of quiet sleep, my friend turned into a chatterbox-drunk who took advantage of his captive audience to loudly critique anything and everything that came to mind. One of his choicer comments almost got us shot: "Hey Aldo, how long you been working for Buchenwald Bonnie? How much she paying you? Conway here's gonna double it, triple it, quadruple it. Hey, I know you can't be bought, but can't we rent you for a couple of hours?"

Aldo stuck the muzzle of his machine gun into my friend's mouth and said only, "Ready to eat lead?" This didn't shut up my drunken companion for long. He turned his critical attention to Conway: "Your investment company, my friend, was but an attractive rumor which ripened into reality only because no one was smart enough to check it out." Conway was too frightened to figure out my drunken friend's comment. He just looked at Wilkes as if he had said something profound.

THE CRITIC

The stream-of-unconsciousness monologue continued right up to the time Maude put us down on the pavement of some small, bumpy runway near Quito. By that time, Wilkes had criticized every book, law, state, country, movie, play, client, lawyer, judge, he had ever experienced. It was all drunken drivel, but Conway was impressed by the vast fund of knowl-edge maintained in my friend's sotted brain. "You should have been a critic," said J. Daniel.

"I am," slurred Wilkes. "Of life." As the plane came to an abrupt halt, my friend's eyeballs slid upward and disap-peared into his forehead. He fell sideways into my lap. Dead drunk.

Conway and I carried Wilkes to the backseat of a waiting car, and we sped off for a short ride to a shack on the outskirts of the city. Maude drove while Aldo kept his ever-present Uzi on us from the front passenger seat. No one said a word. After a day of hearing my drunken friend's babble, the quiet was ominous. I missed Wilkes's chatter. If we were to get out of this pickle, it would take all my clever friend's sober intelli-gence.

When we arrived at our destination and alighted from the car, I got my first good look at Maude in over a day. Somehow she had changed clothes. Now she wore a matching prewashed denim work shirt and jeans and a pair of sneakers. Although tired from the flight, she still looked (even in these clothes) ready for a cover page.

OFF TO THE BANK

"You come with me," she said, pointing to Conway. "We're going to make a withdrawal from the Banco de Quito right now. Aldo, cover the drunk and his friend till we get back."

And off they went, leaving me with the thought that Maude was tireless and beautiful and dangerous, like a black widow spider spinning her web.

We waited for three hours. I sat tied firmly to a rickety wooden chair while Wilkes snoozed away unbound and pros-trate on the floor. Aldo sat in a chair directly in front of the only door to the shack with his Uzi nestled in his lap. Finally, as darkness came, we heard a car roll up and soon saw Maude and J. Daniel Conway come in the door. Maude had her hands full. In one, she carried a small pistol. In the other, a suitcase with the loot. She dropped the money on the floor and pushed Conway toward Aldo. She looked exhausted.

"Tie him up," she said to Aldo. "What about him?" asked Maude, pointing to my unconscious friend on the floor.

Aldo said, "He's been out of it since you left. What're we gonna do with these guys now?" Aldo started strapping J. Daniel to the same wooden chair I occupied.

Maude moved to a corner of the room and slid to the floor. "We'll figure it out after I've had some shut-eye. I need some sleep."

As soon as the words left her mouth, who should leap to his feet, grab the suitcase full of loot, and shoot out the door into the darkness but my friend Wilkes! It was so quick and unexpected, Maude did not know it had happened until she saw Aldo jump for his Uzi and scramble out the door, yelling with apparent delight, "Kill the lawyer! I'll kill the lawyer!"

Maude grabbed her pistol and trained it on Conway and me. Her tired eyes betrayed a look of failure. There wasn't much point in keeping the gun on us since we were tied tight enough to cut off the circulation in our hands and feet. "Aldo better come back with the money," she said.

MA-OO-DAY

As I looked down the barrel of Maude's revolver, I thought of my friend on the loose with a million bucks and running for his life. I wondered why the hell he did it.

About an hour after Wilkes fled, a small Indian boy knocked on the door and said, *"MA-OO-DAY. MA-OO-DAY."* I took this to be Spanish for Maude. The boy continued, *"Una carta para MA-OO-DAY."* Maude backed to the door, still acting as if her bound captives might burst the rope bracelets that bound them and jump her. She took the note from the boy and read it. Here's what it said:

Dear Maude,

I couldn't trust you or Aldo to simply apologize and free
us after the money came into your custody. I have a plan
to trade money for hostages. Tomorrow morning the *autoferro* to Guayaquil leaves at 6:00 A.M. Put Schoonover
and Conway on it, and just before the train leaves, the
money will be delivered to you on the station platform.
No tricks. I'll be covering your every move till then.

Yours truly,
John Wilkes.

That night was one of unrelieved horror. After Aldo returned and read the note, he lobbied Maude for hours to kill
Conway and myself and then try for a kill on Wilkes at the
train station the next morning. For the longest time, Maude
was undecided, her better judgment clouded by exhaustion.
Finally she told Aldo her plan. There would be no killing. Aldo
kicked my chair in disgust at this. They would put Conway
and me on the train, but would not let it leave the station until
the suitcase was delivered. The money was what this was all
about.

I sighed in relief. Conway, who was strapped on top of me,
said, ''God, Schoonover, you've got bad breath,'' to which I
responded with a comment appropriate for our situation,
''Halitosis is better than no breath at all.''

RENDEZVOUS

We were at the train station at five-thirty the next morning.
No one had slept. Maude went in and bought two tickets and
ordered us on the train. We were to sit in the first and second
rows on the window side facing the station so Aldo could cover
us with his coat-covered Uzi.

The *autoferro* is a bizarre thing to behold—a school bus with
train wheels. It looks as out of place on rail tracks as a bear
running the hundred-yard dash. And it is small—there are only

thirty seats to be had—and when Conway and I climbed on board, the inside looked and smelled like an animal farm.

The *autoferro* is an Indian commuter, and the Indians evidently like to take their farm animals with them. I sat down next to a toothless old woman who had a hen tucked under each arm. Conway's seat-mate caressed a baby pig oinking in his lap. But the accommodations were of no matter. We still had Aldo's Uzi staring us in the face just ten yards away, and Wilkes and the money were nowhere in sight.

I saw Maude trying to talk to the train's driver, who seemed to nod very agreeably to her every word. With a minute to departure, he climbed into his seat and started his engine. With thirty seconds to go, he turned toward Maude, who was now by Aldo's side. At exactly 6:00 A.M. three things happened simultaneously: Aldo and Maude ordered us off the train; just as they did, the train started quickly pulling from the station. Then I heard Wilkes's voice from somewhere nearby: "A deal's a deal. Here's the dough." A suitcase fell out of the sky and landed hard on the station platform. It was tied with ropes and belts to keep its treasure safely within as it bounced to within a few feet of Maude and Aldo. They pounced on the suitcase and were frantically pulling off belts and ropes as the train rounded a bend and they disappeared from my view.

CAFÉ OLÉ

We chugged up and down the Andes for about an hour before the train's driver made a sudden stop in the middle of nowhere. He stood, turned to his passengers, and said, *"Diez minutos para café! Vamanos!"* With these words of instruction, he bolted out the door and began a dash for a tiny farmhouse about three football fields away. The passengers rose as one, farm animals and all, and joined in the footrace behind the driver.

"The coffee must be good here," said Wilkes, climbing down from atop the train top, where he had been hiding in the luggage rack. I was surprised and relieved to see him, but Conway immediately chastised him for putting his life in jeopardy. "You could have got us killed! Aldo almost shot us after he came back! You bastard! You're fired!"

Wilkes smiled. "And you're felony-dumb, my friend. The money in my hands was the only thing that kept Aldo from shooting you. Maude couldn't have stopped him; that was as easy to see as the nonrefundable retainer you paid me two days ago." Wilkes pulled a strongbox from the luggage rack and opened it.

THE MONEY

"It's my money!" yelled J. Daniel. "My money! It's all here. Mr. Wilkes, forget what I said. Thanks a million!"

"Not quite all of it," said my friend. "I had to pay the train driver to pull out fast as soon as I threw the suitcase to Maude and Aldo."

"But they'll still be after us," I said.

"I think not. I also paid the local *federales* to be at the station and watch closely as two dangerous gringo revolutionaries received an arms shipment right on the railroad station platform. I was good enough to fill the suitcase full of rusty *pistolas* last night."

"Great work, Wilkes!" said a gleeful Conway. He grabbed the strongbox and caressed it with the same affection that the old Indian on the train hugged his pig.

The balance of the trip to Guayaquil was not one of pleasure. It was incredibly slow. The *autoferro* is the only link many of the Andean Indian villages have with the world, and the driver of the *autoferro* is thus an important and popular local figure. He stopped at every clump of huts along the way (all unscheduled stops) and delivered mail, gossip, and goods— illicit, no doubt—in return for money and favors.

The trip down to Guayaquil is supposed to take ten hours. It took us sixteen. From the bare, rocky Andes to the hot, green, humid jungle plains near Guayaquil, Wilkes, Conway, and I sat planted in our bus seats enduring the smells, the animals, and the heat while waiting for our ordeal to end. Conway was the only one to voice anything positive during the trip. He kept saying, "That jungle green reminds me of my money. At least I got my money." Conway looked at my friend. "Maybe you should have charged me hourly, Wilkes. You could have billed all this. Ha!"

Not a very charitable comment to someone who just saved your life.

INTO THE ASS OF DARKNESS

We finally pulled into the station shortly after nine o'clock amid an incredible storm of flying cockroaches. Billions filled the sky. They were bird-sized and landed on or smashed into everything that moved. We were told by our train driver that this was an annual invasion in Guayaquil. "You get used to it," he said, "You have to. They're here for weeks."

Within minutes of getting off the train, we were all covered by the horrible insects. Conway, wearing a brown coat of the winged roaches, reverted to his terrified babble. "Bugs! Box! Let me out! Box! Bugs!"

Wilkes took this to mean that Conway wanted someone to take hold of the strongbox so he could use his hand to slap the swarming giant roaches away. Wilkes took the box.

"So this is Guayaquil," said my friend. "Gentlemen, welcome to the asshole of the universe." We surveyed the scene before us: the sky filled with billions of huge, man-eating insects; the city not even visible although just a few hundred yards away; the heat and humidity were suffocating. Wilkes said, "Men, if there's a hell on earth, I think we've just entered it. This is worse than the Tombs."

Getting into the city proper from the *autoferro* station requires a short boat trip across the Guayas River, a sludge-filled latrine separating the jungle from the city. As we crossed, I thought I saw icebergs float by. What kind of place was this? Had Mother Nature gone completely crazy here? As the bergs drew closer, I could see they weren't made of ice. They turned out to be

huge foam mounds of industrial waste. Even these were being
dive-bombed by the flying bird-roaches, which plunged like
kamikazes into the white cotton. So thick were the roach clouds
that we never saw the other side of the river. It made the trip
seem endless.

PAPERS

When our boat finally made port on the other side, we jumped
to the ground and into the bug-covered arms of a dozen uniformed men. "Papers, gentlemen?" said the one with the most
ribbons on his chest.

Having been kidnapped to Quito, we hadn't had time to get
our shots and passports. Wilkes said, "Did you capture the
revolutionaries, Colonel?"

"*Sí*, señor," said the colonel. These were the *federales* Wilkes
had sicked on Maude and Aldo in Quito. "Now, your papers,
señor. Perhaps in the box, no?"

"Ah!" said Wilkes. "You must want to inspect those papers!" A lawyer's greed filled the eyes of the colonel. "*Sí, señor!*" he said.

It took about an hour for the colonel to process our papers
by the age-old procedure commonly used on foreigners in trouble—confiscation—and to order us deported. We were taken
to the Guayaquil airport and put on a Braniff flight back to
the States. The flight's first stop was Quito, and who should
board but our former traveling companions, Maude, the fashion plate kidnapper, and Aldo, the Uzi-less hit man. Like us,
they were being deported as undesirables.

The next part of the flight was most uncomfortable as Maude
and Aldo continually gave us the evil eye. This prompted our
courageous client into action. At the next stop, in Bogotá, he
jumped out of his seat and said, "I have decided to emigrate.
Mr. Wilkes, you can wrap up my business and legal affairs in
New York. I'm going to pay a visit to my friend Señor Green

at the Banco de Bogotá. I forgot to tell you about a few other rainy-day accounts I've got down here. Adios!''

We never saw Conway again. Wilkes spent the rest of the long flight home chatting with Maude and telling her how her investors should retain him to get their money back while I spent my time watching Aldo's twitching trigger finger.

11

The Scumbag Speeches

> *These questions [by the judge], like questions put at trials generally, left the essence of the matter aside, shut out the possibility of that essence's being revealed, and were designed only to form a channel through which the judges wished the answers of the accused to flow so as to lead to the desired result, namely a conviction.*
>
> LEO TOLSTOY (FROM *WAR AND PEACE*)

> *The judges of this city are scumbags.*
>
> JOHN WILKES (FROM THE SCUMBAG SPEECHES)

I received the call from Wilkes about four in the afternoon. He was in court, I thought, trying the Paul Rinaldi pornography case in front of Judge Lester J. Throckton. Rinaldi had been a lifelong seller of dirty books. Many times during his career as a professional purveyor of obscenity, Rinaldi got arrested in a "smut sweep" made by New York's finest. Then Wilkes got into the act and beat almost all of the charges with his unusual First Amendment defense.

If he could not get them dismissed on pretrial motions, Wilkes took all the cases to jury trial, where he had tremendous success. He lectured the jury about all the martyrs in history who had sacrificed themselves to permit free expression in America. He told them about the Peter Zenger trial, of his great ancestor John Wilkes of England, and of all the other heroes of history who had fought for free expression. He quoted Voltaire—"I may not agree with what you say, but I'll defend to the death your right to say it!" Most of all, he carefully avoided saying anything about his client, Paul Rinaldi, and the filthy books which lay on the clerk's desk as prosecution exhibits.

Wilkes's favorite quote in these defenses—among many dozen he used in final argument to the jury—was that of Havelock Ellis, who said, "Without an element of the obscene there can be no true and deep aesthetic or moral conception of life. . . . It is only the great men who are truly obscene. If they had not dared to be obscene they could never have dared to be great."

This time Rinaldi was on trial for selling a strange little book from New Zealand which graphically expressed the pleasures of man-sheep bonding. It's American title was *Sheep Never Get Headaches*.

This was to be one of the last, if not the last, trials of Judge Lester Throckton before his eagerly awaited and long-overdue retirement. Wilkes knew it would be a tough case, because the judge hated porn almost as much as he hated Wilkes; and it didn't help much that Judge Throckton was psychotic.

On the phone, Wilkes's voice was barely audible. "Schoon," he said through a cacophonous background of inhuman howling and screaming, "come pick me up."

I had received similar calls in my career with Wilkes. I didn't have to ask his location. I knew exactly where he was.

"What did the old bastard throw you in for this time?" I asked, wondering what slight had prompted Throckton to hold my friend in contempt and put him in jail.

SLIGHT

"Not a damn thing!" howled Wilkes. "The scumbag was on me all day. I heard he hadn't had his shock treatment this week. His clerk assured me he had. The clerk said the old man's antsy 'cause he hasn't sentenced anyone to death for over two years, and with retirement coming, he's angry 'cause it doesn't look like he'll get the chance. So the son of a bitch took his frustration out on me."

It had been common knowledge in the legal community that Throckton was slipping into the abyss of insanity. If you appeared in his court, you knew. But complaints about him were to no avail as none of the other judges would take action to get him off the bench, or even put the guy out to pasture in some unimportant court where he could do no harm. They didn't act because the line between Throckton's conduct and theirs was so fine that they feared establishing any precedent by his removal—after all, it might be used against them. And anyway, if you put a black robe on someone, sit him high up on a throne, and let him rule, you can hardly tell the sane from the insane. With Throckton, there would still be surprising bursts of lucidity punctuating long periods of lost-in-space lunacy. If you focused on those moments of normalcy, the man was as sane as the president of the United States. Lately, however, Throckton's periods of clarity had been further apart. Most of the time, he was preoccupied with the subject of death.

Wilkes continued on the phone explaining what had happened. "During the pretrial motions, he kept asking if it was time to administer the rights to my client. I told him I had explained to Rinaldi his constitutional right to trial and cross-examination, but the old fart paid me no attention. He started mumbling the last rites!

"Well, I got pissed. I shouldn't have. The guy is really out of it. But what to do, Schoon? I gotta get him back to earth, so I respond in kind to his 'ashes to ashes' speech and quote the Scriptures back to him—Romans, two:one: 'Wherein thou judgest another, thou condemnest thyself; for thou that judgest doest the same things.' "

"That's pretty good scripture for an atheist," I remarked. "What about the contempt?"

"Didn't happen till the end of the trial. I'm amazed at my restraint, 'cause the peckerwood was on me, Schoon, really riding me all trial. Anyway, during final argument, I started reading from Rinaldi's book, *Sheep Never Get Headaches*, and telling the jury how it was a bestseller in Australia and New Zealand, when Throckton jumps all over me. 'None of that filth,' he says, 'You just stop it at once!' And I says to the hypocritical bastard, 'You liked it enough in chambers.'

"He cited me for that."

"For that?" I asked. "Given the provocation, it'd never stand up on appeal."

COUNT TWO

"There's more," he responded. "During jury deliberation, we got a note asking to see the illustrated porn books. They were in evidence as exhibits, so they had a right to 'em, but the old geezer said no. Then the jury sends out another note saying they're going on a strike until they get the books. This was too much for Throckton. He calls 'em out, finds 'em deadlocked, and dismisses 'em quick as a wink. Now, this is music to my ears, and I says, 'Thanks, Judge. Too bad you can't try Rinaldi again. Double jeopardy and all that. You can't eject the jury so easily. This is a case of premature ejaculation.' "

"That was citation number two."

I didn't think there was anything legally contemptuous in those words, but in Throckton's court there didn't need to be. He had cited lawyers before for nothing, although usually the contempt sprang from the nutty provocations of the demented jurist. In one trial, Wilkes was contempted for addressing him as "Judge" rather than "Your Honor." Throckton said calling him "Judge" was too familiar and did not confer sufficient respect due his office, so Wilkes called him "Your Highness" and "Excellency" the rest of the trial, which garnered more citations.

I thought of Throckton's coming retirement. He'd miss Wilkes.

COUNT THREE

"There's still more," said my friend. "Throckton started chewing out the jury, calling them names and telling 'em to take a laxative to cure their mental constipation. He told them that with such mental indecision they risked certain death on the highway going home this evening. I interrupted and told them that since they'd been dismissed, court was over, and they didn't have to listen to the judge's lunatic ravings."

My mind raced over the defenses to be asserted on appeal. Court was over, so it wasn't a direct affront to a judge. Merely a vigorous First Amendment exercise in retaliation for judicial misconduct. I asked, "Then what happened?"

"What the hell do you think?" Wilkes fumed. "The necrophilic son of a bitch threw me in the bucket! And he jailed Rinaldi, too, pending retrial. I want you to call every goddamn criminal court reporter and tell 'em to meet us in the press room for an important announcement. Now, get down here and throw my bail!"

PRESS CONFERENCE

"What'll I tell the news boys it's for?" I couldn't imagine the answer. Wilkes getting contempted was about as novel as the DA announcing he'd cleared a cop in a civilian shooting or our most recently convicted senator's announcement that he'd be vindicated on appeal. The news boys wouldn't show for that kind of dog-bites-man story.

"I can't say here," said Wilkes. "Just tell 'em I've got a big story, and if they're reluctant, tell 'em if they don't show, they'll never get a leak of privileged information from me again."

Having bailed out my friend so many other times, I was without equal in throwing bail. I got Wilkes and Rinaldi sprung without a hitch. We marched quickly to the press room of the Criminal Courts Building and entered the small, drab, smoke-filled cubicle. There sat five reporters—which was an amazingly large number since I had only called three. They were a lethargic, alcoholic lot generally, so I figured a couple of them simply hadn't left for home when the others came in on my request.

Adell Loomis, the *Times* reporter, was there. She was the exception to the rule of indolence which prevailed with the reporters who covered the courts. Most of them were spoon-fed all of their news from the press releases or authorized ''leaks'' of information from the DAs or the cops. This they gobbled uncritically, digested, and regurgitated to their papers as news.

Adell was different. Bright, tough, and always full of energy, she could pull a story out of the most tight-lipped attorney or cop. She actually investigated the information she got from whomever.

As far as I knew, she and Wilkes were no more than acquaintances. This would change over the next few months.

THE CANDIDATE

Wilkes wasted no time in getting to the point. ''Lady and gentlemen,'' he stated. ''I am announcing my candidacy for the position of justice of the Supreme Court of New York.'' Everyone, including me, went slack-jawed. Who could believe that Wilkes, the master judge baiter and hater, the man who spoke so often and so publicly about how the job made unfeeling monsters out of even the best of men and women, would think of putting on the robe? A Wilkes joke, I thought.

''Who ya runnin' against?'' asked one of the liquor-breathed reporters as the ash from his cigarette fell and scattered over his chest.

''I'm running for the seat vacated by that malicious scumbag who put me in the pokey today, Lester J. Throckton. As you gents know, the political hacks sold the nomination to his son, Judge Lester J. Throckton, Jr., of the Civil Court, so I'll be running against Junior.''

''Sounds to me like you're out for revenge against the old man,'' said Adell Loomis. She smiled at Wilkes and continued, ''You can't attribute the sins of the father to the son.''

GENES

"I don't attribute the sins to him," Wilkes answered, "just the genes. Two generations of idiots is enough! I'm tired of lunatics like Pops, or brainless nincompoops like Junior, or all the other evil merchants of human destruction running unopposed for the job.

"It's about time someone said publicly what we all know in truth. There hasn't been a contested election for judge in New York in memory. I'm gonna say why. Because it's a fix. The two political parties take turns auctioning off nominations to the highest bidder. This year it's fifty grand, and whammo, some jerk's a judge. And what do we get for it? The lousiest judiciary in the world!"

This wasn't a joke. It was a fit of bad temper. Wilkes was really going to run. He was crazy. He couldn't win against the well-financed efforts of the politicos, and he wouldn't want to unless he'd gone bonkers.

On the other hand, he'd make a great candidate. The paper boys and girl knew it immediately. The same quality that caused them to run to the courts where Wilkes was trying a case would make him a great candidate to cover. The press is attracted to irresponsibly outspoken, free-spirited gonzos because they like to write about controversial people who won't put the reader to sleep.

Wilkes looked like a candidate the media would like: His long, thin frame and brown, bushy hair gave him a commanding appearance; in his voice, strong, deep, and often booming, God gave him a wonderful musical instrument. His face resembled a Norse sea captain's—weathered, tanned, and inlaid with sky-blue eyes, a strong nose, and thin lips. All in all, Wilkes's rough-hewn handsomeness combined with his élan could make him a very appealing and charismatic candidate. If he wanted to be one.

LOST MARBLES?

As we made our way back to the office after the short press conference, I asked him if he knew what he was getting into. I needed to know if Wilkes had lost his marbles. He laughed at my concern over the expense of mounting a campaign. "Hah!" he chortled. "We aren't gonna spend a goddamn cent! I'll just hold press conferences during spare moments at the courthouse and accept invitations to speak. I've got it all figured, Schoon. We can't miss! I'm gonna get my name plastered all over the city! It'll be great for business!"

So that was it. Thank God! He didn't want to be a judge; he wanted to be rich! Getting your name in front of millions of New Yorkers in a futile campaign for office was the old, effective way for lawyers to attract clients. It was the time-honored formula for success: ink equals notoriety, which to the public equals supercompetence.

"But what if you win?" I asked, barely concerned about the possibility.

"No way," he retorted. "Impossible. I just wanna have some fun, drum up lotsa business, and let the folks in the Big Apple know what worms they got for judges."

RUBBER CHICKEN

And so it began in the most unlikely of settings—my friend just out of the slammer on bail and announcing for the judiciary. While the announcement had the taste of sour grapes to it—a lawyer held in contempt was mad at the judge—this was just fine with Wilkes. The less credible the candidacy, the less danger of actually winning.

Wilkes, as promised, limited his campaign appearances to luncheon speeches on the rubber chicken circuit: the clubs—Kiwanis, Rotary, Elks, Masons, and the like. They invited candidates to speak on their qualifications for office. For each appearance my friend delivered his now familiar Scumbag Speech.

The speech had three parts, each intended to serve his reasons for running: attracting business, having fun, and losing the election. The Scumbag Speech included introductory jokes recently stolen from the courthouse corridors, a vitriolic attack on the system that sold scumbags like Junior uncontested judicial nominations, and a little self-deprecation to insure defeat—"Winning? Oh, I don't think about that too much. I take too many prescription drugs to be a judge."

When Wilkes started campaigning in early September, the polls showed Junior 33 percent; Wilkes way under 1 percent; undecided 66 percent. The ratings didn't change much the first few weeks, which was just fine. Wilkes wanted the business, not the judiciary.

TROUBLE

Then a funny thing happened. *Times* reporter Adell Loomis fell in love with Wilkes and began writing pieces in the paper about "this delightful imp who has dared to challenge the Wall Streeters, the judiciary, and the party system of the city." Overnight, her laudatory articles made Wilkes into a legitimate contender. She gave him exposure and credibility. This attracted the interest of the other paper boys, who soon discovered that Wilkes was too entertaining a story to ignore. After all, without my friend, they'd have only Junior to cover.

Junior took the news of Wilkes's candidacy lightly at first. Each time a reporter asked him to comment on one of my friend's charges made in a Scumbag Speech, Junior refused comment: "I won't dignify that hooligan's scurrilous and false charges with a response."

Spoken like a true front-runner. Also very smart. Junior was a stiff on the campaign trail. He carried the courtroom around with him and acted everywhere like the vain, vacuous boob he was in court. Junior knew the less personal exposure he got, the better. The news boys and girls sensed this weakness, and after the first Adell Loomis stories, they did all they could to bring Junior out of his campaign cocoon by building Wilkes into a formidable contender. Obligingly, my friend gave them plenty to write about.

In late September, Wilkes addressed the Kiwanis Club.

HOME-COOKED HUMOR

"The chicken legs and asparagus were not bad. The meal reminds me of a story. Three asparagus are walking down the street when a giant head of lettuce goes out of control and runs one down. The uninjured asparagus, or asparagi, rush their mashed friend to the hospital, where he's taken to the emergency ward. Immediately the medical staff determines it's no garden-variety injury. It's serious. In time, the doctor, a grim-looking zucchini, comes out and says, 'He's gotta brokina stalk.' The two worried asparagus ask what this means. 'Itza so sadda,' says Dr. Zucchini. 'Heeza gonna be a vegetable for da resta his life.'

"So it is with Junior," said Wilkes. "It's in his defective genes. Like father like son. He'll be a vegetable for the rest of his life."

On September 30, the polls read: Junior 40 percent; Wilkes 7 percent, Undecided 53 percent. In early October, Wilkes appeared before the Rotarians.

PLAIN SPEAKING

"People ask me why I'm running for judge. Not for the usual reasons, I can assure you—like winning, or power, or a lifetime of fixed tickets. And I'm not one of those legislator-refugees from Albany who join the judiciary seeking a retirement home or a hiding place from an indictment.

"Nor am I Mob-connected. Yes, ladies and gentlemen, our two parties have auctioned off judgeships to the Mafia. They sell judgeships in this city like madams sell sex. Neither party discriminates based on race, color, or creed against any purchaser of a judgeship as long as they have the dough. Right now I can think of six Mob judges on the bench. There would be eight, but the dons put a couple in the river last summer for conduct unbecoming a bought-and-paid-for Mob judge—finding two Mafia soldiers guilty as charged.

"Which reminds me of the story of the jet full of lawyers on a nonstop flight from here to London. The plane runs into terrible weather at the midway point and loses an engine. The captain announces that they must lose weight if they're to stay aloft. The panicked passengers hurriedly throw out everything they can, but they still lose altitude. 'Not enough!' cries the pilot. 'We've had it!'

" 'Not so!' yells a plucky French lawyer, who runs to the door, proudly bellows, 'Viva la France!' and jumps to a watery grave. 'We're still going down,' the pilot announces. 'I'll do my part,' says a courageous English barrister. He goes to the door, yells, 'Long live the Queen!' and follows the Frog into the Atlantic.

"But the pilot screams, 'No good! No good!' As the plane continues down and nears the water, two other lawyers, an American and a Mexican, run to the open door. They pause and eye each other as if to say, 'After you.' Suddenly the American grabs the Mexican, throws him out of the plane, and screams, 'Remember the Alamo!'

"Well, that maneuver saved everyone on board and is now known in aviation parlance as a Mexican standoff."

MOMENTUM WITH THE MASONS

By the second week in October, the Scumbag Speeches and media attention started something you could feel: Momentum—the Big MO. The polls showed Wilkes with a 20 percent share of the vote; he began drawing big crowds to the lousy chicken lunches. People wanted to hear the outrageous Scumbag Speeches.

Reporters now followed Wilkes-the-candidate around the courthouse seeking interviews, which he gave freely and used to pump up himself and downgrade Junior. The polls had my friend both flattered and worried. "Damn," he said proudly when he looked at the latest glowing *Times* article by Adell Loomis. "This is getting serious."

I told him he had better speak with Adell, and he said he would. I don't know what he said, but it did not have the needed effect. All I know is that they became lovers and her articles became more glowing. Wilkes countered by escalating the nastiness of his Scumbag Speeches to try and make himself less appealing.

In mid-October he spoke to the Masons:

"My opponent claims to be a clearheaded candidate. I concede this. Junior's got nothing in his head. It's completely clear. He's so dumb, he asked me the other day where he was supposed to put his armies once he was elected to the Supreme Court. I told him to put them in his sleevies like all the other judges."

Wilkes then read from a recently published exposé which showed that forty-nine of fifty candidates for judicial office in 1968 had the backing of both parties. To get such dual endorsement, a candidate pays his fifty grand and the path is cleared to a judgeship. "These are the same judges who convict people and send them to prison for price-fixing and restraint of trade," Wilkes said. "These guys are so crooked, when they die they'll have to be screwed into the ground.

"Ladies and gents, Masons and Masonettes: Junior and the Politicians, New York's all-steal band, have been cheating us, using their positions of trust to make a bundle. We gotta throw the scumbags out!"

Loud cheers rang out. A couple of Masons stood, then the whole bunch of them jumped up as if sitting on tacks to applaud my friend.

MIXED SUCCESS

Wilkes's attempt at dampening his popularity by escalating the rhetoric failed, but it was great for business. Clients came in such numbers, we had to refer half to other lawyers—for a modest referral fee, of course. In fact, by the third week in

DO YOU WANT A
CRIMINAL LAWYER
WHO MAKES HIS LIVING
DEFENDING CRIMINALS
TO BE YOUR JUDGE?

THINK ABOUT THIS BEFORE YOU VOTE!

ELECT

JUDGE LESTER J. THROCKTON JR.
Your Friend, Your Neighbor, Your Kind of Judge

October, Wilkes was within easy striking distance of Junior (40 percent to 30 percent).

The days of Junior and the politicos ignoring my friend were now over. They launched a massive media counterattack aimed at painting Junior as the next Cardozo and my friend as a corrupt underworld mouthpiece.

Wilkes realized he was getting into a sticky wicket. "Christ!" he lamented. "If Junior's going to this trouble to win, I'm in deep shit. I might win, Schoon. I've gotta stop it."

But he was dancing on the razor's edge. He had to keep up a legitimate candidacy or face media disapproval and the possible loss of business. At the same time, he had to pop his swelling balloon of voter popularity to lose the election, but his ego would not allow too big a loss. He loved being loved by the masses. He elected not to pop the balloon—just let some air out.

Wilkes spent a whole night writing a new Scumbag Speech for the Croatian Alliance luncheon. The purpose—to offend every segment of New York society by an outrageous talk which would guarantee his defeat. Here's how it went.

GRAND FINALE

"Sorry I couldn't eat your delightful chicken in peanut butter sauce. I can't stand the idea of a cock stuck to the roof of my mouth."

These were the first words Wilkes spoke to the huge audience. The Croats were in shock. They didn't know how to react. Insult humor had not yet come into vogue in the fash-

ionable nightclubs of the city, and the Croats were totally unprepared for it in a luncheon political speech.

Wilkes was only warming up. Grinning with satisfaction, he
continued, "I heard the women of this area recently quit using
vibrators." Wilkes paused to scan the baffled audience and
then served up the punch line: "Too many chipped teeth."

I cringed. That ought to do it. He'd be lucky to get out of
here alive. The discourteous crudity could only be taken as a
horribly tasteless and sexist insult. Right? Wrong! Insult humor was born over the plates of peanut-covered chicken and
Croatian laughter.

"And do you people know what they call a Puerto Rican
with a vasectomy?" Wilkes continued. "A dry Martinez."
More laughs.

On it went. The more ethnic groups, religions, races, creeds,
and political parties Wilkes slandered, the more laughs he got.
The Croats loved it.

"What's green and flies over Germany?—Snotzis." More
laughs. The Croats laughed. The paper boys and girls laughed.
Only Wilkes and I didn't laugh. The more he tried to insult
everyone, the more he failed. Everyone enjoyed the speech.
He was a huge success.

LUBE JOB

A week before the election and despite his hara-kiri attempt,
Wilkes pulled even with Junior in the polls. Junior and the
politicos, of course, were not oblivious to which way the Big
MO was going, and panicked. They challenged Wilkes to a
debate on election eve. Wilkes versus Junior. No holds barred.

We couldn't believe it. Wilkes quickly called a press conference to announce his acceptance. "God! I feel great," he said
jokingly to the assembled newspeople. "My hangover's in re-
mission, business is booming, and Junior wants to debate. I
accept the invitation on behalf of my brother and sister lawyers
of this city. And I'm gonna ask Junior at the debate the most
important question of this campaign."

One of the paper boys asked what the hell he meant by that, and Wilkes answered, "Well, Junior's got a reputation in the civil court as being serviceable, which means if a lawyer greases him, he gets a Cadillac for a result instead of an Edsel. It's called a 'lube job' in the trade—you pull into chambers, and Junior holds out his hand and says, 'Fill 'er up.' "

"So what's the big question for Junior?" asked Adell Loomis.

"Well, for those of us who are occasionally tight on cash, we need to know if the scumbag takes BankAmericard."

—— 12 ——

The Candidate Meets Sal Minchinzi

Those studies of mine . . . were designed to fit me for the law so that I might gain a great name in a profession where those who deceive the most people have the biggest reputation.
CONFESSIONS OF SAINT AUGUSTINE

Per Scaluzzo assai brutta si cunchiusi, centudeci pallottuli chiummusi in corpu. ("It ended up badly for Scaluzzo, 110 bullets entered his body.")
CONFESSION OF SAL MINCHINZI

Election week was as exciting a time as I ever experienced with Wilkes. So much was happening: Wilkes in the papers every day, most times on the front page; a troupe of media types following him around, eager to hear an unprintable joke or a derogatory remark about "Junior," otherwise known as Judge Lester Throckton, Jr.

My friend's colorful accusations and aspersions produced that familiar manifestation of a hard-fought American political campaign—the multimillion-dollar libel suit.

SUE THE BASTARD

Junior's civil suit didn't faze Wilkes a bit. He immediately ordered me to file a counterclaim for double what Junior was demanding. I asked on what grounds we would sue, and Wilkes responded, "File on behalf of the taxpayers. We want the taxes

Throckton didn't pay on all the unreported income he took in bribes the last four years. And file a motion for the prick's deposition. Subpoena his tax records. And tell him to bring his crutches."

"Why the crutches? You gonna break his legs?"

"No. Tell him that after I've finished with him, he won't have a leg to stand on."

Obediently, I filed the counterclaim and the motion. As Wilkes instructed, I also served the newspapers with copies so that we would get more ink. "Never miss an opportunity for free advertising," Wilkes often told me, "especially since it's unethical to take out ads like the dentists do." The papers gave our countersuit page-one coverage, complete with a picture of Wilkes holding the legal pleading I had written and a crutch he was going to give Junior.

Wilkes was feeling thoroughly triumphant that final week. He had already accomplished his campaign goal of drumming up more business than we could handle from the campaign publicity. And as he said he would, he did it without spending a nickel of our money. He had fallen in love with Adell Loomis and was having a rollicking good time mercilessly attacking the judicial system and its black-robed judicial clowns with room-temperature IQs, to say nothing of the vile monsters like Blugeot, who were too eager to dispense punishment for the pure pleasure of it.

A favorite line was, "Pregnant rats don't bear cute little kitty-cats, so don't expect honest judges from the womb of this city." It was so thrilling to hear him speak his mind without inhibition, and so publicly. In no other way could you be free to say such things about judges and not be disbarred.

PERFECTION

It all seemed too perfect: Wilkes skyrocketing from nowhere to catch Junior in the polls; business booming beyond all expectation; Wilkes catching on as a media darling. I can't count the times a newscaster would come on the tube and say something like, "Wilkes says judges even fix city parades. Film at eleven."

There was one campaign goal, however, that Wilkes was failing to achieve: losing. I guess it was during that final week that I began to suspect that he might want to fail in that regard, that he might not mind winning. I could see it was getting to him. You can't be in trial for three months and not come to believe in your cause at least a little bit, and Wilkes, a lawyer's lawyer, couldn't help but believe he'd have been a better judge than Junior. But then, anybody would have made a better judge than Junior.

My concern that Wilkes's ambition was getting the better of him wouldn't last long. The events of that final week put Wilkes back in line so that by election eve, he was trying so hard to lose, you'd have thought his life depended on it. Matter of fact, at the time, it did.

BOB'S CALL

On the Tuesday before the election, I got a phone call from the Reverend Bob Smite, our gold-toothed—with a diamond inset—client from 1962 to 1966. His sodomy charge Wilkes killed with a textbook application of the Old Wine Defense. When we knew him, Bob was just a local huckster with a small following, but in the four years since then, he had become "God's Man of the Hour," the fourth wealthiest Holy Roller preacher man in the U.S.A.

Bob caught on because of his flim-flamboyant style and his attractive message—God wants everyone to be rich. Especially his preacher man.

In the years of his rise to success, Bob attracted one or two million followers to his Church of Ways and Means. He became "God's Deliverer of Cosmic Abundance," "The Way to Heavenly Health and Wealth," "The Healer of Indigence." He was to religion what Wilkes was to the law.

We hadn't heard from Bob since his case was dismissed, so his call was a surprise. After an exchange of greetings, he said,

"Winnie, I've never forgotten the inspired services you and Johnny delivered in my hour of need. I'm gonna pay you back tonight."

"How's that?" I asked.

"Just watch the show at eight tonight."

"The what?"

HOLY GHOST HOUR

"Why, Winnie, you mean you haven't been watching 'Reverend Bob's Church of Ways and Means Holy Ghost Hour' every Tuesday night on channel forty-five? Every week I do a new sermon. Jeez, I've done some good ones. Probably my best was last week on the last buffet that the late J.C. had with the boys."

I interrupted God's Man of the Hour to squeeze in a question. "What're you going to do?" I couldn't see how Wilkes fit in to his Bible stories.

"It's a surprise. You just watch tonight."

That evening, I had to almost sit on Wilkes to get him to watch "The Holy Ghost Hour." He was working on cases and complained he had no time to watch a boob on the tube. I appealed to his vanity. He didn't want to miss a televised testimonial to his lawyering ability delivered by another satisfied client. Reluctantly, he sat in his leather chair and joined me as channel forty-five's Deliverer of Cosmic Abundance appeared on the screen. "This better be quick," he warned.

THE APPARITION

Bob appeared standing alone on a pedestal elevated above an ankle-deep mist covering the stage floor. As the camera moved in, Bob stood in prayerful silence in his stunning white three-piece suit, white patent leather shoes, white shirt, and white tie. Only the bloodred rose in his coat lapel broke the alabaster purity of his ensemble. The camera continued to close on Bob until his powdered, meditating puss filled the screen. Bob opened his eyes and sculpted an angelic smile, revealing his famous gold tooth with the diamond inset, which unleashed a light show of golden sparks.

Wilkes said to the TV, "You look like hell."

"My children," Bob said in his childlike, smarmy voice. "Bless you for tuning in tonight. With your continued support we're saving the lost, whatever the cost. Your financial blessings have made it possible to put God's riches in the hands of the deserving."

"And who could be more deserving than the Reverend Bob Smite?" said Wilkes.

"So keep those love offerings coming in, children. Let's fill God's bank account and give Him the money-muscle to knock old Satan out for good." Bob swished the air with a left hook and a right uppercut.

GIVE TILL IT HURTS

"When's he gonna get to it? Christ, I don't have all night!" Wilkes fidgeted in his chair and swung his body so that his back was on one armrest and his feet over the other. For the next forty-five minutes Bob said, "Give me your money" in so many different ways, he could have written a book of synonyms on the phrase. Wilkes, restless and impatient, hated it, but I appreciated the showmanship and convincing way Bob persuaded the gullible to part with their dollars for nothing in return. It reminded me of Wilkes's final arguments to a jury.

With fifteen minutes left in the "Holy Ghost Hour," Bob said, "And now, children, it's Healing Time, praise the Lord." Wilkes groaned at the thought of further delay, but I was pleased to see that Bob had kept Healing Time as part of his act. Laying hands on the arthritic, the brain-damaged, the bodies racked with disease, Bob would summon all his holy voodoo and dispense miraculous cures. There aren't many places left on earth where you can see this.

"I can feel the surge!" Bob raised both arms to heaven. "Glory be to God, His goodness is within me! Hallelujah! I can feel it! I am His instrument! Hallelujah, watch Him work His miracles!''

Two skinny women in pink muumuus appeared escorting a thirty-year-old man described by Bob as blind, deaf, and dumb since birth. Bob grabbed the man's shoulders and tried to look sincere; instead, he looked like Liberace about to go two out of three falls with Gorgeous George. ''Think of it, children! Thirty years on earth in darkness and silence!''

Wilkes said, ''The man's a fool to want it any other way.''

HEALING TIME!

Bob raised his right hand, placed it on the man's forehead, closed his eyes, and meditated. In a few seconds he said, ''Geeeeeezz-zuhs! Geeeeeezz-zuhs! Lord, life's short-changed this man; he's due a refund. Amen.'' He looked to the man, whose shoulders he held. ''Say, Geeeeeezz-zuhs! Say, Geeeeeezz-zuhs!'' He shook the man. ''Say, Geeeeeezz-zuhs!'' The man said nothing. Bob took his right hand and covered the trembling supplicant's head with it and violently pushed him off his feet into the arms of the girls in muumuus. ''Glory be to God! Hallelujah! Praise Baby Jesus! Believe! Feel! Mend! Heal! Rise and say, Geeeeeezz-zuhs!''

The man rose quickly—pushed by the girls in muumuus. ''Geeeeezz,'' he whispered. Then louder, ''Geeeeeezz! Geeeeeezz! Geeeeeezz!'' Bob embraced him, and the muumuu girls whisked him off camera. Bob, looking stage right, the direction where the man exited, shouted, ''Children, this man believed, not in me, but in Him! Hallelujah! He gave from his pocketbook in order to earn the rewards of the Lord's heavenly stock. Hallelujah!''

''Bullshit,'' said Wilkes.

SCREEN TEST

''We've had so much success with Healing Time on the show,'' said Bob, rubbing his hands together, ''that many of you out there have written requesting that we use the miracle of television to give His healing touch a chance to reach you at home. So, children, yes, you out there in TV land, I want you to bring me your sick babies, your wounded limbs, your lame animals, why, even bring your broken appliances up close to the screen and we'll just let the Lord's Deliverer of Cosmic Abundance work his miracles. Praise the Lord!''

Wilkes and I giggled as Bob put his hand up to the TV camera and began shouting, "In the name of Geeeeezz-zuhs! Reach out, Lord; give the viewers the golden treasure of earthly health and heavenly wealth. Come on, Lord, hand it over! In the name of Baby Jesus! In the name of the Three Rich Kings of the Orient! Glory Hallelujah! Children! I feel the surge!''

Bob's hand shook. "I feel His glorious majesty moving within this flesh and blood and out through these mortal fingers; I feel the power leaving me and moving out through a million miles of wire and through the air and into your homes, children. Believe! Feel! Mend! Heal!''

Bob pulled his hand down and slumped exhausted and sweaty into a divan wheeled out by the muumuu girls. "Well, folks, that about wraps up another show, but before I close, I want to says something real important.''

"Son of a bitch! At last!'' said Wilkes.

PUNCH LINE

"You know, it costs money to put on this show and run our money missions all over the world. We've put our earthly treasure where our faith is. Won't you help me build the Lord's paradise here on earth by just donating a tenth of your yearly income? If you call our eight-hundred number right now, I'll send you a free copy of my popular book *Why God's Children Don't Pay Taxes*. It'll tell you how to make your home a parish of the Church of Ways and Means, thus making all your worldly expenses tax-deductible. Didn't I tell you the Lord would provide? Glory be to God.''

By my watch, the show had less than sixty seconds left, and

not one word about Wilkes. My friend looked at me like I'd just robbed him of his last hour on earth. Then Bob spoke again.

"Finally, friends, as you know, this is election week, and I want to tell you that a member of our church is running for the Supreme Court."

"What!" Wilkes jumped out of his chair and stood in disbelief in front of the TV. He kicked the wooden TV cabinet.

"His name is John Wilkes, a lawyer who has done a world of good for me and many others. He doesn't save souls, of course, but he's saved many a rear end. Hee hee. So when you go to the polls, friends, vote for my friend and yours, John Wilkes. He's on God's team. God bless and good night."

AN INTERRUPTION

Bob's endorsement cut Wilkes's rage to a few muttered epithets. There wasn't time for much grousing anyway, because a knock on the office door made us forget all about the Reverend Bob. "Who the hell could that be at nine P.M.?" asked the Church of Ways and Means' new candidate for the Supreme Court.

I walked to the door in the reception area of the office. "Probably just another reporter," I said. I opened the door and found a swarthy man impeccably attired in black—the suit, the shirt, the shoes, the sunglasses, even the hat cocked to the right. Only his white tie and the purple hanky in his breast pocket broke the theme. I am prone to instant first impressions. My initial assessment was that this was no reporter. This was the Mob.

"You Wilkes?" His voice was strong, deep, and gravelly.

"Who wants to know?"

"I'm Frank Bollo, and I'm carrying a message to Wilkes from Sal Minchinzi."

GREETINGS FROM THE BOSS

"I know of Mr. Minchinzi," I said respectfully. Indeed I knew of him. He was the most powerful Mafia boss in the country, head of the infamous Five Families, *Capo di Capi*, Boss of the Bosses. Men like Costello, Luciano, Genovese, Gagliano, Profaci, Mangano, and Anastassia jumped when he said move. When he spit, these guys swam; he was that big. No one was more powerful or feared. He had thousands of soldiers ready to do his bidding without questions. Anyone who broke the rule of obedience to the don (*e a lu so capu sempri ubbidiente*— "always obedient to the chief") slept with the fishes that night.

Yes, I knew Minchinzi, and my knees began to shake. And where was Wilkes, the man Frank Bollo wanted to see? "Mr. Wilkes isn't in at the moment," I lied. "I'm his partner and would be happy to deliver the message to him."

Bollo handed me the note. "Tell Mr. Wilkes it would be a good idea to accept the invitation. And no artillery." Bollo stood in silence in the doorway as if to emphasize his point. I think he was staring, but I couldn't see through his lenses. After a few seconds, he turned and walked down the hall.

THE LETTER

Before I could close the door, Wilkes was out from his hiding place and opening the note snatched from my sweating, nervous hands. I looked over his shoulder as he read the message:

> Dear Mr. Wilkes,
>   As you know, I am very interested in the government of this city and am desirous of talking to you to see if you are the kind of candidate I can support for the Supreme Court. Please come to my house tomorrow night at eight.
>   Yours in Good Government,
>   Salvatore Sciortino Minchinzi

Wilkes turned to me. His eyes were wide and unfocused, and he gulped audibly before saying, "Jesus, the American Bar Association didn't even give me the courtesy of an interview before they endorsed Junior." It was a joke of desperation.

"I wonder what it's all about," I said. "After your Scumbag Speeches about judges on the Mob payroll, I can't believe they want you. Junior's gotta be their boy."

Wilkes looked at the note again. "It's obvious. Junior's already on their team. The don wants to make it clear to me that I'd better take a dive in the last round and let Junior win."

"In other words . . ."

"I'm gonna be made an offer I can't refuse."

Wilkes went to the credenza and slid the door open just enough to withdraw my bottle of Jack Daniels. He slowly unscrewed the cap, lifted the bottle, and chugged at least a half pint. He stood waiting for the effect to take hold, and when the room began to sway, he dropped into the nearest chair, bottle in one hand, note in the other.

Wilkes, usually a teetotaler, was worried, as he had every right to be. When the number one Mob man in the country beckons, you come. There was no refusing unless you wanted to be fitted with cement shoes and spend eternity in the East River. I went over to my friend and interrupted his trancelike staring at the floor just long enough to pull the bottle from his hand. At the moment, there seemed no better way to deal with the problem than numbing the medulla.

WAITING FOR BOLLO

The next morning Frank Bollo called to say that he would pick Wilkes and me up at seven for the ride to the don's home. This cheered Wilkes somewhat: "It means they probably won't kill me. They don't like to make messes in their own homes." Wilkes was grasping at straws. He knew such rides often didn't reach their destination.

The mood was grim that day as we waited for Bollo. It was like waiting for a jury to return a verdict in a hopeless case. Wilkes was half-panicked. He refused all press interviews; he took no phone calls; he wouldn't even talk to Adell. He spent the afternoon pacing his office, cursing himself for getting into this predicament and babbling on and on about Minchinzi. He was like a fly in a spiderweb.

Bollo's black Cadillac pulled up in front of the Woolworth Building, and we went down to meet it. On the way down in the elevator, Wilkes continued his soliloquy about Minchinzi. "He's responsible for more executions in one year than the worst South American dictator. And do you know what his record is? One conviction for grand theft auto when he was a kid, and one arrest ten years ago for—get this—registering to vote; for being a felon who registered to vote! They indicted him for doing the only socially responsible thing he's ever done in his life! Of course, by this time, he was much too big for the likes of the DA's office. They dismissed the case shortly after the prosecutor was found castrated."

"I remember that one," I said. "The papers made a big deal about that one. Poor guy died without a will or testicles."

"It's what the Mob means when they say, 'He died intestate.'"

THE AUDIENCE

Bollo said not a word to us during the thirty-minute trip through Manhattan and over the bridge to the Bronx. It was dark, so I couldn't see much of the house as we pulled into the driveway except to note that it was huge, surrounded by a tall iron grille fence, with snarling dogs roaming the grounds. Bollo escorted us into a small anteroom, patted us down, and disappeared. In a few moments he returned. "The don will see you now."

He led us through a grand hallway and into a moderately sized room off the gigantic, beautifully appointed living room. I was struck with the darkness of the room we entered. Only

one small lamp with a low-wattage bulb was on to illuminate
the entire room. The heavy floor-to-ceiling maroon curtains
shut out whatever light could have come in from the outside.
As my eyes adjusted, I could see that the walls were covered
with huge religious pictures in ornate gold frames. I recognized
a few El Grecos and wondered if they were originals. The irony
of Don Minchinzi as a religious killer-crook struck me so funny,
I almost laughed aloud.

Next to the lamp was a thronelike overstuffed chair which
held the stout body of Don Salvatore Minchinzi. "Mr.
Wilkes," he said, "itza pleasure to meet you. Pleaza, you and
yer friend, sitta down."

ON THE SPOT

Wilkes and I found our way to the sofa that was directly across
from Minchinzi. Bollo pulled up a wooden chair and sat to the
don's right. There was an unnatural silence, like in an elevator
full of strangers. Then the don said something in Italian to
Bollo, and Bollo said that the don felt more comfortable talking
in his native tongue, and so he would interpret. "The don has
a few questions to ask you."

The fat man and Bollo talked for a few minutes in Italian.
Then Bollo asked Wilkes, "The don wishes to know if you
have ever represented anyone from the Maranzano Family."
Maranzano was Minchinzi's hated enemy and archrival for
power over the Five Families that ran New York. Just the year
before, the two gangs had gone to the mattresses in a struggle
for supremacy over the Mob. Minchinzi won, but his rival
lived, and the don was still wary of him. I heard him say to
Bollo something about *"un confidenti di la famiglia Maranzano."*

"Never," replied Wilkes.

"Fine," said Bollo. "The don is also concerned about your
fitness to be a trial judge. He wants a judge who is reliable,
with an unblemished reputation and intelligence. You fit the
latter requirements, more or less, but the don is worried about
your reliability."

RELIABILITY

More Italian exchanges between Bollo and the don. We knew exactly what the don meant by "reliability." He meant that when one of the Family soldiers came before the court accused of some heinous crime, the reliable judge delivered a reasonable-doubt acquittal. It was a joke around the courthouse about the Mob judges. They delivered a reasonable doubt for a reasonable fee.

Wilkes said nothing, and Bollo continued, "The don hears things that displease him about your campaign speeches. He hears you talk about judges on the Mob payroll. He wonders if what he hears is accurate."

"Well," said Wilkes, "uh, er, ah, I may have made a few jokes on the subject, but nothing serious, and let me say that—"

The don leaned forward over his tummy and cut Wilkes off: *"Non scherrare giovantto ardita! Rassettarsi la testa o su famiglia na sira torno dintu senza ali!"*

Bollo interpreted. "The don says you are a daring young man who shouldn't joke about such things. You should keep your mouth shut or one night your family will come home very sad."

DISMISSAL

The don looked Wilkes over with a slight scowl on his face and said, *"Stu travagghiari ti fa mali."* Minchinzi gave a look to Bollo which meant the interview was concluded. Bollo informed us that the don appreciated our coming to the house and that he would now be giving us a ride home. He quickly ushered us out without an exchange of good-byes to the don. It wasn't something we forgot. You don't worry about such niceties when you think you're going to be shot.

We were in the car and back on the road before Wilkes could ask Bollo what the don's last words were. Bollo said, "The don has concluded that this kind of work, the judging, is not good for you.''

We knew that the don had not been pleased, but this was cold and ominous. Wilkes and I exchanged glances of concern. I wondered if we were going to make it back to Manhattan and half expected Bollo to pull out a .44 and blast us right there in the car. But nothing happened. Instead, as Bollo pulled in front of the Woolworth Building to let us off, he said, ''Mr. Wilkes, I think it would be a very good idea if you lost the election.''

Wilkes got out after me and turned to Bollo. ''I've been trying to do just that for the last three months.''

''Try a little harder,'' said Bollo. He floored the Caddy, wheeled it into the Broadway traffic, and disappeared into the night.

13

Wilkes *v.* Throckton, Jr.

There are so few trial judges who just judge, who rule on questions of law, and leave guilt or innocence to the jury. And Appellate Division judges aren't any better. They're the whores who became madams. I would like to be a judge just to see if I could be the kind of judge I think a judge should be. But the only way you can get it is to be in politics or buy it—and I don't even know the going price.

MARTIN ERDMANN, *LIFE*, MARCH 12, 1971; SEE ALSO *IN RE ERDMANN* (1973) 33 NYS 2D 559

COURT: *Next case. Motion to Evict.*
TENANT: *I ain't paying no rent till he gets the rats. . . .*
COURT: *Think of them as pets.*
TENANT: *. . . and fixes the leaks in the roof.*
COURT: *Try using an umbrella.*

FROM THE COURT FILES OF
JUDGE LESTER J. THROCKTON, JR.

The morning after our audience with Don Minchinzi, I busied myself in the office shuffling papers, reading new appellate court opinions, answering correspondence—anything to keep my mind off the death threat of Sal Minchinzi, Boss of the Bosses. Nothing worked. I kept thinking of machine-gun bursts from passing cars, or a couple of thugs emerging from the shadows, and Wilkes—Wilkes! I looked at my watch. It was past two in the afternoon. He was supposed to be in hours ago. Thinking of Minchinzi, Frank Bollo, and machine guns, I called Wilkes's home number. No answer. I called Adell's. No answer.

SEARCH AND SEIZURE

I ran out of the office and began a methodical search of every bar and restaurant within walking distance of the Woolworth Building. At half past five, I found Wilkes at the Guadalajara Café facedown in a bowl of slop. He wasn't moving. I gave him a little pat on the back and said his name. He popped up for an instant—his eyes sunken and dark like two holes burned in the snow—then his head plopped noisily back into the bowl. I pulled him out before he became the first man in history to drown in a bowl of chicken noodle soup.

Here was John Wilkes—indomitable courtroom guerilla fighter, terrorizer of prosecutors and their witnesses, slayer of overwhelming trial odds, judge baiter and hater, sometimes teetotaler and prescription drug abuser, prankster and imp, lover of laughter, money, and acquittals, premier self-promoter, and leading candidate for the Supreme Court of New York—as far down in his cups as I'd ever seen him. I half carried him back to the office.

JAVA TALK

After six cups of coffee, Wilkes started coming around. He was lying on the sofa in the reception area, bleary-eyed and haggard from his night of boozing and aimless walking about town. The first coherent thing he said was, "We gotta do something about Minchinzi before he makes good on it."

I agreed. "We've gotta make it clear you're doing your best to lose the election."

"I've been thinking of nothing else all night. I gotta plan that can't miss," he replied.

The plan was in two parts, the first aimed at popping Wilkes's balloon of voter popularity. I was to let slip in an "off the record" story with a preselected, slimy, untrustworthy reporter—of which there was no shortage in New York—that our own poll showed us slipping badly in voter preference because of Wilkes's "drug problem." Wilkes knew this was the kind of story that would spread like wildfire in the media—bad news travels fast—and that such a scoop would prove irresistible to the reporter we picked. So what if it was off the record? It was news, wasn't it?

What surprised me was the swiftness with which the plan paid dividends. An hour after the call, I started getting heckled by paper boys wanting confirmation. I answered, as Wilkes suggested, in a way to make sure they'd absolutely believe the rumor about the poll was true. I said, "No comment." To others I said, "Have to take the Fifth to that," or even better, "We unequivocally deny it."

PHASE TWO

Phase two of the plan was more desperate, but more certain to kill Wilkes's chances in the election. At ten in the morning we marched to the Criminal Courts Building, where Wilkes had a suppression motion scheduled for a client in a drug possession case. We spotted Narcotics Task Force Officer Pete "The Flake" Tchamkoff, the state's star witness, standing out in the hall. Like any cop who'd been taken apart on the stand by Wilkes—and my friend had carved up Tchamkoff on numerous occasions—Tchamkoff hated him.

"Hi, asshole," says Wilkes.

"Beat it, prick," says Tchamkoff.

Wilkes maneuvered himself directly in front of the cop, reached in his briefcase, and pulled out his file on the case. "I just wanna ask a few questions about your illegal arrest, unlawful search, and the rubber-hose job you did on my client to get his statement. By the way, Tchamkoff, do you own your home?"

There was nothing to provoke a cop, especially a crooked one like Pete the Flake, like the threat of a lawsuit. Most coppers would rather empty death row than face ten dollars of personal liability for their misconduct. Tchamkoff had often uttered the policeman's credo: "Better ten guilty men go free than I get a lien on my house."

Wilkes's threat to Pete the Flake was thus ill received, and Tchamkoff's anger unrestrained. He grabbed Wilkes by the lapels, pushed him across the hall, and screamed every obscenity in the book. Wilkes dropped his file and briefcase in the struggle and fell to the floor to pick up the debris. Something very unusual rolled out of the briefcase.

EUREKA

"Aha! What do we have here! I don't believe it!" As Wilkes scrambled to put his files back in his briefcase, Tchamkoff lifted off the floor a small cellophane bindle of white powder. "So the great John Wilkes really is a dope fiend! I don't believe it! Son of a bitch! It gives me the greatest of pleasure to announce that you, prick, are under arrest."

Tchamkoff was in ecstasy. He cuffed Wilkes while he was still on all fours, stood him up, frisked him, and led him off to the holding tank. I went downstairs to arrange bail.

Everything had gone as planned.

As planned, you ask? Did the Great One and old Schoon take leave of their senses? All this to avoid a Mob hit? Why not just withdraw from the goddamn election?

Good questions. But it was too late to withdraw. Wilkes's name couldn't be stricken from the ballot, and if he quit, he'd still probably win given his lead in the polls that final week and all the media hype which pictured him as the next Harry Truman, a give-'em-hell, tell-it-like-it-is underdog about to clobber an Establishment stuffed shirt.

We had to make sure not only that Wilkes lost, but that Lester Throckton won. Only a disgrace, a colossal embarrassment, or a monstrous indiscretion would do, and we figured a felony drug bust would do it all.

THE REAL THING

It was real Peruvian cocaine that Tchamkoff picked off the floor that morning. Thoughts of using baking soda or some other drug substitute in the bindle were dismissed as too dangerous. The coppers might do a field test, and that would blow the whole bust. So that morning Pete "The Flake" Tchamkoff seized one gram of the purest snow then being sold on the streets of New York.

Pete Tchamkoff got his nickname "The Flake" because he was one of many New York cops who practiced the art of flaking a suspect. This happened when Pete grabbed a guy he thought was a crook or whom he just didn't like. If the guy happened to be clean when Pete made his ill-timed, illegal arrest and search, Pete "flaked" his suspect, that is, planted official police contraband stolen out of the police evidence locker on the poor soul. Then he would seize it and make the arrest. All legal for court.

Flaking was going to be our defense at the trial to save Wilkes from the slammer. It was why we picked the Flake as our cop to make the bust. In the meantime, however, Tchamkoff's bust was necessary to save Wilkes's life.

SCANDAL

The news of Wilkes's arrest made headlines that afternoon. This ended any chance of his election, the news boys said. Throckton naturally held a press conference to call for Wilkes's immediate withdrawal from the campaign and, given the "overwhelming evidence of guilt," his resignation from the bar—this from a man who took an oath to uphold the constitution's presumption of innocence.

Although he was exactly where he wanted to be, Wilkes was not happy with his predicament. Sure, his candidacy was lost and his life insured by that fact, but there was the prosecution looming, which was no sure thing to beat even with Pete's reputation for flakery. And now we were sure to lose business.

It was with such mixed emotions that we retired that evening both too tired and demoralized to go home, refusing to answer the dozens of calls that poured in, but confident that our miserable plan was working. Throckton would win. Wilkes would live. Sal Minchinzi would be pleased.

The next morning I got up and got the paper, not letting myself outside our office for more than a minute for fear of being mobbed by reporters and evil-wishers. When I opened the *Times*, I expected to see the lurid headline "WILKES CAUGHT ON DOPE CHARGE." Instead—and to this day I still can't believe it—I read this:

NY COP INDICTED BY GRAND JURY

FOR PLANTING EVIDENCE.

LATEST VICTIM JOHN WILKES.

DA REFUSES ALL CHARGES ON JUDICIAL

CANDIDATE.

Story by Adell Loomis

The Knapp Commission investigators have turned up yet another crooked cop in their ongoing investigation of police corruption. Peter Tchamkoff, Sergeant of Detectives for the Narcotics Task Force of NYPD, was the subject of a 57-count indictment unsealed by the special grand jury yesterday afternoon. The grand jury, according to prosecutor Turk Villon, has been looking into Tchamkoff's activities for months. Villon said the jurors heard testimony from hundreds of witnesses before secretly indicting Tchamkoff over a month ago. "We saw a definite pattern. It's called flaking, planting evidence on a citizen to make an arrest and assure a conviction," said the prosecutor.

When asked about the sensational arrest of Supreme Court candidate John Wilkes, Villon said, "It's what got us to go public with the charges. We wanted to continue our investigation to catch others, but after the Wilkes arrest, it was clear to us that this cop had to be stopped. Everyone knows of Tchamkoff's dislike for Wilkes. It was the same old thing. Hopefully it won't disrupt the campaign."

New York District Attorney Frank Hogan has refused to process any complaint on Wilkes. "All we can do at this point is tell the public no charges have been filed and hope that Tchamkoff's criminal conduct does not affect the campaign," he said in a press release issued at 6 P.M. last evening.

As for Wilkes, he is in seclusion and has made no statement concerning the bizarre events which led to his arrest, release, and vindication in just eight hours.

SHOCK

When Wilkes got up and read the story, he went into shock. He dropped the paper and said, "Of all the rotten luck, I can't even get arrested." Then he disappeared into his office. Those were the only words I heard him say for the next three days.

Just as well. During those three days while Wilkes wallowed alone in the depths of a black depression, he received an anonymous daily telegram, each a chilling reminder of what was in store if Wilkes defeated Throckton on November 2.

The first was almost humorous: ENTER EAST RIVER MARATHON BREATH-HOLDING CONTEST NOV 2ND! BEAT WORLD RECORD HELD BY JUDGE CRATER!

The second continued the watery theme: WHAT'S THE DIFFERENCE BETWEEN A FISH AND YOU-KNOW-WHO? ANSWER: ONE SWIMS, THE OTHER DON'T.

The third was equally ugly: NOTICE OF LIQUIDATION: NOV 2ND. I tore them all up before my friend could see them.

DEBATE

On the fourth day, I convinced Wilkes to go home and clean up. It was election eve, the night of the debate between Wilkes and Throckton, our last chance to do something to throw the election. Despairing and depressed by the prospect of inevitable victory, we drove to Founders Hall, where the battle of the candidates was to take place.

Walking into the hall with Wilkes, I expected to see a mostly empty cavern, with a few political types and reporters maybe filling the front row. Instead, it was like a Knicks play-off crowd. The place was packed with thousands of loud, back-slapping, laughing people, swilling liquor from the no-host bar, obviously having a good time.

ANXIETY

Wooden chairs were moved about to enable groups of friends to circle and chat. Occasionally a chair folded as it was being moved and fell flat on the hardwood floor with a BLAT! that sounded like gunfire. Wilkes and I jumped instinctively at the noises. Our eyes wheeled about the room, looking for the assassin sent by Minchinzi. Even the soft pop of falling plastic liquor cups—and thousands fell that night, making the place sound like a huge popcorn machine—had us thinking of the smoking muzzle of a silenced machine gun. Within minutes, we were both drenched in a stinking, nervous sweat.

I don't know why we worried about the don that night. Not when we could worry about the sickening green fog which hung in the air of the hall like poison gas. Everyone was smoking like tobacco prohibition started at midnight, and there was no ventilation to carry out the choking fumes.

THROCKTON SPOTTED

Through the haze, Wilkes noted something and elbowed me to look in the area of the hall just beneath the stage. There was Lester Throckton, Jr., in a receiving line shaking hands with everyone coming within arm's length. Junior's movements were mechanically brisk, sudden, and jerky, as if meeting real people was completely unnatural to him. If he were naked, he couldn't have looked more awkward and out of place.

Wilkes immediately picked up on this, and it lifted his spirits. "Let's go through the line. I'll bet the bastard doesn't even recognize us." I joined him as he went to the end of Throckton's receiving line.

I'd never seen Throckton in person and was surprised to see how small he was. Instead of the burly giant depicted in newspaper ads, billboards, and TV, the schmuck was a little runt of a guy, so skinny, a sneeze would blow him off his feet. As we drew closer in the line, I heard his wimpy-voiced greeting to each well-wisher: "Good to see you. Thanks for coming. Thanks for coming. Good to see you."

And so on. His light, powder-blue rodent eyes were glazed and unfocused as he shook each hand and mouthed his meaningless greeting. Of course, no human being could personally relate to the scores of admirers, groupies, hacks, and hangers-on who flashed by, but that was the difference between Wilkes and a guy like Throckton. Wilkes wouldn't even try.

CONFRONTATION

Junior continued his monotonous "Good to see you, thanks for coming" right up to Wilkes. My friend stuck out his hand to envelop Junior's and pump it vigorously like a tire jack. Throckton, still in his trance, gave his usual insincere greeting and tried to withdraw his hand, but my friend held it firmly. Then Junior's powder-blues focused, the glaze disappeared, and fear took its place.

Wilkes stuck his nose within an inch of Junior's and quietly said, "Listen, you sadist. Your friends with all the vowels in their names are making me take a dive. So I'm givin' the robe to ya, understand? I'm givin' it. I could kick your ass! I could kick your tiny little tight ass!"

The pressure of the past week releasing, Wilkes was on the verge of punching out Junior right here in the receiving line, which wasn't a bad idea. Might lose a few more votes. I elected not to interfere.

"Wilkes!" said Junior, his eyes darting about like a frenzied rat. Perspiration the size of goose bumps squeezed through the makeup on his face.

"That's right, pimp." Wilkes was hunched over like a cobra in order to be nose-to-nose with Junior. He grabbed Junior's clothes in the vicinity of his chest. "I'm gonna kick your ass all over this place, you two-bit scumbag. You son of a bitch."

With his free hand Wilkes arched a beautiful high right hook toward Junior's jaw. I thought about diverting the punch for an instant, but I was as angry as my friend about our ridiculous situation and let it pass. The sounds of Junior's scream and the dull thud of the blow landing home were followed quickly by at least a dozen bouncer-types jumping Wilkes and flattening him on the floor.

SPEECH

It took about thirty minutes to restore order and get the candidates conscious and on the dais to begin the debate. Lester J. Throckton, Jr., charged the podium like a mad bull. His angry supporters screamed their heads off for him for ten nauseating minutes. Junior's campaign speeches had been dull enough to put a convention of insomniacs to permanent rest, but God bless him, he was giving this his best shot, and what he was saying was pretty potent stuff. We needed him to make a good impression to insure our defeat. Here's a bit of what he said:

"My opponent is unfit for the judiciary. In fact, he's unfit for any responsible position. He calls me a scumbag. Well, let me tell you this. I'm no scumbag. I think Wilkes has confused me with himself and the people he represents. Sure he has a right to represent murderers, dope pushers, pimps, hijackers, and burglars. But you, the people of New York, have rights, too. To safety. I want to say this: I'm so law-and-order, I can't even utter the words 'not guilty' without choking."

PIMPING FOR JUSTICE

After twenty minutes of such rousing rhetoric, Junior sat down to great applause. Then it was my friend's turn. In a debate under ordinary circumstances, Wilkes could have annihilated Throckton, but that wasn't in the cards this evening. Wilkes had to take his dive. He dove.

"I rise to speak tonight to say I'm glad I'm not gonna win this lousy election. I'm glad I'm not gonna sell out and be a black-robed pimp in the whorehouse of justice! I don't want to spend all day plotting the number of tricks I can turn, trying to get defendants to lie down and give up their rights so I can screw them real good with a sentence, and all the while demanding that they honor me for it. Pimping for justice ain't my bag, man."

The audience was silenced by Wilkes's curious talk. This was not the man they had read about. Where was the free spirit, the insult comic, the imp? A lot of people sensed the oddness of my friend's demeanor as much as his comments. Many looked puzzled.

Wilkes continued, "And I wanna apologize to the many prostitutes among you for the analogy I just made. You are better any day than the three-piece-suited sluts Johnny Politician gives us for judges.

"I suppose trying to beat a party man for a judgeship in the whorehouse of justice was just a futile effort. Like giving an enema to a corpse—in the end, nothing changes. The polls seem to reflect my defeat. But that is okay with me. I am proud not to be a judge.

"So I just wanna thank my supporters tonight for all your backing and suggest you protest Throckton's certain victory tomorrow by staying away from the polls. I ask you to do that. Let the small voter turnout be the message to the party bosses that you are sick of the whores they pick to be judges. Thank you and good night."

A couple of boobs in the audience started booing and throwing things. Wilkes's supporters jumped on these disrupters,

and this incited the whole damn place, which erupted with
angry people screaming and throwing chairs, bottles and cups.
Fights broke out everywhere. Wilkes ran off the stage after two
large ladies in fur coats came up and started clobbering him
with their handbags.

All in all, the debate went very well indeed.

ELECTION RETURNS

The following day, Wilkes and I got up early and were the first
persons to vote in our precinct. Junior got two quick votes.
We spent every minute of the balance of the day driving all
over Manhattan offering rides to the polls to everyone we could
entice or cajole into exercising their franchise.

If we couldn't get them into the car, we explained how a
vote for Junior was a vote for their self-interest. To the bums
in the Bowery, we said Throckton loved to imbibe the distilled
nectar of the grape and would be a compassionate bail setter
on their next arrests.

To the Wall Streeters, we said Junior was heavily invested
in the market and thus either would conflict out of their favorite corporation's suits or hear the case and vote for big business.

In Little Italy, we made vague references to all the Italians
backing Junior: "All the heavy hitters want Throckton," we
said. In the Village, Throckton became a closet bohemian poet.
In the garment district, he was a friend of Dior, Coco Chanel,
and Rudy G. In Times Square, he was a generous patron of
the arts. And so on. We got Junior a lot of votes that day.

When the polls closed at seven, Wilkes and I grabbed a bite
to eat at Jack Dempsey's and returned to our homes in the
Village, exhausted and ready to collapse into bed. We had
done everything we could to lose the election, and I went to
sleep thinking Wilkes would lose and we would be safe.

I slept twelve hours that night, awakening at nine the next
morning only because of a call from a hysterical Wilkes. He
tried reading me the Adell Loomis story of the election results

from the *Times*, but I couldn't understand him through all his
blubbering and screaming. I ran outside to grab my paper and
read the front-page story:

> In one of New York's most stunning political upsets,
> upstart independent lawyer John Wilkes has narrowly
> defeated Judge Lester J. Throckton, Jr., for the judicial
> seat on the Supreme Court recently vacated by Throck-
> ton's father. Throckton refuses to concede, charging vot-
> ing irregularities. He demands an investigation. The only
> comment to date from victor Wilkes has been a hand-
> delivered letter to the Registrar of Voters demanding a
> recount.

14

"Dinero the Profit"

Taking legal advice from Clinton Rexrout is like receiving flying lessons from a kamikaze pilot.

JOHN WILKES

All you get from the law is what you take from the other side.

PERCY FOREMAN

When times are bad, there's nothing like an insanity defense to take your mind off things. Times weren't so hot for John Wilkes. Despite making every effort to lose the election to the Supreme Court, Wilkes won by a narrow margin. Now he was doing everything he could to avoid being sworn in. Fortunately, his opponent, the dishonorable Lester J. Throckton, Jr., the candidate of a peculiar coalition of the Bar Association, the two major political parties, and the Mafia, gave my friend the excuse he needed to rationalize his refusal to put on the robe.

The day after the election, Junior publicly claimed voting fraud and demanded a recount and a full investigation of his charges. Unquestionably, there had been voter manipulation. Wilkes and I had hauled at least fifty bums out of the Bowery gutters and dragged them to the polls to vote for Junior.

RECOUNT

To give Junior the time he needed to buy off the elections commissioner, Wilkes called a press conference and magnanimously announced to the assembled paper boys and girls that he would refuse to be sworn in until after a recount irrefutably secured his victory.

"It's a matter of conscience," he explained. "After all, I'd feel terrible acquitting all those defendants only to find out after the recount that if I lost the election, my verdicts weren't worth a cup of warm spit."

Comments like that were sure to have their intended effect with the Establishment powers, and within hours of Wilkes's announcement came word that an official recount would commence to determine the winner. Which brings me to the insanity business. Despite all the campaigning during the months prior to the election, our law practice was booming. This was due to the millions of dollars of free publicity Wilkes got running for office.

Now our phones rang incessantly. If anyone had heard me answer the calls, they'd have thought we were running a bookie joint. "You want Mr. Wilkes on the tenth. You gotta ADW, eh? Ten grand by noon." And so on.

DINERO THE PROFIT

Two days after the recount announcement, I got a call from a polite, well-spoken woman beseeching me to convince my friend to take the case of Dinero the Profit. The poor woman spoke as if the name were a household word when, in fact, I'd never heard of the guy. The Profit was in the Tombs, it seemed, having just fired his attorney, Clinton Rexrout.

Well, I thought, Wilkes isn't about to go see some nut in jail and waste time listening to a drooling, Thorazine-bombed psychopath rant on about the Conspiracy between J. Edgar Hoover, Pope Paul, and Lady Bird Johnson to kill him.

I gave the lady the stock answer to such inquiries. "Please deliver thirty grand by way of certified check and I'm sure we can take the case."

And what d'ya know, that afternoon we got a thirty-grand check. Now, money talks, and this fee screamed, "Go see Dinero the Profit."

Had Wilkes and I been following the papers closely in the previous months—other than the campaign coverage—we would have known all about Dinero the Profit. He robbed thirty-seven banks in just ninety days—a record of some sort. Each robbery, according to the tellers, was the same: A middle-aged, bearded man wearing a tweed suit and smoking a calabash pipe pointed a chrome-plated Smith & Wesson .38 at them and handed them a withdrawal slip on the back of which was the following handwritten message:

> Don't be stupid and press yer alarm
> An I won't do you no harm.
> If you think I'm jokin
> My gun'll start smokin
> An you'll gain weight
> From all the lead
> But you won't care
> Cause you'll be dead.
> Don't get funny
> Just hand over the money.
>   Remember Nothin,
>   Dinero the Profit

Most bank robbers are crazy, and from what little we knew of the case before seeing Dinero, our new client seemed no exception. He had committed thirty-seven of the most serious federal crimes in a manner that would assure identification. Yet his appearance, dapper and intelligent, belied his crude MO. Wilkes and I went to the Tombs expecting to see a client as schizoid as his crime methodology. Actually, we hoped for it. We wanted a client hopelessly crazy and wonderfully defendable.

SURPRISE

Were we surprised!

Instead of a blubbering psychotic, we met our old friend Dr. Lorenzo Pound, noted psychoanalyst, head of the psychiatry department at Columbia, founder of the controversial Primal Yawn Explanation of All Human Behavior, and one of the most frequently used forensic psychiatrists in the city. Had we paid attention to the news the past months, we'd have known all about it: the sensational arrest after a shoot-out at the Morgan Trust Bank; the shocking revelation of the Profit's true identity by an inmate at the Tombs (Dr. Pound had testified for the prosecution in the con's case; the latter decided to return the favor by ratting on the doc, but only after beating the crap out of him first); the hiring and firing of his first attorney, Clinton "Deathhouse" Rexrout.

Each story had been page-one news, but Wilkes and I, being wrapped up in the campaign to lose the election, missed it all.

On the way to the Tombs, I filled in Wilkes on what little I knew about the case. He was delighted to hear that Dinero had hired Clinton Rexrout. The man was to law what bubonic plague is to medicine. Rexrout was the quintessential V-6. Sadistic judges routinely appointed him to defend capital cases in order to insure electrocutions. Rexrout ended up escorting more men to their death than the chaplain at Sing Sing. Thus his moniker, "Deathhouse."

Said Wilkes as we entered the jail, "Anyone who'd hire that necrophiliac must have extensive brain damage. We've got a great defense!"

THE DEATHHOUSE STRATEGY

Deathhouse, of course, had completely overlooked the insanity defense and, true to form, attempted to cop Dr. Pound out to the indictment, thirty counts of armed bank robbery, at the first appearance in federal court. Deathhouse's motto was "When in doubt, cop 'em out." Only the protest of the Useless Attorney—Wilkes's tag for the U.S. attorney prosecuting the case—stopped the plea.

The prosecutor objected that the plea was premature in that he had seven more counts to add and needed a new grand jury indictment. He told the judge, "Your Honor, the grand jury convenes today at two. If we could reconvene here at, say, ten after, I'm sure I can be ready with the new charges."

At ten after two that afternoon, Deathhouse had Dr. Lorenzo Pound pleading guilty to thirty-seven counts of armed bank robbery. Fortunately, Mrs. Dr. Lorenzo Pound walked into the court just as the judge asked Deathhouse, "Does your client understand that he could receive a sentence of nine hundred twenty-five years for these offenses?" Before Deathhouse could answer, Mrs. Pound intervened. She complained that her husband was obviously too deranged to understand what was going on. She fired Deathhouse. She forbade Pound from speaking. And she phoned me and hired Wilkes.

FIRST BLUSH

"What the hell am I doing here?" asked a downcast Lorenzo Pound at our first meeting. Wilkes said he thought it had something to do with the number thirty-seven. "They've got thirty-seven big glossy color photos of you. They've got thirty-seven

tellers ready to tell a jury about your thirty-seven cash withdrawals. They've got thirty-seven fingerprint IDs of you. And
they've got thirty-seven demand notes made out in your hand-
writing.''

"Well, I'll be damned," said the doctor. "It's news to me."

Wilkes looked at me. I was as puzzled as he was. I asked,
"Don't you remember the Dinero the Profit routine? Christ,
you just about pled guilty to those bank jobs."

"Sir, I'm telling you, I have no memory of any of it."

I looked at Wilkes. He no longer looked puzzled. He even
seemed pleased by Dr. Pound's answers. He said, "Doc, of
course you didn't commit these ridiculous crimes. Why, the
thought of it's preposterous! We'll figure it out. Don't you
worry. You just hang in there and we'll have you out on bail
in a jiffy."

STUPID STORY

We left. I was still confused and let Wilkes know it: "He's
guilty. Jesus, that amnesia bit is the stupidest story I every
heard.''

"Schoon, most of our clients aren't too smart. That's the
primary reason they're our clients. But this one's different. He
is very smart. I think he's quite capable of pulling off thirty-
seven. God, an untrained orangutan couldn't lose this case."

It wasn't at all clear to me. "Thirty-seven what? Crimes?"
I asked.

"Perfect crimes," answered Wilkes.

The defense of the psychiatrist was to be psychiatric. When
we got back to the office, Wilkes had me hire ten psychiatrists.
I commented that ten seemed quite a few, and Wilkes said,
"Our guy's loaded. Ten's a good stat. If they don't find him
nuts, we'll hire ten more, and so on. And make sure you pick
all of the prosecution whores first."

This was an old Wilkes ploy for which I needed no explanation. Confidentially hiring all the shrinks the prosecution looks to hire is a can't-lose maneuver. If the shrink says the client is sane, it's no great loss, because then he can't say it for the Useless Attorney at trial. The attorney-client privilege would prevent that. And if he says your guy's nuts, well then, that's really something coming from a prosecution marionette.

FIRST WAVE

The reports from the first wave of psychiatrists were as bad as the recent election returns. Every shrink, even the defense whores, opined that Dr. Lorenzo Pound was the sanest bank robber they'd ever seen. None believed his amnesia story.

Wilkes, undaunted, had me hire a second wave of ten to shrink Pound's head. But again, all concluded that our man was perfectly sane. I couldn't believe it. Twenty shrinks agreeing on anything was medical history. Lorenzo Pound was still without a defense, and trial was closing in fast.

"Great," said Wilkes when I told him of the latest shrink reports. "Subpoena each of those bastards for trial."

"Let me get this straight. You want twenty shrinks available to testify that Pound, the erstwhile Dinero the Profit, New York's most dangerous bank robber, is sane?"

"Precisely," said Wilkes. "You don't expect a jury to cut loose a crazy man, do you?" My friend suggested it was time for me to go see Pound again. "He's got it all figured out. Go ask him."

THE INTERVIEW

I went to Dr. Pound's office, found out what was going on, and came away from the meeting profoundly impressed that we had a solid defense, although not nearly as confident as Pound or Wilkes that it would work. After all, we were in federal court—more defenses are rejected and rights violated there in a day than Roy Bean trashed in a lifetime. Worse, we were trying to persuade the jury to buy an insanity defense, which is about as easy as selling sunshine to Count Dracula.

Our only advantage was that in federal court the government has to prove the accused sane as well as guilty beyond a reasonable doubt. "Hell," said Wilkes on my return to the office, "to win, the Useless Attorney's gotta *convince* twelve good and true people Pound is sane. I just have to *confuse* one dumb son of a bitch."

The day following my visit to see Pound, we appeared in federal court for trial setting. The judge handling the calendar was a grumpy old fart given to involuntary loud snorts from some unknown affliction of age. The courtroom was packed with people holding handkerchiefs to their faces as Dr. Pound's case was called.

WHAT'LL IT BE?

"All right, Wilkes, what'll it be?" asked the judge.

"We'd request a date for trial," responded my friend.

"Judge or jury, Wilkes?"

"Both, Your Honor, if you don't mind."

The judge smiled slightly at Wilkes's joke. "Well, the court is very sensitive to all the defendant's precious constitutional rights. I will grant the defense motion for trial by jury with a judge. Mr. Clerk, draw a judge."

As bad fortune would have it, we drew Judge Julia Cunninger, the judge who tried to take Pound's pleas of guilty when Deathhouse represented him. Wilkes objected that Julia the Just couldn't be fair to Pound after hearing him try to plead guilty to the charges. He asked for another judge, but the malevolent bastard presiding said, "That'll be denied, counsel. You know how to challenge a federal judge. File your affidavit with Judge Cunninger." The judge smiled and leaned back in his chair.

He was right, unfortunately. To get a federal judge off a case for prejudice, you had to write a statement under oath swearing to the judge's bias against your client. Then that judge would decide whether your affidavit made out a case of prejudice. And when you lost the motion, you had to try your case in front of the same judge you'd just called a venal bigot. Such is federal justice.

Wilkes made the motion anyway. As he told Julia, "What if I want to waive jury and have a court trial? My client must have an unfettered option of trial to the court in this case, where the psychiatric testimony may be very complicated."

MOTION SICKNESS

Julia Cunninger, fiftyish, graying, hair pulled back tight and rolled into a doughnut, looked at Wilkes's motion papers as if they were a notice of eviction. She bit her lower lip with her ferret's teeth. She knew he'd sooner die than waive jury in front of her.

"In all my years on the bench, no one, not one person, has ever challenged my fairness." This was probably true. Most lawyers believed her numb from the neck up and thus incapable of a predisposition on a case. She shook the motion papers in front of her bobbed little button of a nose. "This is garbage."

"I've made my case, Your Honor," replied Wilkes. "I think your quarrel is not with me, but with the law."

Julia the Just's face turned crimson. She threw down the paper and stood. If looks could kill, Judge Cunninger would have been up on a murder rap.

Wilkes asked solemnly, "I take it my motion is—"

"*Denied!*" shouted the judge. She bounded off the bench and into chambers, leaving an atmosphere of mustard gas in the court.

"Jackass," said Wilkes loudly to Julia's chair. The court reporter dutifully took down the comment. And we were off to trial.

OPENING ARGUMENT

Wilkes gave his opening argument to the jury after the prosecution presented eight days of unimpeachable evidence that Pound had committed thirty-seven armed bank robberies. His first words must have surprised them.

"What we have here is actually a 'whodunit.' Is Wilkes crazy, you ask? Sure, the prosecution has proven that the corporeal manifestation of Dr. Pound committed the bank jobs. But what you are about to see and hear is truly mind-boggling. I will show you that there are two people inhabiting the flesh of Pound. Two exact opposites: one kindly, articulate, dogooder, with traditional American values; the other is mean, talks like a West Side street tough, does bad things, and values only himself.

"The gentleman you see before you now at the table is the sanest man I know. Dr. Lorenzo Pound. The cunning other who lives like a leech in Pound's body is the villain of this piece, Dinero the Profit.

"The doctors who will testify will explain the how and why. We will learn how this other spirit takes control of Pound's body and why it seeks to destroy Dr. Pound. When Dinero is in control, Dr. Pound has no conscious awareness of what is going on, which is why he has no knowledge of the events in the various banks. That was the Profit's handiwork.

"Ladies and gentlemen, Dr. Lorenzo Pound has been a solid contributor to our community for the past twenty-five years. The doctors will tell us how his imagined failures have created a terrible sickness in his mind, like demonic possession. This multiple personality affliction is nothing new. Remember Jekyll and Hyde? *Three Faces of Eve?* And what about Richard Nixon?"

DEFENSE EXPERT

I listened to all this and wondered where in hell we were going to come up with our experts. I had twenty shrinks in the gallery under subpoena ready to say Pound was sane.

Wilkes answered my question quickly. He announced to the court, "I call as my first witness the eminent forensic psychiatrist and professor at Columbia, my client and friend, Dr. Lorenzo Pound."

Pound looked every bit the professor as he ambled to the stand in his gray tweed suit. He walked slowly and gingerly, like a man twice his age. During the first hour of testimony, I had great satisfaction watching two pros at work. When you hear such a tandem, it's what I imagine listening to a Mark Twain Chautauqua was like—great storytelling. The jury was as involved as I was. Some leaned forward, some turned to face the doctor better, and all paid close attention.

Pound said it took him three months after his release from jail to figure out what had happened to him. He was self-destructing, he knew, but why? In a desperate attempt to find out, he locked himself in a room for six days with tape recorders going all the time save for sleep periods. When he replayed the tapes, he met for the first time his nemesis, Dinero the Profit, who was all that Pound despised—a selfish, callous, remorseless crook.

CRIMINAL INTENT

"I ask you, sir," said Wilkes. "Did you intend to rob those banks?"

"No. I have no memory of ever even being in them."

"I ask you this as a forensic expert who has testified, as I'm sure the judge will agree, many times for the court and prosecution. Did Lorenzo Pound have the intent to commit bank robbery?"

Judge Cunninger didn't even appear to hear Wilkes's question. But Pound did. He said, "No. I was legally insane and unconscious of my actions. Dinero is the villain. That cunning viper who hides inside me who, who is, who—uh—argh!"

Pound clutched his throat for a second and then slumped in

his chair. "I'm having—attack, it's—him, ahg! It's . . . Dinero, it's . . . yeah . . . yeah, man, it's me, man, the conqueror worm, yeah, Dinero the Profit appearing in person. Ha! Dig it, man!"

The change we saw was fantastic. The mild-mannered professor transformed into an arrogant street tough. Pound's face was a blank compared to Dinero, who talked out of the side of his mouth and mugged for the press. Either Pound was the world's greatest actor or we had actually witnessed the decomposition of one personality and ascendancy of another.

Wilkes appeared stunned. He turned to the Useless Attorney and said, "You take him."

CROSS-EXAMINATION

"Well, Dr. Pound, or is it Dinero?" asked the prosecutor.

"The wimp headshrinker ain't here, man. It's me, Dinero."

"State your true name for the record, sir," demanded the Useless Attorney.

"Francis Kafka, man. No, wait. He's my uncle. Just call me Mr. Profit."

"Do you know where you are right now?"

"Sure, turkey, ain't dis the B&O Railroad?" Dinero made his hand into a gun. "Take me to Cuba, man. This is a hijack."

"Very funny, Mr. Profit," said the Useless Attorney. "Now, would you mind bringing back Dr. Pound so I can talk to him?"

"Forget it, man; that fucker's nowhere. Really, you can search me, man." Dinero stood and started disrobing. "Take a look, man," he said.

"Stop that. Tell me this, sir. When Pound is in control, can you hear what's going on? Do you hear voices?"

"Sure, man, I hear da voices," said Dinero.

"And just when is that?" asked the prosecutor.

"When people speak, man."

"Dr. Pound, Mr. Profit, or whatever you call yourself, it was you who robbed all those banks, wasn't it?"

"Naw, man, I just made a few withdrawals, man. Don't call it no robbery, man. This ain't no federal case, man."

"And your motivation in entering these banks was to take money, wasn't it?"

"It's where they keep the money, man. Where else ya gonna go? It's like they say, man, money talks, and in the banks, man, da money comes on to me like it wanna make love. 'Take me, I'm yours,' it says, and I do, man."

Sign of the Times

Criminal lawyers are rarely artists enough to turn the beauti-fully horrible aspect of a crime to the advantage of the criminal.

NIETZSCHE

I love the smell of Dinero in the courtroom. He smells not guilty.

JOHN WILKES

Dinero the Profit was the crudest, loudest, most insulting and entertaining defense witness John Wilkes ever put on the stand. God love the bastard, he didn't give an inch to the Useless Attorney during cross-examination. Instead, he was thoroughly disrespectful and nonresponsive to the prosecutor's plodding, predictable questions. Okay, so maybe he did confess a little bit to the bank robberies, but this was fine—we were defending the hapless Dr. Pound, not this loathsome street hood inhabiting the good doctor's body.

USELESS ATTORNEY

After several hours of questioning Dinero and getting a lot of "dunnos" and "beats mes" and "I forgots," the Useless Attorney got tired and gave up. "What is it with you, mister?" asked the angry prosecutor. "Are you just totally ignorant?"

"Dunno," answered Dinero.

"Apparently," said the Useless Attorney.

After a moment's pause, Dinero recalled something. "Oh, I know somethin'," he said excitedly. Everyone in the courtroom paid close attention as Dinero made his first narrative statement of the day.

"I just remembered when I was pulling all the grocery store jobs last year—that was way before the bank jobs. I used to pull them with a buddy name of Beanpole—a tall, skinny kinda guy. He was a cool dude with the iron. Know what I mean?"

Few people in the court knew that he meant that Beanpole was handy with a .357 magnum revolver. Everyone could tell, however, from Dinero's stylistic description, that Beanpole was up to no good.

"One day we go into the store and Beanpole pulls his iron like he did on all the jobs and says it's a stickup. Whatdayaknow, out of nowhere comes this stakeout type copper, and then bango, Beanpole gets shot dead and I get arrested. So we goes to court, and like the cop says on the stand that he was hiding in the store and when he heard Beanpole say 'stickup,' he comes out from the back room with his gun pointed at Beanpole. The copper testifies he yelled, 'NYPD! Freeze!' and says Beanpole turned his gun toward him. Then he shot him in self-defense.

"So in my defense, I hop up here just like I am now and testifies, and they ask me what happened and I says it's almost like the copper said except I didn't know nuttin' about no robbery Beanpole was plannin'. My attorney—ugly guy with a big red boil on his neck—just sits down, and the DA gets up to ask me a lot of stupid questions. Like he thinks he gonna trick me into sayin' I'm guilty and put me right into a felony murder beef. Hah! Fool!

" 'So you admit you were in the store when Beanpole pulled the gun and announced it was a stickup,' he asks. 'Yep,' I says. 'And then the officer came out from the back?' 'Yep,' I says. 'And the officer told Beanpole to freeze after announcing his identity?' 'Somethin' like that,' I says. 'Well, what exactly did the officer say then?'

"I tells the DA, 'Cop comes out with his big gun pointed at Beanpole and says, "Adios, motherfucker," and just shoots Beanpole dead on the spot.' "

Dinero preened for the jury. "Got me acquitted in that case."

"Well, Dr. Pound, or Dinero, whichever, you are an arrogant fool if you think you can trick this jury with the fantastic story you are telling," said the Useless Attorney. "You are excused."

"I don't give a fuck what you think, man," said Dinero. "And nobody excuses me for nothin'. I ain't done nothing to be excused for, man. Like you think I done something wrong, man? What, man? Digame!"

The Useless Attorney smiled at Dinero's apparent misunderstanding. "Excused means I'm finished with you. That is all. Scram."

Dinero's face lit up with understanding. "Oh! You mean get off like when my ol' lady tells me we are done screwin'. Sure man, I'll get off."

THE SMELL

Dinero the Profit leaped off the stand and ran full speed toward the rear doors. As he passed me, I was overwhelmed by the penetrating, nauseating, nostril-searing smell of BO. My smeller is not particularly noted for sensitivity, but this odor had the power of ammonia and the staying quality of skunk. It was a smell I associated with the courtroom holding tanks, where dozens of nervous men are kept all day waiting their turn to cop a plea or receive a sentence in accommodations rivaling the Black Hole of Calcutta. It's a smell you never get used to and don't ever forget.

I guess what struck me about it was that I'd worked with Dr. Pound on cases before, had him on the stand testifying for my clients, seen him interview dozens of inmates at the Tombs, and he always smelled like a cologne commercial. Dinero's stench erased all doubt in my mind. I became a believer. The multiple personality defense wasn't the postarrest concoction of my friend Wilkes and his desperate client. No one fakes BO that raunchy.

As Dinero headed toward the doors, I noticed people in the gallery instinctively putting their hands to their noses in self-defense; others looked around their immediate areas for the nearby spectator who might have secretly unleashed the ghastly stink. One woman gagged and bent over with dry heaves.

I paid particular attention to the twenty shrinks I had subpoenaed. Every one of them had been a doubter of the defense. Now some looked like true believers. There was one thing no one could deny. Dinero the Profit had the worst BO ever emanating from the armpits of a human being.

ADIOS!

Wilkes picked up on the shrinks' reactions. "Get those entrail readers out of here!" he ordered. "See if any of them changed their mind about Pound's sanity."

As he said this, Dinero reached the courtroom exit, abruptly turned around to face us all, shrieked, "Say hey! Adios, motherfuckers!" and disappeared out of the swinging doors.

I got up from the defense table and hustled the twenty headshrinkers out of the courtroom just as the Useless Attorney was asking the judge for an opportunity to make some motions outside the presence of the jury.

Judge Cunninger, fully understanding the nature of the motions about to be made and granted, told the jury to call it a day. Meanwhile, I started buttonholing the psychiatrists in the corridor one at a time to see if they'd had a change of heart after seeing and smelling the change in Dr. Pound.

The very first shrink I talked to was Dr. Akmed Ben-Mohammed, who was duly impressed with what he had seen. He said he changed his mind. Pound's insanity was real. "This has to be authentic," he said. "A change in smell like that could only occur in a true multiple."

I used him to talk to the next shrink. I figured that if any of the shrinks were going to stick to their guns and say that Dr. Pound was legally sane, I'd just tell them to take a hike. But if one agreed, then he joined me and Dr. Ben-Mohammed in questioning the next one. In this way, I had the weight of peer pressure, consensus, and BO working for me. No shrink likes to stick his neck out for a defendant in a notorious case, but if all his pals are doing it, well then, it isn't so tough.

SHRINK BREAKDOWN

After interviewing all twenty of our experts—who were once unanimous that Dr. Lorenzo Pound was the sanest bank robber who ever lived—I drew the following division of opinion:

NO CHANGE (DR. POUND IS SANE): 13
CHANGE TO INSANITY (POUND IS NUTS): 5
REFUSED TO STATE CURRENT OPINION: 1
COULD NOT BE REACHED (FLED COURT DUE TO STINK): 1

So now we had six experts—I include in this count our own defendant, Dr. Pound, who testified magnificently as our first witness to his own insanity—who agreed that Dr. Lorenzo Pound was truly possessed, an authentic multiple personality, and eminently insane when under the possession of his other self, the loudmouthed rogue, Dinero the Profit. I scribbled the names of the five other helpful alienists on my yellow pad and added my personal evaluation about their usual forensic allegiance in the courtroom—that is, if they were routinely witnesses favoring the defense or the prosecution.

1. Dr. Akmed Ben-Mohammed (Defense Whore)
2. Dr. Salvador Tostada (Defense Whore)
3. Dr. Virginia Graham-Waterstock (Whore)
4. Dr. Michael E. Meely (Defense Whore)
5. Dr. Renata Tenebruso (Prosecution Whore)

Getting Dr. Renata Tenebruso on our side was about as likely an occurrence as Judge Julia Cunninger granting a defense motion. Tenebruso was all the prosecution could ask for in an expert: bright, articulate, and full of common sense, she could persuade the most dubious juror—of which there were all too few—of the perfect lucidity of the most schizy defendant.

So effective was Dr. Tenebruso that she was celebrated in prosecution circles for convincing a judge that a six-year-old child had the criminal capacity of an adult. This paved the way for the kid's conviction of extortion and his incarceration in juvenile hall for a long time.

Tenebruso was attractive, early fiftyish, and so virulently antidefendant that she had never to my knowledge found a criminal defendant insane. Her standard opinion to me was, "Mr. Schoonover, your client is as sane as you or me."

We had confidentially retained her solely to keep her out of the case as a prosecution expert. By placing her in our camp, the attorney-client privilege meant that she was ours as a matter of law. We owned her expert opinion. If it was good, as we never dreamed hers would be, we'd use it. If it was bad, as we expected it to be, the other side would never know. She was on our side, whatever she thought.

To get her on our side was a coup. As I rushed back into court and slipped Wilkes the list of the five chameleons who were ready to join the defense, I thought that maybe Renata had a very refined olfactory sense. Maybe that is what turned her nose our way. I also knew the moment Wilkes's eyes caught Tenebruso's name on the list, he'd be shocked. His knees did buckle a bit when he read her beautiful name. He looked at me, and I nodded that it was true.

LUNACY AND TOMMYROT

"Mr. Wilkes," asked Judge Cunninger, "what say you to the motion of the United States attorney to revoke your client's bail and have him examined by a court-appointed psychiatrist?"

"That all depends on whose bail you're revoking and which client you want examined," Wilkes answered. My friend noted the puzzlement on Cunninger's puss; it had "Huh?" written all over it. "You see, I represent Dr. Pound. Dinero the Profit, who just left, is at this point unrepresented, and I certainly can't speak in his behalf, since I'm pinning the rap squarely on his shoulders."

"Pure lunacy," interjected the Useless Attorney.

"Tommyrot," agreed the judge.

"It's a conflict," said Wilkes, "a patent conflict of interest. Unusual, yes. Unprecedented, surely. But as actual a conflict as one lawyer can have. You should appoint separate counsel to represent Dinero. As far as I'm concerned, you can do what you want with him."

"Thank you for your abiding concern for the legal interests of Mr. Profit," said Judge Cunninger. "Based upon the in-court confessions of the defendant Pound, also known as Profit, the motion to revoke bail is granted. As far as the prosecution request for a psychiatrist to rebut, er, uh, to explore the possible insanity of the defendant, that'll be granted, too."

Cunninger looked at the prosecutor with a knowing look, a product of years of collaboration. "I suppose you want Dr. . . ."

"Renata Tenebruso. Yes, indeed," said the Useless Attorney.

"That'll be granted," replied the judge. "Prepare the order."

LET THE RECORD REFLECT

"Let the record reflect the absence of Dr. Pound and Dinero the Profit," said an aroused Wilkes. He always said, "Let the record reflect" when making a futile motion, one calculated not only to fail, but to accomplish an ulterior purpose—in this case, to object to the appointment of Tenebruso, but not so strongly as to succeed in his protest.

Wilkes knew, as all good defense attorneys do, that a moderate protest of a judge's anticipated action, unsupported by citation to any authority other than the law of the state or the voice of God, would be certain to fail. By such protests against the judge's action, you would be certain to entrench the judge in her position and get her to do exactly what you wanted.

My friend continued: "Neither of the defendants, Dr. Pound or Dinero the Profit, is here. Only one has counsel. The prosecution motion is made without notice to the defense and granted without an opportunity for the defense to be heard. We must protest the procedure as a denial of basic constitutional rights. . . ."

And so on. Wilkes objected for twenty minutes—anything less for him might have made the judge suspicious—but he didn't say a damn thing. When the judge cut him off, he cried, "But, Yer Honor, I have important points to make which you must hear!"

Cunninger got up from the throne behind the bench and said, "I've heard enough out of you, buster," and vanished into chambers. The Useless Attorney, having gotten his way by winning all his motion requests, was ecstatic. He merrily left the courtroom, too. But Wilkes stopped the young court reporter, Cynthia Midriff, from leaving by asking her to stay put. Then we waited for the court to clear of spectators.

When the court was empty, Wilkes dictated the following for the record:

"Let the record reflect that the judge has left while I was in the midst of my objections to the appointment of Dr. Renata Tenebruso. If the court had not walked out, I would have stated why it should not appoint Dr. Tenebruso. Long ago, Dr. Tenebruso was retained as my expert. Nevertheless, in a spirit of comradely cooperation and out of a keen sense of economy for the taxpayers of this state, I assent to the appointment of Dr. Tenebruso if that is the court's desire as well as that of the prosecutor. I now declare these proceedings adjourned."

WHAT ABOUT MIDRIFF?

What about the court reporter, you ask? How could we trust her not to spill the beans? We knew that like most reporters who worked Cunninger's court, Midriff thought the judge a bitch. The reporters called her the Ice Queen, because she was as cold and harsh to them as dry ice held to the tip of the tongue.

Cunninger never learned the names of her reporters, never greeted them, and never gave them a break when their fingers got tired. The only direct communication she had with them was when an appellate court reversed one of her convictions for judicial misconduct, usually because of one of the judge's intemperate remarks berating a defendant or his attorney. When news of the reversal got out, the communication between the judge and her court reporter grew immensely. But it was all one-sided—the judge berating the poor reporter by claiming, "I never said that! You took it down wrong! Misquote! Misquote! Misquote!"

They hated her. And when my friend was up to his old legal tricks—being his charming self to the lovely lady of the stenograph—she'd not want to spoil the fun. Anyway, she was just doing her job reporting the goings-on in a court of law.

When Wilkes finished his soliloquy to the empty courtroom, a delighted Cynthia Midriff clapped her hands and laughed. "Sheeeee-it!" she said.

NIGHT MOVES

Wilkes spent that night with Renata Tenebruso to prepare her for testimony the following day. I was with them for the first few awkward hours; they seemed uncomfortable working on the same side. But after a few drinks—Wilkes made another exception to his teetotaling rule—they warmed to each other. In fact, they got downright cozy working out her planned testimony and giggling over the anticipated furor of the judge's and the Useless Attorney's discovery that Renata was our expert.

I got up and left unnoticed. I knew that soon after I got out the door, Wilkes's preparation of his witness would be consummated on a mattress—nothing like a good roll in the hay on the eve of battle. Wilkes did it as often as possible: "I want 'em to feel comfortable as possible up on the stand. A romp in the sack's the best thing I know for it."

But this was a damned dangerous approach to witness prepping. It could lead to devastating cross-examination. Fortunately, no prosecutor ever had the chutzpah or the imagination to ask one of Wilkes's "lay witnesses"—as my friend called them—if they'd been balling the defense attorney.

RENATA CALLED

"I call as my next witness, Your Honor, the psychiatrist appointed by the court to examine my client for the Useless Attorney, Dr. Renata Tenebruso." This is how my friend opened the court proceedings the next session. All hell broke loose.

The Useless Attorney demanded a chambers conference to find out what was going on. When Renata told him that she was going to tell the jury that Dr. Pound was so insane, his brain ought to be pickled and saved for study as the classic example of cerebral meltdown, he just about collapsed. But when she told him in chambers she'd been on the case for a couple of weeks as our expert, he went through the roof, yelling that Wilkes had to be disbarred for deceiving the court, screaming that my friend was "the biggest fucking shystering liar-lawyer that ever infested a courtroom." Then he said some real nasty things about my friend.

"Let the record reflect," said a calm Wilkes, "there had been no deception, no intrigue, no cabal. If Cynthia will please read my remarks to the court yesterday, you will see that I made full disclosure that Dr. Tenebruso was my expert."

Cynthia the court reporter was only too happy to oblige. She pulled out her last fold of steno paper and read Wilkes's remarks of the day before. Judge Cunninger did not say a word to question what was just read—her memory was so short, she wouldn't have remembered whether Wilkes said it or not, and she knew it. More important, she knew we knew it.

The Useless Attorney, however, was not so reticent. "Bullshit! You never said that, Wilkes! I know you never uttered a word about Dr. Tenebruso. You perjuring prick!"

Wilkes stood and went to the door to return to the courtroom. He turned to the Useless Attorney, pointed to Cynthia, and said, "Look, mister, if you are accusing that wonderful little lady of falsifying the record, you just go right ahead, and I'll represent her for nothing and sue your rotten ass for everything you got. And when we finish, you'll be lucky if you've got enough money to pay bus fare to go collect your food stamps."

Cynthia Midriff brushed aside a little tear as she gave my friend a quick smile and nod of thanks. Wilkes walked back into the court saying, "The Useless Attorney is denying Dr. Pound his right to speedy trial by these delaying tactics." Cunninger got up without saying anything and followed Wilkes into the courtroom. The prosecutor, alone with the reporter, pounded the table and said, "I'll kill that bastard."

Cynthia Midriff, moving her fingers with the elegance of Liberace on the keyboard, typed the comment into the record.

Renata Tenebruso did the killing that day. She did in the prosecution. She told the jury this was the first true case of multiple personality she had ever seen. She added that she knew Dr. Pound quite well and, although at first skeptical, was convinced of the authenticity of his illness. No fake could so genuinely change his entire demeanor, voice, inflections, jargon. More important, "Dr. Pound has always smelled good even in times of stress. The man who ran out of here yesterday afternoon had as foul a body smell as I've ever had the displeasure of inhaling. That was not Dr. Lorenzo Pound. There is truly another person living in Pound's body.''

SMELLS LIKE VICTORY

The stink became the key corroborative point in the case, and Renata Tenebruso, the court's own witness, underscored it for the jury. She turned that noxious, suffocating stench into the sweet smell of success. She also mentioned that five other doctors completely agreed with her findings. Wilkes rested.

The Useless Attorney asked no questions of Tenebruso. He knew he'd get drilled by her answers. Instead, he asked, or rather begged, the court to appoint another expert to analyze Pound, call him sane, and thus create some prosecution rebuttal evidence. "Otherwise," he told the judge, "this guy's gonna take a walk on this case."

Judge Cunninger didn't need the threat. She didn't deny prosecution motions; she was a team player. She looked at Wilkes, who was about to go into his filibustering objection, and cut him off. "Motion granted. Wilkes, your objection is noted so the record can reflect it."

The Useless Attorney selected Dr. Malcom Venturi, a solid, well-credentialed prosecution whore. "Sorry," said Wilkes, "we've confidentially retained him as our expert."

"Then I choose Dr. Lauren Mendlejohn," said the prosecutor.

"Try again," said Wilkes. "He's on our team."

The Useless Attorney went through thirteen more names— every prosecution whore within fifty miles of the city—and Wilkes claimed them all. There was no one left on the list except for the defense whores, and the prosecutor wasn't about to take one of them.

Wilkes tried to pimp one on him anyway. "Well," said my friend, "I see about a dozen other names on the court's list. Your Honor, I suggest that if the court is going to appoint an expert, you should pick one. All these people are professionals.

They have no bias one way or the other. Let's not insult them. After all, this is the court's list of experts."

ANYONE YOU WANT

Cunninger would have none of it. "I see what has been done here by the defense. You've hired everyone on the list." She told the prosecutor to just go out and get anybody he wanted and have him ready to testify by the next afternoon. That evening the prosecutor went to NYU and grabbed a professor of psychology, Dr. Brooks Skuz, and drove him down to the Tombs to see Dr. Pound. But Wilkes and I had already beaten them there. Dr. Pound, who was now himself again, was advised to say nothing to the NYU professor. He complied.

This did not dissuade Dr. Brooks Skuz from coming into court the next day to opine that Dr. Pound was sane, "based upon my detailed observations of his nonbehavior. After all," said the prof, "if he won't talk, what better proof of a guilty mind can you get?"

Wilkes spent the entire next day trying to dismember the professor on cross-examination. Although a virgin on the stand, Dr. Skuz was an impressive, convincing witness.

It was one of the few times I saw my friend ineffective on cross-examination. It was worse than that. He took a clobbering. Every question he'd ask served as a platform for Skuz to vilify psychiatry. Dr. Skuz said there was no such thing as a multiple personality. In fact, he said all mental illness was a myth created by elitist doctors anxious to establish a new psychiatric priesthood with an impenetrable jargon. They do it, he said, to lord it over us and make a fortune doing it. "And now they say this man, Pound, one of their own tribe, is ill—mentally sick. Hah! What they see is the actor creating a role for his own ends."

What was so appealing about Skuz's testimony is that he was debunking a profession everyone loves to hate. Just get someone to run a flag up a pole that says psychiatry is hokum and you'll get a million arms raised to salute it. Not that there was anything scientific or valid about what Skuz had to say. He just said it was all BS, that shrinks were doctors of voodoo, and that their high priest, Dr. Freud, "was a cocaine addict who loved to make extraordinary extrapolations about all human behaviors from the nuttiness of a few Viennese old ladies."

TAKING TURNS

It got so bad that by midday, Wilkes turned to me and said, "Who *is* this guy? You try to take him apart. I need a break."

I took over the cross for an hour, but it was me that got dismembered, and I told Wilkes I was doing worse than he and that he should take the questioning back. And so the afternoon went, each of us taking an hour or so questioning Skuz, trying and failing at rehabilitating the science of psychiatry, and then giving him over to the other guy. We were a sorry tag team taking turns getting our brains beat out.

The jurors loved it. I saw a couple of them elbow each other in the ribs in gleeful agreement with Skuz's statement that "When it comes to accuracy, if a psychiatrist says anything, the odds are ninety percent that the opposite of his opinion is correct." And so on. Dr. Skuz single-handedly was pulling a conviction in for the Useless Attorney.

After Skuz left the stand, Judge Cunninger, seeing the momentum shift, called for the attorneys to immediately commence final argument. The Useless Attorney readily agreed and jumped right into his speech. As he droned on about the rug that had just been pulled from under the "phony, self-serving defense," I looked at the worried face of my friend as he sat waiting his turn. I watched and saw him thinking— thinking that this case was about to go down the drain barring a miraculous intervention.

I watched as his mind ran down the corridors of his vast imagination looking for the appropriate maneuver. He ran by his daring old tricks, his flamboyant speeches, his reliable last-minute stunts, but none seemed right to rescue this case.

PROPS

Then he got it. The cloud of preoccupation evaporated. He leaned over to me and said, "Go to the nearest hardware store and buy a compass, a level, a square, and a plumb bob. And hurry!"

I didn't wait to ask why, but ran out of the courthouse, purchased the needed goods, and beat it back to the court. I arrived just as Wilkes was beginning his address to the jury. He nonchalantly walked over to our table, where I had placed the implements he ordered, and picked up the compass. Then he went over to the easel and drew several circles. He got the square and drew some right angles; he got the plumb, held it in front of the easel, and drew a straight line; the level he used just to make sure his lines were perfectly true.

JOHN BELCHER

He looked at his drawing and said, "Here, as John Belcher would say, is the human mind." He looked at a juror named Andrew "Cutter" Conner, a construction contractor. Our pre-trial jury investigation had uncovered that Cutter Conner was head of the Blue Masonic Lodge, a fraternal order of Free-masons.

John Belcher was the first Mason on the North American continent—around 1704—and the ridiculous drawing Wilkes made was nothing more than a ritual that Conner couldn't miss—the most secret rite of initiation of the "Bronx Broth-ers of the Ancient Arabic Order of Nobles of the Mystic Shrine."

Wilkes was making a play for this one juror to carry his case into the jury room. He gave a good final argument, too, telling the jury again about Pound's insanity, which was so palpable, you could smell it. He was, said Wilkes, "pound for pound, the craziest man I have ever seen."

The jury paid close attention, as they always did when my friend closed his cases. But Cutter Conner was particularly attentive after Wilkes's opening ritual, and the clincher came as Wilkes was sitting down. "Is Conner watching me?" he asked.

I nodded. Wilkes wheeled in place, mumbled something in no language I ever heard, and gave what looked like a sign of the cross. Then he sat down and whispered to me, "It's their sign to render aid to a brother in need. And brother, we need a lot of aid."

CUTTER COMES THROUGH

The jury was out for seven days. Seven days of bitter division and argument caused by our man Cutter, who through force of personality persuaded a jury, initially eleven to one for guilt, into a unanimous verdict of acquittal based upon Pound's insanity.

After the verdict came the inevitable blast of bad press and prosecution scapegoating. The Useless Attorney was quoted in the *Times* saying, "This is what happens when you combine stupid laws, jurors who don't know their back ends from their front, and a shyster lawyer like John Wilkes."

Several jurors called a press conference the next day to claim that they voted not guilty only because of "the law"— whatever that meant—and because Cutter Conner threatened to cut their heads off if they didn't vote for acquittal.

MORE GOOD NEWS

It was just after Dinero's acquittal and the uproar it brought about that the Election Commission announced its long-awaited recount of the results of the Wilkes-Throckton election. Wilkes was still basking in the glow of that most satisfying verdict when we received the telegram from the commissioner. It read:

RE: WILKES-THROCKTON ELECTION. SIR, INVES-
TIGATION HAS REVEALED THAT YOUR NOMINATING
PAPERS WERE NOT IN PROPER ORDER AS PETITIONS
DID NOT CONTAIN SUFFICIENT NUMBER OF QUALIFIED
VOTERS. RECOUNT DEEMED UNNECESSARY. YOU LOSE.
SORRY.

VICTOR GOODPOINT,
NEW YORK ELECTION COMMISSIONER

Wilkes stared at the yellow rectangle in stony silence. I said, "Jesus, you must have won by a huge margin. Too many votes for the Mob to phony up to beat you, I guess."

Wilkes still said nothing. I filled the void again. "The verdict in Dinero's case must have pushed them to get it over with quick during the uproar. I'll bet they figured with you getting off a bank robber–nut, that there'd be no protest over this."

Wilkes still said nothing. I chimed in again, "Damn, aren't you relieved? They'd have killed you if you beat Junior and took a seat on the Supreme Court away from them."

Wilkes looked up from the telegram and said, "Huh? What? Did you say something?"

I said that I thought the news was good. It was what we wanted. He would live.

Wilkes laughed. "You're goddamned right it's good news. I'd have hated being a judge. There's no fun in it. I was just thinking about how close I came to ending the best time of my life by being put in a lousy, boring job, every minute of which would have cramped my every instinct."

"Including your survival instinct," I added to remind him of the Mafia threat to take him out if he beat Junior and took their seat on the Supreme Court from them.

"Yeah, that, too," said my friend as he crumpled up the little yellow message and tossed it into the waste bucket. "And I couldn't have taken the big pay cut either."

POUNDED OUT

As for Dr. Pound, he made a miraculous mental health recovery within a month of the verdict. "Acquittal will do that to you," claimed Wilkes. "There's no better tonic." But Pound was all washed up as a forensic shrink and was fired from his job at Columbia University. He moved to Beverly Hills, opened an office in a nearby canyon, and is reportedly making a fortune listening to the babble of rich neurotics.

—16—

Joe Guts

An advocate who has been well paid in advance will find the cause he is pleading all the more just.

PASCAL (1661)

If you've got cancer, you don't go to the free clinic.

JOHN WILKES (1951)

The first time I saw Eddie "Pogo" Ridley was at the NIT finals in that Garden. Wilkes had been given two center-court seats by that most rare form of the human species, the grateful former client. Knowing of my love for the sport and curiosity about Pogo, basketball's latest sensation, he invited me along.

It took exactly six seconds to see what all the hoopla was about. Pogo got the opening tip ten feet in front of his own key, tore up the right side of the court weaving between defenders, dribbled behind his back to change direction, and cut to the top of the opponent's key. Only two forwards remained between him and the basket. He paused long enough to pound the ball three times into the hardwood and then made his final charge up the middle toward the basket.

BACKPEDAL

The defenders backpedaled into the center of the key, hoping to jam his route and slap away the shot. They never got the chance. Seeing the tall timber planted under the bucket, Pogo instantly converted his lateral motion into a tremendous vertical leap, a jump so remarkable, he seemed to suspend himself in the air high above the two defenders. It was as if Pogo were excused from the laws of gravity. At the peak of this leap, he arched a rainbow shot. The ball rotated slowly backward as it passed untouched through the iron rim and caught the net for a score.

For the rest of the game, Pogo put on a one-man show of helicopter dunks, rebounds, steals, no-look passes, twenty-five-foot one-hand set shots, and fast-break lay-ups. He fouled out late in the game with thirty-seven points, exactly half what his team eventually scored in winning the tournament.

He was a helluva ball player. And he was just a nineteen-year-old college sophomore.

POGO NAMED

After the NIT, Pogo was named All-Big East at guard. His junior season he had an even more spectacular year and was an easy All-America selection. His final year, he was a consensus All-American—everyone named him on their all-star team. The People of the State of New York even got into the act.

They named him in an indictment.

The charge was point shaving. Pogo took racketeer money to make sure his team never beat an opponent by more than the posted odds. In the era of televised games, the hoods called point shaving ''doing a Gillette job''—so named for the razor company which was the innocent sponsor of the TV games. A good many gamblers got very wealthy betting on Pogo to keep his team under the odds makers' point spread.

Pogo was the perfect man for the job. No one controls point production better than a play-making point guard who's also the team's high scorer. The fact that Pogo played on a good team made it easier on him since the point spread was usually comfortable, at least six to ten points, so the shaves he gave his team's point production didn't have to be done so close as to risk losing games.

Pogo wouldn't have gone that far. He would later testify to his code of honor, ''What counts is whether you win or lose, not whether you beat the Vegas spread." As he saw it, he was just a gentlemanly winner who never rubbed another team's nose in humiliating defeat. And actually, it was a sacrifice for Pogo to shave points, because doing the Gillettes cut into his point production. But Pogo's diminished point production led to one helluva income.

STARTING FIVE

Named along with Pogo in the indictment were four small-time hoods from Jersey. Each had a record—for bookmaking, numbers racketeering, extortion, and the like—but there wasn't a big fish in the bunch.

Pogo's explanation for how he hooked up with such underworld sleaze was disarmingly forthright: "Some guy comes up to me before a game and says he's gonna give me a grand if we win by eight or less. We did. And he did. I hadn't even tried to make it happen, but the next time he says it, I think about it a lot on the floor and kind of unconsciously let it happen, and the money comes in, which I liked, and after that I began doing it purposefully. For the money."

Pogo wasn't alone. In the early fifties, so many ball players were doing Gillettes, it seemed every game was fixed. It was especially bad in New York. All the big B-ball colleges (Manhattan, NYU, Seton Hall, Long Island University) had kids taking money to beat the spread—or worse, the ultimate disgrace: to dump the game itself.

The scandal broke the year after City College of New York performed its miracle grand slam. In 1950, CCNY won both the NIT and NCAA championships, a feat never duplicated by any team before or since. When it was learned that during its magnificent grand slam season, three players on the team were actively doing Gillettes and dumps, the bottom fell out of college basketball.

PRESIDENTS, COACHES, ALUMNI

The scandal hit the sports world like a gonorrhea epidemic. Players were called "contaminants to innocence," "defilers of the purity of college athletics," "pestilences to be quickly wiped out." University presidents demanded swift convictions; coaches called for maximum punishment; and alumni moved to make examples out of players by banning them from sports for life.

Players not involved in the fixes didn't say much. Especially quiet were the gifted ball players who were illegally recruited, or on undeserved academic scholarships—given to the gifted jocks with sixty-watt minds when the school ran out of the athletic variety—or riding around in "signing bonus" cars, or taking weekly checks for nonexistent jobs provided by university presidents, coaches, and alumni.

Such was the virginal sport that was now being defiled by the guys doing Gillettes.

Amid the uproar, the prosecuting attorney on Pogo's case, Miles Landish, said, "Twenty years in prison ought to give the basketball world the example it wants and Pogo enough time to think about what he's done."

CAFÉ TALK

Wilkes and I read Landish's ominous words in the *Times* over a couple of bowls of greasy chicken noodle soup at the Guadalajara Café, our favorite dive near the Woolworth Building, which posed as a purveyor of edible food. Between spoonfuls, I recalled to Wilkes that it had been two years since we had seen Pogo at the Garden.

The article noted that Pogo had retained a defense attorney, Wilmot Finster, a red-nosed V-6 who pleaded clients guilty faster than most people shake hands. Pleading defendants guilty was like a religious rite to Finster. He raced to the DA's office to offer up his clients as a kind of human sacrifice.

The most odious part of the ritual was the bargains he got.

For the defendant to earn his promised sentence reduction, not only must he give the prosecutor a soul-baring confession, and later a sworn guilty plea, but he also had to identify the next sacrificial lamb for slaughter. This is called "making" a case—naming names, snitching off a friend, becoming a stool pigeon. It was the price of dishonor all of Finster's clients paid for the privilege of committing hara-kiri in court—with Wilmot Finster holding the sword.

CODE BLUE

Naturally, none of Pogo's four hoodlum codefendants even considered such a course. Their Code of Silence saved not only their personal dignity, but their lives as well. A violator of the Code, an informant, weaves himself into a snitch jacket, which invariably targets the wearer as a rat. The Code dictates the extermination of such chatty rodents.

Pogo knew none of this. He was just a naive, scared kid who made the fatal mistake of hiring the most dangerous—to his clients—criminal lawyer in the state. People in trouble spend more time looking for a place to park than investigating which lawyer to hire. The only reason Pogo picked Finster was that he was listed first in the phone book. Wilmot had convinced the telephone company to run his name as "AAAFinster" in the attorney's section of the yellow pages. Being first got him a lot of business, and many a client went to his doom because of it.

THE MAKING OF A CASE

With a few arm twists by his attorney, a frightened Pogo Ridley agreed to cop a plea and, after a little coaxing from Finster and the prosecutor, to "make" a case. DA Miles Landish convinced Pogo with the following words: "You can tell me now and walk away from this mess, or you can tell me later in Sing Sing on the front end of a twenty-year prison scholarship."

All over the world, this has been an accepted way of making

cases—torturing a suspect physically or mentally until he comes up with what the interrogator wants. In India, the police have a way of doing this. They say, "It is far pleasanter to sit comfortably in the shade rubbing red pepper into a poor devil's eyes than to go about in the hot sun hunting up evidence."

In America, defendants are tortured with incompetent defense lawyers and extortionate plea-bargains.

SPILLED GUTS

Between slurps of soup at the counter of the Guadalajara Café, Wilkes talked about Pogo's predicament. He observed that the moment Pogo attached his fate to Wilmot Finster, he perfected his own destruction. Now he was probably in a small cubicle at the DA's office making a case.

My friend turned in his stool and looked at me. He was about to tell a story. "Did I ever tell you about the time Wilmot actually tried a case?"

I said no but thought that maybe he had told the story. It was a story I've heard lots of times since then. In fact, years later I happened to be doing some research in the *Times* archives and read about it. But Wilkes told it better, and here is how it went.

"Finster was appointed to represent a hooker named Coreen North for plying her trade in the streets of New York. At this time in his career, Wilmot would not ever go see his jailed clients, as he found the surroundings too depressing. Going to see a slut in the slammer was an outrageous notion—out of the question for the urbane Wilmot Finster. But not going to see the woman in jail prior to the trial meant he couldn't arm-twist a plea of guilty out of her. Many of his clients thus had their right to jury trial preserved in this fashion.

"As the trial began, of course they brought out the defendant and sat her down next to Finster. Then the DA called two undercover cops to the stand, who both positively identified Coreen North as the hooker who propositioned them with the estimable goal of getting their rocks off. For money, of course. When the DA finished, Wilmot did not cross-examine. When the DA rested his case, Finster, already resting, rested, too.

"The DA argued for a finding of guilt on two counts. Wilmot told the jury, 'Ladies and gentlemen. The DA's done his job. Now I've done mine. The judge is about to do his, and then it's your turn. Good luck and thanks for your attention.'

"The jury came back in five minutes with guilty verdicts. The judge called the next case, and before Finster could leave the courtroom, the clerk called out, 'Yikes! Hold on, everybody! This one's Coreen North!'

"Turns out that the bailiffs mistakenly brought out a hooker from the harem of hookers in the hooker tank named Charlotte Goins. She was up on the same charges, but with different cops, and Wilmot was not her attorney. So they just sat her down in the defendant's throne during Coreen North's twenty-minute little old trial, and Charlotte took two guilty verdicts without knowing what hit her.

"When Finster assessed what had happened—that he had represented the wrong person into a conviction—he bellowed out like W. C. Fields, 'Your Honor, another case of mistaken identification by the constabulary. I move for a judgment non obstante verdicto.'

"The judge asked Wilmot just how it was that he sat through the trial next to a woman who was not his client yet defended her as if she were. Wilmot answered quite truthfully, 'Judge, until I met the real Coreen North twenty seconds ago, I never laid eyes on her.' "

Wilkes laughed, "So not only does the hooker get her jury trial—albeit in absentia—she gets her case dismissed by the judge based on the perjury of the cops in identifying the wrong hooker as the defendant."

Wilkes handed me the newspaper and said, "That was Wilmot's finest hour as a trial attorney. Happened years ago. I think the experience frightened him so much that he became dedicated to never trying a case again. Now he's raised the cop-out race to the DA's office into an art form. Plead 'em and bleed 'em. Too many cases are made, not solved, in the DA's office with Wilmot leeching his clients for names of others to trade for a plea of guilty. Right now some poor slob's about to get clobbered 'cause Pogo Ridley has Finster steering him to make a case to save his butt. And Pogo's pretty good at putting the fix on things when properly motivated.''

I folded the paper in half, swilled the last of my coffee, which looked and tasted like it was retrieved from an oil slick, and wondered about the conversation in the prosecutor's office and on whom Eddie ''Pogo'' Ridley was spilling his guts.

JOSEPH GUTZNIK

Basketball was played in the Olympics for the first time at the 1904 St. Louis games, but only as an exhibition. The sport first officially appeared in the games in Berlin in 1936. Joseph Diahgenov Gutznik was there. He saw Dr. Naismith, the American inventor of the game, throw up the first ball and then watched as the Americans easily won the tournament.

Gutznik was the twenty-four-year-old captain, center and star of the Rumanian National Basketball Team. But they weren't entered in the games, because as a team they couldn't beat a squad of blind pygmies. However, Gutznik was an able player and a fanatic about the game. He read every book about basketball. He followed the U.S. college games and taught basketball every day as a grade school coach in Bucharest. He attended the '36 Games at his own expense to see the world's best play the game he loved.

Gutznik was deeply affected by what he saw the Americans do in Berlin. He had never dreamed basketball could be played so well. In routing their five opponents, the Americans routinely sank beautiful hooks and long sets that would have been declared miracles if made in his country. Gutznik was amazed by the patterned offense and pressing defense. Most impressive were the plays and the way the players moved without the ball to set picks and double screens to allow teammates unobstructed shots.

In the Olympic finals, played outdoors in a miserable, driving rainstorm which kept the score low, the American guards were able to control the ball against their Canadian opponents. Final score: America 19, Canada 8.

Gutznik went home after the games and brooded about what he had seen in Berlin. The memory of the brilliant American team made him feel bad about the Stone Age level of the game played in Rumania. In 1938 he made the most important decision of his life: he would go to America, become a citizen, and play on the 1944 U.S. Olympic team.

BEST-LAID PLANS

Joseph Diahgenov Gutznik arrived at Ellis Island in February of 1938 and was greeted by a representative of the Immigration and Naturalization Service. This gentleman, in the great tradition of the INS, was quite helpful to Mr. Joe Gutznik's entry into the United States. He took one look at his passport and immediately renamed him with the moniker he would carry for the rest of his life—Joe Guts.

Joe quickly found out that it wasn't so easy to become a basketball star in the United States. Most good players were in college, and Joe Guts had already been to college. College teams supplied the talent to play on the Olympic squad, and Joe marveled at the quantity of great college players as he watched double-header games held at the Garden in New York. He saw the first NIT games played there soon after he arrived in 1938, and also the first NCAA national tournament, which was played the following year in Evanston, Illinois.

ONE-HAND SHOT

There was only one place where Joe could make it in America, learn English, play basketball every day, do no work, get fed and housed and paid, and most important, perfect his considerable raw skills in time to play basketball for the 1944 Olympic team.

The United States Army.

After boot camp in 1939, Joe was assigned to a post at Fort Wood, Missouri, where he tried out for the base basketball squad. The coach must have been surprised when he saw the tall, skinny, sunken-cheeked Rumanian sink his first twenty-foot one-hand push shot. The shot had just been invented by Hank Luisetti at Stanford, but Joe Guts, a consummate student of the game, picked it up immediately and added it to his repertoire. It didn't take long before Joe was leading his team to a string of victories and eventually to the army championship.

His teammates nicknamed him "The Count," because when Joe started speaking the Queen's English, he sounded just like Bela Lugosi. What do you expect from a Transylvanian transplant?

When the war broke out, Joe's team became part of the Third Army. When he was informed he was headed for the European theater, Joe said to the base commander, "Dis is vonderfull news. I love the French stage."

Joe saw a lot of France, but no stage plays and no basketball. Instead, the Third Army under General Patton in late 1944 made a spectacular sweep across northern France straight into the Battle of the Bulge. Three miles south of Bastogne, Corporal Joe Guts took a burst high in the legs from a Nazi machine gun. He was saved by his size. Had he been shorter, this story would end here.

Joe Guts was captured by the Germans and sent to Poland, where he spent the rest of the war as a POW.

HOMECOMING

After the war, Joe Guts returned to New York with a Purple Heart, a wooden leg, and a piece of paper that said he was now a U.S. citizen. But the dream was gone—there would be no Olympic games in his future, at least not as a player.

Joe set his mind to coach a future American Olympic basketball team. He was still a dreamer.

Thanks to his old army coach, Joe Guts got a teaching job
at Iona College and became the assistant basketball coach. The
team went winless that year, just as it had for the previous
three seasons. The head coach quit after learning that the school
planned to drop its basketball program. But Joe Guts pleaded
for one more year to make the team competitive. The school
relented only when Joe said he'd take the coaching duties for
no pay and that no scholarships need be given to any player.

With no talented players, no scholarships, no "signing bonuses" to high school prospects, and no illegal gifts of cash or
cars to stars on the team, Joe Guts still turned the Iona program around. The first year the team won seven games, the
second year eleven, and the third year they won their conference title. It was tremendous coaching achievement, a product
of the unique way he taught, disciplined, conditioned, and motivated his scrappy players to win games.

Joe said there was no secret to his success. "You must teach
the boys hard vork, teamvork, and the vill to vin, that's all."

Joe Guts was a helluva coach.

VILL TO VIN

Inevitably, a big New York basketball school with a flounder-
ing record made him a Godfather offer he could not refuse,
and soon Joe came to the Big Apple to continue his quest to
become U.S. Olympic coach. Again he turned the school's
program around.

He instituted two-a-day practices, weekend distance running, and preached discipline, fundamentals, and "the vill to
vin." The players began playing together like parts of a fine
machine. He tolerated no hotdogs or slouches, just kids who
wanted to play team basketball.

Once his story got out, the New York media made a hero—
and rightfully so, for a change—out of Joe Guts, the gimpy
war hero who talked like the heavy in a horror movie and

motivated kids to play great team basketball. The school loved
him, because in his first four years, Guts's teams won three
conference titles and one NIT championship. And he did it
without the aid of a single All-American.

Until Eddie "Pogo" Ridley came along.

WOOLWORTH INTERVIEW

A week after lunch at the Guadalajara Café, I got a call at the
office from a man with a heavy East European accent. He
didn't identify himself. He said only that he "vood like Mr.
Vilkes" to represent him in a criminal matter. He said he
would come to see us at the Woolworth Building that night
around seven, and hung up.

I joked to Wilkes that Dracula just called, wanted him as his
lawyer, and insisted on an interview that night. I said, "He's
overdrawn at the blood bank again."

That evening at seven he came. Tall and thin, eyes sunken
and black, his big nose leaking a bit, he looked worried and
nervous—like a guy who'd just been indicted for seven counts
of murder. He sat down heavily and said, "Gentlemen, I am
Coach Joe Guts. I tink I am vith beeg problem."

As he spoke, his big red tongue darted out serpentlike. He
sounded like Dracula, all right, and the thought passed through
my head that if we did get him as a client, he could never take
the stand. He'd scare the hell out of the jury. Maybe the judge,
too.

SIXTH MAN

Guts said that DA Miles Landish had called him into his office
that morning to say that his name was to be added to the five
basketball point shavers who had been indicted the week before. Landish also said that one of the defendants had been
secretly indicted a year ago and had been cooperating with the
prosecution by making cases on the coconspirators. In that effort, the informant had taped all his conversations with Guts.

Landish said the tapes revealed his participation in the scheme. The prosecutor said he was giving him this chance to confess, hire a lawyer—Wilmot Finster was suggested—and work a deal. Otherwise, he'd get twenty years.

Guts said he told Landish that if he had tapes, they were phony, because he would never have had any part in fixing basketball games. Landish responded, "I have reels of tape of a man who talks funny, like you do, giving instructions to a player on the point spread. And I've got an All-American witness to verify that you made the statements. This case is a slam dunk."

Joe Guts asked, "Who vood say such tings?"

Landish answered, "Pogo Ridley."

FEE SIMPLE

"Mr. Vilkes," said Coach Guts slowly, "basketball is my life. I vood never do what they say. You vill help me?"

"Of course," said my friend, "but first there is the matter of my fee." Wilkes quoted a five-figure retainer, which for the time was big bucks. Hell, it's still big bucks. Guts looked like he'd just been hit with a techanical foul and ejected from the game.

"Yes, it is a great deal of money, but in America you pay for what you get," said my friend. "Like if you've got cancer, you don't go to the free clinic." This was a line that always impressed clients with the seriousness of their plight and the need to fork out for self-protection.

"But I have family to feed," protested Coach Guts. "You vant more than year's salary."

Wilkes picked up a framed photo of a matronly woman cuddling four young children and held it out for Joe Guts to see. It was a picture of a former client's family presented to Wilkes during a similar haggle over fees to convince Wilkes to lower his price. Now my friend, a bachelor, regularly used it for the reverse effect. "I have my obligations, too," he said solemnly.

Joe Guts sat up a bit and forced a smile of defeat. "Okay, Mr. Vilkes, you vin. But I tink it misleadink for you to have office in dis buildink."

"Why's that?" asked Wilkes.

"Because Voolverth's is supposed to be for the discount, Mr. Vilkes."

17

State *v.* Joe Guts

Pain is transitory. A loss lasts forever!

COACH JOE GUTS

Extremism in the defense of a client is no vice, and moderation in examining a state's witness is no virtue.

JOHN WILKES

I had just come into the office after spending the entire week with Uriah Condo investigating our new client, Joe Guts. As with all of Wilkes's cases, this one had to be meticulously investigated, starting the moment the retainer check cleared the bank. He had given us one week to check out Guts's story. The balance of the pretrial time—and there was precious little of that—was to be spent on Pogo Ridley.

Wilkes, impatient and anxiously waiting at his desk, wanted the low-down on Coach Joe Guts. We found him leaning back in his chair, feet on his desk. On seeing us, he straightened up. "Well, come on, out with it. What have you got?" His voice was unusually apprehensive. He suspected what I was about to tell him and knew he would both love and loathe it. The news was going to make the next four months of his life miserable.

I started my report with the good-bad news. "Joe Guts is innocent or my name isn't Winston Alfred Schoonover."

Uriah Condo added, "I'll bet my home, the Condo condo, he's not guilty."

For the next hour, we gave Wilkes the details of our detective work, which had kept us nearly sleepless for the last seven days investigating every aspect of the case.

RAVAGING INNOCENCE

"To sum it up," I said, "everyone we interviewed loves and respects the coach. They all want to testify for him."

Condo added, "Yeah, looks like you got one decent, honest-to-god innocent, fee-paying Transylvanian on your hands. He may talk like Bela Lugosi, but he's a better American than most Americans."

Wilkes looked across his messy desk at me. Pain showed in his face. He said, "Shit, I was afraid of that." He got up and left us, saying he was going for a walk.

I had seen the agony before. I understood the rising tide of terror filling my friend's soul. He had assumed responsibility for the defense of what we call in the business a "ravager"— a man wrongly accused and facing the probability that the false accusation would be confirmed in a court of law. Guts's entire future now depended on the ability of John Wilkes to right the wrong being done in the name of justice.

Innocents like Joe Guts are ravagers because their cases eat lawyers alive. You win their cases or you become an accomplice in a horrible crime, the ruin of an innocent man. Your job is to make sure that that never, ever, ever happens. But if it does, it means no peace or rest. It means you continue working the case through appeals and writs and clemency applications until the ravager is exonerated, or dies, or you die.

Wilkes defended all of his clients to the hilt, of course, but most were guilty, and he knew it, and they knew it, and they knew he knew it. It made representing them a pleasure. If the case was lost, they knew they received the best defense money could buy and now had a bloody good appeal ready to go, with Wilkes again defending. If the client won, as often happened, so much the better.

Wilkes's motto was that no defendant should fall as long as

the thinnest strand of reasonable doubt supported his innocence, and Wilkes was the master spinner of that delicate
thread. His ability to tie prosecution cases in little knots earned
my friend the enmity of his adversaries and the nickname "that
devil Wilkes."

Doing absolutely everything in your power to defend a client
is enough when it is clear enough he's guilty, but winning is
the only acceptable result with a ravager. You can prepare a
year for trial, file every conceivable motion, make all the right
objections, put on credible witnesses, brilliantly argue like
Daniel Webster to the jury, but it is not enough if the ravager
falls to a guilty verdict.

You can't look a grief-stricken wife in the eyes after such a
verdict and tell her of your superb presentations and add, "Oh,
by the way, he'll be out of prison in about twenty years."

The hulks of many good trial lawyers are shipwrecked at the
bottom of the dark watering holes and flophouses of the city
today because they were destroyed by the agony of losing
these cases. The human body, even the body of a defense lawyer, can be ravaged only so long by such losses before it crum-
bles.

WILKES IN MOTIONS

Wilkes came back from his walk in an hour. "Schoon," he
said, "I want the following motions prepared tonight and filed
tomorrow."

I had every right to protest that I hadn't had twenty hours
sleep the last week investigating our client's illustrious life, but
I knew Wilkes was in no mood for hearing it. He was preparing for war. It was a time for sacrifice.

"First motion. Move to dismiss the charge of bribing a participant in an amateur sport. Second motion. Move to strike
the aliases from the indictment. Third motion. Move for a
continuance."

Usually Wilkes didn't need to explain the reasons for the
motions. After working a couple of years for him, they had all

become self-evident. We would move to strike the aliases because the indictment charged our new client under the names
of "Joe Guts, alias Joseph Gutznik, alias 'The Count.' "
Aliases are things only guilty people use to hide their identity;
prosecutors like to charge them to dirty up the defendant in
the eyes of the jury. Because an immigration official renamed
Joe Gutznik Joe Guts, I would argue that the state could not
now use that as evidence of criminality. The nickname "The
Count" was hung on Joe by his army basketball-playing bud-
dies. It was irrelevant.

Actually, the state missed on the right alias. The indictment
should have charged Joe Guts with the alias of "Coach."

By now you know the reason for the continuance motion.
The DA had spent a year meticulously preparing this case and
now insisted on the defendant getting his right to speedy trial
jammed down his throat like a slam-dunked basketball. They
prepare a year. We get a couple of weeks. No fair. We wanted
more time.

OLD WINE DEFENSE

Time is the defense's best witness, my friend would often say.
Then he would recite his favorite Ralph Waldo Emerson quote
on the subject. "Ralph Waldo," he said, "captured the Old
Wine Defense in one sentence when he wrote, 'Time turns to
shining ether the solid angularity of fact.' "

Time. We were going to need plenty of it what with the
mountain of tape-recorded evidence we had yet to review. I
needed no coaching to implement Wilkes's Old Wine Defense
motion.

But the one motion he insisted on that had me stumped was
the motion to dismiss. I asked Wilkes, "What's our ground to
dismiss the charge of bribing a participant in an amateur
sport?"

"College basketball isn't an amateur sport," said Wilkes.
"Hell, half the kids are on someone's payroll doing dumps or
Gillettes. The other half are taking signing bonuses, cushy jobs,

cash gifts, and phony grades. If that's amateur athletics, bribery's not a crime. It's part of the business."

Wilkes was only slightly exaggerating. Between 1947 and 1950, eighty-six college basketball games were known to be fixed. Seven colleges—CCNY, Manhattan, Long Island University, New York University, Bradley, Toledo, and (say it ain't so!) Kentucky!—were caught at it. These were the *known* fixes. How many others escaped detection—and there had to be plenty—we'll never know.

JUDGE HENRY "RED" FOX

On Monday Wilkes and I walked to the court of Judge "Red" Fox. I must have looked pretty strange matching strides with my friend while pushing a bright red wheelbarrow in which we had dumped the motions I had written, the reel-to-reel tapes we had just received as discovery, and a number of relevant law books. We thought we needed a little show-and-tell if we were going to have a chance to get our continuance.

Prior to his timely suicide, Red Fox was a hate-filled judge whose only job-related pleasure was sentencing defendants to the maximum possible prison sentence. Since good lawyers were often an impediment to this joy, he hated them more than the clients they represented. Thus, he hated Wilkes more than any of us.

"What's this telephone book about, Wilkes?" asked Judge Fox when the session opened. He lifted my motions with his arm stuck straight out to keep them as far away from his face as possible, as if he were holding a plate of rotten fish. With his other hand he was rubbing the top of his skull, a tic that had given him a pink bald spot on the top of his head by age forty and the nickname "Red" from the lawyers he hated.

"Huh?" said Wilkes.

"I said, what's this all about?" repeated Red Fox.

"It's about time," answered my friend.

"Huh?"

"I need time to prepare this case. I need a reasonable continuance."

Fox dropped the motions onto the floor in front of his bench and said sarcastically, "What'll it be, Wilkes? Shall we set the trial in this or the next century?"—Fox was familiar with the Old Wine Defense—"By God, that's not a bad idea! Then I won't have to try it!"

"Look," said Wilkes, "the DA was kind enough to provide me—on Friday—with five hundred hours of tapes he says have my client's voice on them. If I do nothing else but listen to them for the next six weeks, which is what it will take, I won't have a chance to do anything else in preparing this case for trial."

JUSTICE DELAYED

Fox pulled out a handkerchief and wiped away a few invisible tears. "Oh, Mr. Wilkes, you poor, poor man."

Wilkes shot back, "They've had a year to prepare their case. I've had these tapes one day and the case for a week. Just look at what's to be reviewed."

With that, I went out in the hall and wheeled in the tapes. I rolled them to the front of the court and tipped the wheelbarrow over so the tapes spilled onto the floor into a large mound. The gallery, especially the paper boys and girls, were amused. Even the DA gave us a wink. But not Fox.

"Well, well," said Fox. He leaned over the bench and took a quick look at the tapes. Then he leaned back in his throne, stared at the ceiling while rubbing his head with both hands, and said, "Our system will break down unless the defendant and the People have their trials in the speedy fashion that the law says they're entitled. Justice delayed is justice—"

"Denied the DA," interjected Wilkes. "Fast justice is like fast food. It's junk. I ask for one year."

"That motion must be denied," said Red Fox. The pink spot on his head grew redder than ever. "Mr. Clerk, pick a date in the normal course."

"I ask for six months."

"That'll be denied."

The clerk pushed a few pages of his calendar while Wilkes continued peppering the judge with dates.

"I ask for four months."

"That'll be denied, as will any other request you may make."

Finally the clerk said, "We have an opening in three weeks, Your Honor."

"Wait," shot Wilkes. "What about my other motions, the one to strike the aliases and the other to dismiss?"

"Those'll be denied, counsel," said the judge. "Trial in three weeks. Okay with you, Miles?"

DA ELOQUENCE

The DA, who had been enjoying the show in silence, was now moved to make an eloquent contribution to the hearing. He lifted his corpulent frame from his wooden chair to address the court, but as so often happened, his bulging hips caught the arms and he lifted it off the floor.

"Fine with me, Judge," he said, half rising out of the chair. But he stopped midway when the back of the seat jammed into his spine. Ignoring his predicament, Landish turned his flat, almost featureless moon face to Wilkes, gave him a wide grin, and plopped back down.

Judge Fox spat out a "So ordered" and flew off the bench and back into chambers, leaving Wilkes angry and the floor strewn with unlistened-to tapes. It was bad enough that this was a ravager case, but now we had to review five hundred hours of tapes, investigate Pogo, and prepare a defense in three weeks.

Wilkes walked over to Landish and stuck his face to within an inch of the DA's. "See this puss, turkey? Better learn to love it, 'cause it's gonna be in yours every day for the next six months! This is gonna be the slowest quick trial you ever mistried!"

And so we were off to trial.

The next three weeks were as crazy and hectic as any I ever spent working for my friend. By dividing the tapes between Wilkes, Condo, and myself, we managed to hear them all in time to spend a week chasing down leads on Pogo Ridley. One of those leads came as a result of Wilkes's assigning Condo to pay a visit to all of Pogo's teammates.

LANDISH OPENS

Landish's opening argument was short and simple. This was a case of corruption and greed, he said. A coach of a basketball team and his star player, Pogo Ridley, conspired to win games by keeping their margin of victory under the odds makers' point spread. This way the crooks who paid them could bet a bundle on the underdog, take the points, and win big. He used a chart to illustrate the five games in which Coach Guts and Pogo did a Gillette on the score:

OPPONENT	DATE OF GAME	POINT SPREAD	WON BY	GUTS ON TAPE
Manhattan	12/21/51	+ 9	+ 4	"Nine's fine."
Bradley	1/7/52	+ 7	+ 5	"Seven's heaven."
C.C.N.Y.	1/19/52	+ 3	+ 1	"Three's a squeeze."
Kentucky	2/12/52	+ 4	+ 2	"Four's the score."
L.I.U.	2/24/52	+ 8	+ 3	"Eight's great."

Landish said he had tapes of Coach Guts giving Pogo the spread just prior to tip-off before each game. "These," he said, "would destroy any fabricated claims of innocence which the accused, Joe Guts, alias Joseph Diahgenov Gutznik, alias 'The Count,' may make. We will show that in an effort to make a quick buck, Joe Guts corrupted a gifted athlete and helped kill big-time college ball in this city."

When Landish sat down, Wilkes announced that he would postpone his opening until after the DA's case was in. "In about six months," he whispered to me.

The DA's direct examination of Pogo Ridley took about an hour. Landish got Pogo to say that he and Guts agreed to do Gillettes on five games, the ones on the DA's chart. Just before opening tip-off, said Pogo, Guts would find out the latest line of the game and pass it on to him in a rhyme like "Eight's great." This would be the number the team had to stay under.

"It wasn't too difficult to do; the Gillettes, I mean," explained Pogo. "We had a real good team, and I was the playmaker and high scorer. I also led in steals, assists, and rebounds, so I could easily control the tempo of every game. If we scored too much 'cause someone else got a hot hand, Coach Guts could substitute one of the Pine Brothers like Snyder or Mowbry. They'd put our hot streaks in the icebox real quick."

Pogo said he got paid a grand after each game by one of Sal Sollazzo's men. He assumed Joe Guts got more, but he never saw him take money.

GUTS ON TAPE

"These little rhymes Coach Guts would give you before tip-off," asked Landish. "Did you do anything to preserve them?"

"I recorded them at your request, sir," said Pogo.

Landish pushed a button on a recorder he'd set up, and in the next thirty seconds we heard the five rhymes in the voice of a man who sounded very much like Count Dracula.

"Can you identify the man whose voice that is?" asked Landish.

"Yes, it's Coach Guts, sitting right over there."

The DA smiled and turned to Wilkes. "Your witness." He lumbered over to his wooden chair and squeezed into it.

My friend approached Pogo's cross-examination with the extremist zeal of a religious fanatic, and although he hadn't had much time to prepare, he felt he could skewer Pogo with the tapes. The tapes were supposed to be the downfall of Joe Guts, but Wilkes embraced them as one does a keepsake from a lover. They would show Joe Guts to be framed.

Wilkes quickly got Pogo to admit he taped every practice lecture, pregame pep talk, halftime evangelical soliloquy, and post(game) mortem during the entire basketball season. It amounted to five hundred hours of tape, and Wilkes proceeded, after the inevitable objections from Miles Landish, to play every minute for the jury.

Wilkes explained to the judge that the thirty seconds the DA played were lifted out of context. The jury needed to listen to what came before and what after.

COACH TALK

It took three months. Coach Guts gave us a clinic on disciplining young men and molding them into a team. It was a rare opportunity to hear a jargon meant only for the jocks on the hardwood floor spoken by the most knowledgeable Transylvanian basketball coach in the world. Here are a few representative excerpts:

[Practice]: ''Snyder! Vhere'd you play ball? School for the deaf, dumb, and blind? Look for picks, Snyder! Your man's goink baseline 'cause you're gettink picked. Cover him like a rash, Snyder. Like a rash. If he goes to drinkink fountain, you turn water for him. If he goes to john, you hold his think. If he goes baseline, you block his ass off the court.

[Pregame]: ''Vee vill not vin by just showink up, boys. You think like that and vee vill be in a vorld of hurt. Remember the three D's out there—discipline, desire, and defense. They're key to vinning.

[Halftime]: 'Boys, I vant to congratulate you. You're two points behind shittiest team in league. You, Snyder, you must love the floor out there. You never leave it! An you, Mowbry, vhat's the matter? Rigor mortis set in? Show me you're not dead out there, man, move! And you, Curtis, how many shots of yours vere blocked in your face? What a disgrace! Here's a toothpick. Get the leather out of your teeth. You guys play like you're unconscious. I vant to see desire out there. Hustle till it hurts, boys. Vake up or you get whipped! Remember, pain is transitory. A loss lasts forever!''

[Time out in game]: 'Boys, boys, vhat is it out there? Feel-ink sorry for other side? What? This isn't bullrink, boys. Stop with the matador defense! And you, Snyder, pick your opponent out there, not nose. Mowbry, spray your hands with glue. You drop balls too often. Now, listen up. Let me introduce you all to league's leading scorer, Pogo Ridley. You boys play like you never saw him before. This is a five-on-five game, boys, so how's about gettink ball to Pogo so he can shoot us back into the game? Now, let's get out there and play ball!''

TALE OF THE TAPE

After three months of listening to Guts on tape exhorting his boys in every conceivable manner to victory, it seemed obviously, hopefully even to the jury, that Joe Guts was no crook. No one who cared so much about the success of his team would risk defeat and his personal ruin by doing Gillettes.

The endless tape playing clearly had an effect on Pogo. He seemed much less confident and ill at ease as Wilkes readied for the kill.

JW: "I see you were talking to Mr. Landish this morning."

POGO: "Yeah."

JW: "What'd he tell you to say?"

POGO: "Nothin' but the truth."

JW: "That would be refreshing. Wonder why he had to tell you that?"

It was a nasty little start, but Wilkes was out for blood. He next sought to bring out Pogo's motivation for turning on his coach.

JW: "Since you didn't mention it when Mr. Landish was questioning you, I assume you decided to secretly tape Coach Guts for a year and to testify against him out of a spirit of good citizenship?"

POGO: "That's part of it."

JW: "We're all anxious to hear about the other part."

POGO: "Yeah, well, I was doing Gillettes last year, and some coppers saw me meeting some of Sollazzo's men for the payoff, and they questioned me and I told 'em everything."

JW: "Everything? You told them you were doing Gillettes on the scores and getting a grand per game from Sollazzo?"

POGO: "Yeah."

JW: "And that was the whole truth?"

POGO: "So help me God."

JW: "And when those cops questioned you, you didn't mention a word about Joe Guts, did you?"

POGO: "I didn't want to get him in trouble."

JW: "But something changed your mind about that, obviously. What?"

POGO: "Mr. Landish. He said tell everything or I'd get twenty years. He said if I'd make a case on someone else, he'd let me go free."

JW: "So initially you lied to the cops by saying no one else on the team was involved, but when told to finger someone else or get twenty years, you told this fairy tale about Joe Guts!"

Wilkes yelled the last accusation, and it prompted Miles Landish to shout out an objection—"He's badgering the witness."

COURT: "Restrain yourself, Wilkes, or it'll be contempt for you."

JW: "My apologies to the court and the jury, but it's difficult to be restrained when examining a man who's trying to perjure my client into prison."

This drew more venomous objections from the DA and threats from the judge, but Wilkes didn't care. He'd made a point with the jury.

MOVING IN ON POGO

Wilkes moved in on Pogo. He pulled from his pocket a photo of the team and asked, "Who's your best friend on the team?"

POGO: "Ernie D., the other guard."

JW: "You've been seeing a lot of him lately, haven't you?"

Pogo squirmed a bit on the stand, uneasy with the notion that this change in direction of the questioning was leading somewhere he would regret going.

POGO: "Yeah. After court each day we been going to Toots Shor's to relax, Ernie, me, and Ernie's friend Uri."

Wilkes pulled another photo from his pocket and showed it to Pogo. He asked, "Do you recognize the people in this picture?"

POGO: "Yeah, that's me and Ernie and Uri at Toots. How'd you get that?"

JW: "You got to be pretty friendly with Uri, didn't you?"

POGO: "Just pals. Say, what's this all about?"

DA: "Yeah, I object. This seems irrelevant."

COURT: "That'll be denied."

JW: "I suppose you wouldn't mind telling us about the confession you made to Uri last night telling him that you decided to perjure yourself to save your lousy hide."

POGO: "That's a lie!"

JW: "Oh, is it? You sure? You know this man?"

Wilkes pointed to a man seated in the back row of the gallery. The man stood up, and my friend asked him to identify himself.

MAN: "My name is Uriah Condo, known to the witness as Uri. I'm a private investigator for John Wilkes."

Pogo nearly fainted. The jig was up. Acting on Wilkes's plan to check out Pogo's teammates, Condo befriended Ernie D., Pogo's best friend, and convinced him to help us get Pogo to own up to the truth. Ernie believed in his coach's innocence and readily agreed to help. The rest was easy. Pogo was anxious for companionship after the endless hours on the witness stand listening to the tapes of the Knute Rockne of college

basketball coaches imploring his team to excellence and victory. He welcomed the meetings with Ernie and Uri for free
drinks and ball talk and more free drinks.

JW: "That's the man you knew as Uri?"

POGO: "Yeah, so what?"

POGO'S LAST FOUL

Wilkes pulled from his coat another reel-to-reel tape and put
it under Pogo's nose. "Mr. Condo knows how to operate a
tape recorder, too, Pogo. Wanna hear it?"

Pogo sank in the witness chair. He was caught and he knew
it. Suddenly he grabbed the tape out of Wilkes's hand and
made a fast break for the doors to escape. Wilkes turned and
yelled, "Stop the bastard!" I jumped up and set a perfect pick,
which Pogo crashed into, sending both of us to the floor in a
heap.

Wilkes picked up the tape and stood over a prostrate Pogo.
"That's the worst charging foul I've seen in a year, Pogo. You
must be losing it."

What Pogo lost was his credibility. Condo's tape revealed
that Pogo set up his coach to make a case and get his outlandish
deal from the DA. The incriminating rhymes, it turns out,
were a product of Pogo asking Guts if he thought the team
could win by the posted point spread, and the coach innocently
responding in rhyme that winning by such a margin would be
fine.

After hearing the tape of Pogo's confession, the jurors
stopped listening to the evidence. Their ears clogged and their
eyes froze over, but the DA still made an effort to convince
them that Pogo's confession was a defense trick played on a
naive kid plied with drinks and overbearing pressure. He might
as well have been talking to the wall.

Coach Joe Guts was acquitted by a jury that didn't even
leave the room to deliberate. They just looked at each other,
and when one said, "We've decided. He's innocent," they all
nodded in agreement.

At this, the gallery jumped up and applauded Wilkes and his client for fifteen minutes. Joe Guts beamed. He looked like he'd just won the NCAA tournament.

Wilkes looked exhausted. He sat through the ovation smiling a little and shaking a lot. He had survived the ravages of four months of nonstop worry and work. As we left the courtroom, he said, "Thank God the cops catch a few guilty people every now and then. A few more Joe Gutses and I'm a goner."

—— 18 ——

The Earnie Libido Story

All thieves who could my fees afford
Relied on my orations,
And many a burglar I've restored
To his friends and his relations.

W. S. GILBERT

My fee, if I'm to be hired
(and fatten my treasury's girth)
Measures how much I'm desired
And not how much I'm worth.

JOHN WILKES

It was an usually hot morning when Earnie Libido came into the office dripping sweat on his rumpled suit jacket and moaning the first words to be heard from this garrulous man in distress.

"Jesus Christ, is Mr. Wilkes in? Jesus, I need help. Boy, oh boy, do I need help, Mr., uh, er, what's your name? Oh, well, okay, Mr. Schoonblower, huh, er, oh, pardon, uh, Mr. Schoonolder, or whatever. Say, I'm in real trouble, Mr. Schooner. Yessirree, real one hundred percent authentic no-bull trouble. With a capital T. I need to talk to a real lawyer, Mr. Schoon, 'cause you are looking at a man about to walk the plank, and the buff-headed, money-sucking mouthpiece I got is helping the two-headed team of Blugeot and Landish send me to destruction. I speak of my alleged defense attorney, Charles Alvin Seneca Hardson. He's helping 'em ruin my life, Schoonower. It's a damned conspiracy, an unholy alliance, a troika of terror, I tell you! And read this! My God in heaven, just read this!''

He thrust a document, crumpled and soaked with perspiration, into my hand. I recognized it as the probation department's presentence investigation report to the judge. Earnie Libido paused just long enough for me to take possession of the report and then continued.

''I really need to see Mr. Wilkes. I really, really do. I'm in serious trouble, Mr. Shoonshower. They're trying to ruin my life. Destroy! Finish! Kaputsky! You get the idea, Mr. Schoon?

''I *gotta* see Wilkes! I know he can straighten this thing out. But don't worry, no sirree, I know what it's all about. I can pay right now. Up front, Mr. Spoonover. I know that's the way it is, and how Earnie Libido knows! God, does Earnie Libido know! I've been fleeced by the best and the worst—Charles Alvin Seneca Hardson being the number one fleece artist. A good thief maybe, but a disgrace to your alleged profession. I mean, I'm just another ignorant consumer when it comes to picking a lawyer. How was I to know the man is a no-good? The man said he was a great lawyer! I'm a victim of fraudulent advertising! He's a shyster! Please let me see Mr. Wilkes! I'm a desperate man, Mr. Spoonblower. I've been, uh, I've been, er, con-con-convicted!''

He choked as he said the word ''convicted.'' And there was no question that Earnie Libido was a desperate man. He talked like a desperate man. And he had good reason to be. Earnie Libido had been convicted by a jury of his peers. Refusing to plead guilty is risky business. Going to jury trial and being convicted is a disaster—the ultimate offense in the American criminal courtroom.

But I did not feel much compassion for Earnie Libido as he stood before me panting nervously, drenched in sweat, and babbling almost incoherently. Maybe he deserved this anxiety state. I didn't know. What I did know was that his current lawyer could soon look forward to squiring Mr. Earnest Libido to a legal massacre conducted by the forked-tongued Judge Joseph Blugeot. What could be done for him at this point? I asked myself. He's a goner. Why take such a case? Why volunteer for the rack and screw?

In my own way, I expressed these concerns to our prospective client: "Mr. Libido, as you are undoubtedly aware, Mr. John Wilkes is an extremely busy attorney. And because of his vast experience and skill, his fee is considerable, particularly where he is expected to drop everything and devote full attention to a client's emergency. At the moment, he is in court. Your current situation sounds most unfortunate and legally quite difficult. However, as you may be aware, no case has proven too difficult for Mr. Wilkes, and I'm sure he could serve you well if he can squeeze you into his schedule. Why don't you leave me your documents, come back at four this afternoon, and I'm sure Mr. Wilkes will be able at least to spare a few moments to talk to you."

Earnie Libido looked at me. His eyes moistened as he gave me his surprisingly limp hand to shake. As I took hold of his wet, spongy hand, he said, "A million thanks. You can bet I'll be here at four on the dot. We need to act quick. We gotta put off that sentencing date. Move for a continuance, right? Maybe sometime in the twenty-first century, eh? Ha!"

I asked our eager-to-be client when he was scheduled for sentencing and was shocked to hear his answer.

"Tomorrow."

FACT OR FICTION

"Goddamn! Son of a bitch! Unbelievable! What an asshole!" For the twenty minutes it took Wilkes to read the presentence report of Earnie Libido, he gave a running commentary of expletives which assured me that this presentence report was no different from the hundreds he had read during his legal career.

Except for perhaps police reports, no legal document is so filled with bias, distortion, and libel. Churchill could have been speaking of them when he said, "I should think it impossible to state the opposite of the truth with more precision." Mark

Twain would have said, "You've got to take them with a ton of salt." Yet few writings have more impact on a person's life.

These works of fiction are concocted out of the minds of inadequate personalities fronting as objective truth tellers; they are written by so-called probation officers, an institutional title which has few rivals for classic Orwellian Doublespeak. The only persons who get probation in the justice system are those who should never have been prosecuted in the first place.

Wilkes had little respect for the probation officers who prepared these short works of character assassination. They always worked to the detriment of his client by invariably characterizing the defendant's humanity solely in terms of his act of social deviance. By focusing entirely on the crime and making it the single standard by which to measure a human life, it was inevitable that each defendant's biography would be just another portrayal of evil and a justification for unrestrained societal revenge. What made it so hard to swallow was that all this venom was packaged as the objective observations of a neutral professional—the probation officer, the court's designated hit man.

My friend, despite his anger at Libido's report, cautioned me. For I became outraged at the slander of the probation officer and condemned them all. "Calm down, Schoon," he said. "They're not all this bad. It's the rotten ninety percent who give the others a bad name."

But Earnie Libido's probation report was even too much for Wilkes. "The guy who wrote this was born too late. He'd have made a perfect train guard on the Auschwitz Express. He calls Earnie—and every poor slob he analyzes for all of thirty minutes—subhuman sewage fit only for permanent segregation from society. You'd think Libido was a strong-arm stickup artist, a gang leader, or a triple ax-murderer instead of a two-bit telephone solicitation chiseler."

Libido's report matched the worst we had seen. It was filled with a thousand little cruelties about the "subject defendant"—the PO's hygienic term for the human being he was deriding with his poison pen. The report triggered in Wilkes the anger that fueled many of his unrestrained retaliatory strikes against these cowardly ghostwriters of judicial barbarism. I was always amazed at Wilkes's painful sense of justice, which, no matter how many years went by and how many courtroom atrocities he witnessed or fought against, never subsided. He may have been hyperbolic and crazy in his way, but his passion generated from injustice helped him survive and succeed.

An injustice done against a client was taken personally. Wilkes didn't ignore it or accept it or tune it out like so many of our colleagues did in psychic self-defense. A clinically dispassionate and impersonal approach—otherwise known as avoidance or neglect—saved lawyers the horror of absorbing the pain recklessly inflicted on their clients by judges, prosecutors, and probation officers whose busy schedules and malevolence prevented rational, sensitive treatment. Sure, our clients often did naughty things, but that was no excuse for treating them like societal rubbish.

Wilkes suffered from no lack of an instinct for self-preservation; he just could not help interpreting the attacks by the justice system functionaries on his clients as personal attacks on himself. He was ready to wage unrelenting war on those who would do him harm. Clients were the inevitable beneficiaries of Wilkes on the warpath.

As Wilkes continued ranting about the report, I thought it time to interject an important point. "My friend," I said, "there is no sense getting up in arms just yet. Mr. Earnie Libido is not our client, and given the short time between now and his sentencing tomorrow, it appears unlikely that he will be."

PERPETUAL MOTION MACHINE

No sooner had the words left my mouth than in walked Earnie Libido, looking just as anxious and sweaty as when he had departed hours earlier. It was precisely four in the afternoon. Earnie's forehead was beaded with so much perspiration, it looked like he'd broken out in a heat rash. His chubby little cheeks, glistening with moisture, looked made of porcelain. But it was Earnie's mouth I noticed most of all, because it was the closest thing to a perpetual motion machine I'd ever seen. Without so much as a "How do you do?" Earnie's motor-mouth was off to the races.

"Thanks so much for seeing me, Mr. Wilkes. I appreciate it, and man, do I need to talk to you. Mr. Scopehoover undoubtedly told you about my situation, which is bad; you don't need to tell me just how bad what with sentencing tomorrow and that stupid report and me without a good mouthpiece, er, counselor, I mean that guy Hardson is walking malpractice, and Jesus, he's all that is between me and the slammer; and then there's that black-robed serpent they call a judge. All he does is speak dago, *'e pluribus unum.'* Out of all the asshole judges in the world, how come I get the biggest? And that jury! I can't believe they convicted me. I'm as innocent as a bystander. Never should have happened, Mr. Wilkes. No sirree! That jury would have convicted Jesus Christ himself. Yessirree! Don't get me wrong, I may not be a saint, but I sure as hell am not guilty. Know what I mean?

"Sure, you know, don't ya, Mr. Wilkes? You're the best. I know. I asked around. Wish I'd have done it before trial and came to see you instead of that bald-headed bum I got."

FEE TALK

My friend looked at our prospective client with the friendly gaze of a pickpocket unobtrusively working a crowd. Wilkes said to Mr. Libido, "I dislike entering cases at this stage. It's like a neurosurgeon taking over a brain operation after his colleague has accidentally severed the brain stem. There just ain't a helluva lot I can do."

"I'll pay!" protested the desperate Libido. I appreciated his getting to the point. So did my friend.

"I know, but it's so very late. Sentencing is tomorrow," said an uninterested Wilkes.

"Whatever it costs!" said Earnie.

"Well then, how about this figure?" Wilkes jotted down a number on a pad. All I could make out were the zeros, of which there were many. Libido's eyes widened as he looked at the number.

He sat down and made noises as if he were gasping for air. After a few moments of pained silence, Earnie spoke. "All this for just a few hours work tomorrow?" He looked to Wilkes in disbelief. "I knew it was gonna be empty-my-wallet time when I walked in here, but I had no idea you'd want this much. I'll have to hock the family jewels. All this for a few hours?"

Wilkes was still standing. He smiled slightly at Mr. Libido and walked behind his chair. "The painter Whistler was asked a similar question in a court case once. He was asked how he could possibly ask a small fortune for a painting he had completed in one afternoon. Whistler replied as I do, 'I ask for the money not for the work of an afternoon, but for the wisdom of a lifetime.'"

"This is too much, way too much," said Libido.

"Not really."

"The customer is always right," smiled Libido.

"Not in my professional experience," replied my friend.

They were like two prizefighters feeling each other out in the early rounds. Having witnessed these fee-haggling disputes many times in the past, I knew Libido didn't have a chance. No one could beat Wilkes at fee talk.

"Look, Mr. Libido, I don't charge you based on the idea that your case will take a few hours. They never do in my experience. Further, when you hire me, you hire a trial attorney, not a plead-guilty lawyer. You're hiring me for a trial whether you want one—or more accurately in this case, whether you're lucky enough to get another one—or not.

"Last, Mr. Libido, you came here because you know the kind of work I do. I quote another great man, Aldo Gucci, who said, 'Quality remains long after price is forgotten.' Think about it."

The enthusiasm of the talkative Mr. Libido waned quite a bit after he received the blow from the note with the number followed by all the zeros. Wilkes's fee speech further quieted him. I suspected there were very few times in his life that Earnie Libido was lost for words. He knew that there would be no conning John Wilkes. This depressed him, but not being one to give up without a fight, Libido regrouped and proceeded to regale us with a multitude of fee promises: "Look, I've got this great business I've just started. Already incorporated and everything. It's a winner for sure. Let me put you down for half of the shares.

"No? Well, look, today is your lucky day, Mr. Wilkes. Yessirree, it sure as hell is. Let me make you a millionaire. I got this one big account receivable, which you can have now, and I'll assign all the future income from that account to you; it's got a growth potential like you can't even imagine.

"No, well, man, you drive a very hard bargain, Mr. Wilkes, so how about this? I'll give you my entire telephone solicitation business; it's a surefire money-maker once new ownership takes over and gets the law off its back. There's millions to be made in that business for sure. Jesus, it is so easy to sizzle those folks on the phone. You can sell anything for a thousand percent markup and never leave your office. Just sit on your ass and watch the money roll in. How about it?

"No? Well I can see you're a tough man to please, Mr. Wilkes, but I think I've got just the thing you and your associate Mr. Snoozover will love; just look at this guaranteed diamond and gold Cartier watch I'm wearing. Ain't she a beauty? You know what these little babies cost, don't ya? I just happen to have sixty more like it in my car. You could sell them for monster big bucks, and the car I've got sitting in the lot of this building, it's yours."

As Earnie stuck out his left wrist for Wilkes to inspect the beautiful watch, my friend delicately touched the crystal with his index finger, made a sound like flesh on the griddle, and retracted his finger as if it had been badly singed. This was to signify the watch's certain unsavory origin.

Earnie Libido got the message. He concluded his fee offers. "No? Well, how about all my assets, the rights to my internal organs, unlimited quantities of my blood, and my firstborn son?''

To this generous offer, Wilkes responded by observing that we were a cash-only business. ''It appears we have reached an impasse,'' said my friend to the almost prostrate Earnie Libido. ''Now I must be going.''

Without saying a word, Earnie Libido reached for his briefcase. He quickly unlocked it and unloaded on Wilkes's desk enough greenbacks to match the enormous scratch pad figure Wilkes had presented him a few minutes before. I asked him if he wanted a receipt. Libido responded scornfully, ''A receipt? Hah! What I need is a surgeon to stop the hemorrhage.''

Wilkes was staring at the mound of money on his desk. Without lifting his eyes, he said to the money, ''Yes, of all operations, the walletectomy is by far the most painful.''

As I put the money in our little safe, I thought of the complete success of the surgery.

NIGHT SHIFT

Taking this case at the last minute warranted the outrageous fee Wilkes charged. Kamikaze duty should be high-paying at least. The all-night work vigil that followed was nothing compared to what we were headed for the next morning with Judge Joseph Blugeot, the many-tongued man who had put Wilkes and me in the Tombs for contempt in Johnny Wad's little pot case.

We had to attack the probation report, and this meant taking on the probation officer, a confrontation loathed by judges as much as the probation department. I never met anyone who welcomed critical examination of their work. The problem with challenging judges or probation officers is that they have the power to not only rule on your challenge—and dismiss it—but also to retaliate with the full force of their vindictive wrath.

I reminded Wilkes of the judge before whom we would appear the next morning. ''It's Judge Blugeot, Wilkes. The guy you called a racist honky motherfucker the last time we were in his court. He'll probably give Libido a hundred years and suggest you do the first fifty."

My friend was not the least bit worried. He said, "You know, Schoon, we couldn't have had a luckier break than for Blugeot to be Libido's judge. It's gonna give us all the time we need to prepare."

Wilkes looked to our puzzled client, who rightfully believed Blugeot to be a wicked man and evil judge. Wilkes explained: "Yep, put a man in authority and his defects are magnified a hundred times. It makes prediction of behavior so easy. I may get thrown in jail again, but, Libido, you'll get your continuance."

Our new client grinned. I don't know if he believed Wilkes or not, but having paid a king's ransom for his services, he wanted very much to believe.

DAWN OF DESTRUCTION

"Your Honor, I have been recently retained by Mr. Earnest Libido for purposes of filing a new trial motion, a motion to strike the presentence report, other related motions, and perhaps for sentencing if the new trial and other motions should somehow fail. I will need a reasonable continuance for all this, of course." This was Wilkes's opening salvo to Judge Joseph Blugeot. The second round quickly followed the first.

"And since you and I, Judge, have had a most unfortunate history of interaction, I must also move for your disqualification from this case based on your established track record of misplaced animosity toward me and my clients. I could expand on this, but I think you know what I am talking about. So, I suppose to put first things first, you should rule on the sufficiency of the recusal motion as the first order of business."

You could see the blood pressure soar in Blugeot as he listened to this. Here he was looking forward to dishing out a few decades of prison time to the vulnerable Mr. Libido, who had been virtually undefended by the V-6, Charles Hardson, when in steps this disgusting intruder intent on taking away all the fun. I saw hate in the man's eyes as he attempted to compose himself and say something that would avoid the legal booby traps he rightfully suspected my friend of laying.

"Where are your moving papers? I see no motions on file, Mr. Wilkes." The judge thought he had us there.

"An excellent point, Your Honor, but one which makes my point for a continuance. With all due respect to Mr. Hardson, Mr. Libido's former counsel, the fact that he has neglected to file anything demonstrates the need for conscientious counsel to fill the vacuum. There clearly needs to be a motion for new trial, a motion to strike the mistake-ridden, biased, and slanderous probation report, and an investigation to pursue an ineffective-assistance-of-counsel claim. At this point we are quite ready to go into chambers and have Mr. Libido explain the promises made to him by Mr. Hardson as to the filing of those pleadings. Yet nothing was done. We cannot proceed, and neither could Mr. Hardson. Now, with the able assistance of my colleague, Mr. Winston Schoonover, whom incidentally you also held in contempt and threw into the Tombs in our last appearance before you, we were able to put together last evening a one-hundred-page affidavit to support our motion to have Your Honor step aside in this case."

Blugeot, being a bright bully, knew Wilkes had just made an arguable point—meaning a record that could bring about appellate intervention in Wilkes's favor unless the judge did something to fix things. I could see the wheels spinning in the man's head. Blugeot looked for help from Earnie's ex-lawyer, the incomparable Charles Alvin Seneca Hardson, who had been sitting in the front row paying very little attention to the proceeding. "What say you to this, Mr. Hardson?"

Hardson said, "Yeah, well, maybe I am a little late in filing my papers, Judge, but now it looks unnecessary since I have been deposed as Libido's lawyer. And I might say that this is the first I heard of Mr. Wilkes coming into the case. I mean, these people could have had the decency to let me know so I could be at my other appointments this morning."

Hardson was thus no help to the judge. By his pathetic admission, he had expected to appear to represent Libido this morning, yet he was totally unprepared. Wilkes seized upon the point, which the judge knew was growing better by the minute.

"There," said my friend. "Mr. Hardson would have been asking for a continuance anyway, because, by his own statement to the court, he believed he would be handling this hearing this morning, yet was unable to do so due to the press of business, or other good cause. I'm sure he wants to file those legal papers he has so diligently been working on."

Hardson could only nod as if in agreement. He had no choice—either he was a lazy, unprepared, incompetent slouch, or, as Wilkes so generously lied, a very busy man unable to meet the demands of his hectic schedule.

Since Hardson was no help, the judge looked to the prosecutor, the slovenly Miles Landish, who lifted his huge frame out of his chair to belch, "I see this as a ploy to deny the state its due in a timely fashion. We oppose all delay. We urge immediate sentencing. The public safety demands no less."

"Yes," said the judge quickly in response. "I agree. All motions for recusal, for new trial, for striking the probation report, and for anything else you might conjure are all denied as of this moment. Now, Mr. Wilkes, are you ready for sentence?"

He said this as if he were about to sentence my friend again. Much as he might love the opportunity, my friend reminded him that the rules would not allow anyone to be sentenced this morning.

"Clearly not, Your Honor. For as you know, a recusal motion must be heard by another judge. Your job is to pass on the sufficiency of the showing. I have my affidavit complete with exhibits and case law right on point. Will you not even look at it, sir? I believe that you are without jurisdiction at this point to do anything else."

As he did in moments of volcanic anger, Blugeot blurted out an angry comment in Latin, *"Pluet super eos laqueos,"* which loosely means, "He shall rain traps upon them." It was a reference to the wily moves of Wilkes and his apparent check-mate—at least for this day—of the judge.

Wilkes immediately responded in kind, "Remember, too, Proverbs, thirty:thirty-three: *'Qui fortiter emungit, elicit sangui-nem,'* " which in this case meant, if you punched a beast hard enough in the nose, you would eventually draw blood.

From previous experience, Blugeot knew he was no match for trading barbs with Wilkes, no matter what the tongue. Perhaps thinking another contempt citation was the way to solve this obstacle to moving Libido's case along, he then tried to bait Wilkes: "Sir, are you once again demonstrating your contempt for this court?"

"Absolutely not!" shouted Wilkes at the judge. But to me in a loud stage whisper he said, "I'm concealing it!"

19

The Return to Judge Knott's Chamber of Horrors

It was the improvement of the splendid Techtronic Cranial Infiltrators, or TCI's as we've come to know them, that led to society's ultimate victory over crime. When the JUST US DEPT. first used TCI's in satellites, their capacity was technologically restricted to monitoring the moronic mumblings of the earth-bound populace. It took the discovery of the brain print—every human's unique brain wave pattern—and particularly the sociopathic wave which permitted JUST US DEPT. technicians to detect instantly criminal thought patterns from the orbiting TCI's. Henceforth, good and bad thoughts of all humans could be continually monitored from cradle to grave, or in other cases, from test tube to vaporization chamber.

Round the clock surveillance of all human thought was quite an advance, but it merely provided knowledge. There was never time for the JUST US DEPT. to process the criminal's thought pattern in time to neutralize the villain before he could strike his foul blow. While termination of the barbarians invariably would come speedily after the criminal act, this was not soon enough, for history teaches that incapacitation may well lead to some degree of deterrence, but never prevention.

For many years, JUST US DEPT. scientists labored to find the celestial solution—a means of not only detecting the criminal thought pattern, but also a way to strike the malefactor down before he could do his contemplated dirty deed. Finally, after many failures (including the unfortunate liq-

uidation of Des Moines, Iowa—which led to the bloody "TCI riots" following the error), success came with the invention of a marvelous supplement to the orbiting TCI's. Now scoundrels on earth could be terminated by microwave from space within twelve nanoseconds of their criminal thoughts (with a very acceptable mistaken liquidation rate of less than 1%). We know this wonderful invention today as the Cerebral Mushmaker.

EXCERPT FROM GROTEK'S
"ORBITAL TECHTRONIC CRANIAL INFILTRATORS:
SATELLITES IN SPACE-AGE CRIMINAL JUSTICE."

It's difficult to argue logic in the temple of reason when the high priest is off his rocker.

JOHN WILKES

Wilkes knew Blugeot would not easily excuse himself from the Earnie Libido case. Blugeot never granted defense motions, particularly if it would deprive him of the intense satisfaction of sentencing a criminal defendant such as Earnie Libido to many years in prison. There was the audacity of the man in demanding trial by jury—another insult to Blugeot—an implicit statement that this judge could not be fair. And then there was his towering animosity toward Wilkes.

There would be no convincing Hizoner about the correctness of our legal position. The more Wilkes argued for the judge to allow another jurist to look at whether Blugeot ought to be off the case—which was, after all, the law—the more determined Blugeot became to refuse what Wilkes requested. Getting anything from the judge was a long shot in any case. As Wilkes would say after hearing Blugeot make one of his famous Latin comments—*"Ut puto deus fio"* ("I suppose I am becoming a god")—"It's difficult to argue logic in the temple of reason when the high priest is off his rocker."

Wilkes knew what he was saying in court was for the record only. There would be no persuading this lunatic. So many judges develop a similar form of insanity, it makes you wonder if it's the job. Or maybe it's the kind of person who'd want the job. Whatever the reason, if you want a test of a person's mental health, just put a robe on him.

Blugeot's craziness was the worst of them all because of its insidiousness. To the outsider looking in on his courtroom, the bastard appeared sane as hell—a paragon of mental health. But he was not just crazy in the invisible way only judges and priests can be, he was also bright and evil to boot. The other judges knew, but they weren't about to do anything about it. After all, they could be next.

BLUGEOT SPEAKS

"Now, Mr. Wilkes, I have reviewed thoroughly your papers supporting the motion to have another judge hear this case," lied the judge, who had about five minutes of uninterrupted time to view our papers.

"I might say that I find the papers extraordinarily libelous in the extreme and, if not protected by the absolute privilege from lawsuit, would have brought about a speedy verdict against you. I mean the use of such epithets as 'Judge Blugeot demonstrated this venomous hatred toward attorney Wilkes by first ordering him to break the law by revealing attorney-client communications and then, in a diabolic reaction, arbitrarily holding him in contempt and throwing him in jail for merely restating his client's comments as ordered.' "

Wilkes seemed pleased with the track Blugeot was on; he could see that our well-crafted papers were unconsciously pushing the judge down the garden path to disqualification.

Wilkes said, "Well, that's the way it happened, Judge, and don't forget it drove you to file that baseless complaint against me with the Bar Association. That is why you and I should never be in the same courtroom together."

"Lies! Monstrous lies!" said Judge Joseph P. Blugeot. "How dare you say—" Hizoner turned his eyes to read some more from our scandalous papers—" 'On information and belief and personal experience, the judge is bigoted against the following who have been or will be represented by John Wilkes:

the young, the old, the middle-aged; individuals of any race, color, creed, or religious denomination; persons charged with felonies, misdemeanors, infractions; all witnesses; litigants in civil suits.'

"This is slander, Wilkes! This is outrageous! This is typical of you and your ilk! But cunning as you are, you'll not taunt this judge into the recusal you seek."

Shit, I thought. All that work last night dreaming up ways to masterfully bait Blugeot out of the case. All for naught. But my resourceful friend was not done yet.

"I see that Your Honor has reviewed our papers. But I don't think Your Honor has accurately addressed the important factual assertions which by law require another judge to at least pass upon whether you should hear this case.

"Look," said Wilkes, faking sincerity and respect with all his might, "I don't expect you to find the assertions made to be truthful, even though I believe with all my heart they are. You're too involved. After all, how many lawyers have called you a racist honky motherfucker before, Judge? No, no, no, you are just too emotionally involved. If not in reality, then by appearance. That's why the law in its majesty demands in these instances that someone else look at the allegations."

SPEAKING IN TONGUES

At this Blugeot started speaking in the many tongues at his command. He looked up from his throne to empty space and muttered to himself a self-pitying *"Extinctus amabitur idem"* ("The same man dead will be loved").

To which Wilkes responded, *"Omnium consensu capax imperii nisi imperasset"* ("If he had not ruled, people would have thought he could rule").

"Mr. Wilkes, I speak the truth," replied the judge. "Remember, *'Veritas, a quocunque dicitur, a deo est.'* ('Truth stated by anyone like me is from god')."

"Judge, I think Bracton said it best, *'Veritas habenda est in juratore; justitia et judicium in judice'* (In context: 'Give me a little less truth and a little more justice')."

Wilkes could talk Latin-jive with the best of them. Matter of fact, he was the best I ever saw. He made mincemeat out of Blugeot, who visibly got wobbly on the bench after this humiliating exchange with my friend. The funny thing about it was that they were the only two in the courtroom who understood what the hell it was they were talking about. But Blugeot was too out of touch to know this; he acted like it was a national humiliation.

He said with great bitterness in his voice, "No, Mr. Wilkes, it was Bacon who said it best, 'There is no worse torture than the torture of laws.' You've made your record, and now I'm going to, er, to think a moment, yes, whether to grant your fervent wish that another judge review these papers to see if they make out a case for my recusal."

And so the court was silent, very silent, for several minutes until a strange, sickly smile appeared on Blugeot's puss. He rose from the bench slowly and put both his hands together as if he were a priest about to lead us in prayer. "Mr. Wilkes, there is both good news and bad news I have for you. Which shall it be first?"

Wilkes said nothing.

"Cat got your forked tongue, Mr. Wilkes? Hah! Well, the bad news is that you shall appear before the Honorable Yulburton Abraham Knott tomorrow morning at nine to learn of his decision on your motion to depose me from this case."

Our client, Earnie Libido, anxious for a kernel of hope (it was his liberty on the line, after all), thought this was good news. It meant the judge had granted our motion. He had allowed another judge to pass on our affidavit of recusal. Thinking that if this was the bad news, what came next couldn't be too bad, he interjected, "But what is the good news, Judge?"

Blugeot smiled broadly at our pathetic lump of Libido and

said, "If Judge Knott rules as I expect, sentencing shall take place in this department immediately after that ruling. *Magna est veritas!* (Truth is great!) This court will be in recess."

Y. KNOTT

Talk about out of the frying pan and into the fire! Appearing before Judge Knott, another nut cake Wilkes-hater, would be like appearing before Blugeot's clone. Knott was the Ivan the Terrible of the criminal bench. He was Blugeot without the veneer of civilization. He was openly callous, cruel, and bigoted on the bench, and some said that these were his best qualities.

Knott was the best evidence that a genetic change takes place when lawyers put on black robes. Rational attorneys mutate into intolerant, people-crushing dispensers of despair. Either that, or the robe strips away the patina of compassion and reveals the true nature of the being placed in power. Either way, when it's a Blugeot or Knott who is revealed, you fear for your future.

Because the Honorable Yulburton Abraham Knott was the most often avoided and challenged judge, he was less busy than his brethren. Thus he was the judge held in reserve for assignment to cases when another judge had been successfully challenged.

Knowing Knott was hovering in the wings as the backup had a chilling effect. Few lawyers would be so foolish as to challenge their judge knowing that they would be delivered into the clutches of Judge Y. Knott. No sense taking another step into the inferno. This meant Knott had a lot of leisure time on his hands. He spent much of it in chambers writing futurist essays under the pen name of Grotek—his vision of the day when there would be no more crime, no more freedom, and no more defense lawyers.

Wilkes and Knott, of course, had done battle before. It was with Wilkes that Knott had long ago tried his first case as a judge—the disastrous trial of the pimp, Hank "The Lizard"

Gidone. Then there was the more successful defense of Whiz Kid gang leader Lyle Diderot. From these awful courtroom experiences Wilkes would say, "I reel in horror when I draw Judge Knott. You get more justice from the KGB."

I pointed out to my friend as we left the courtroom of Joseph Blugeot that afternoon how bleak things were looking. I did it not so much to inform him of the obvious as to get his reaction.

"Sure it looks bad," grinned Wilkes, who acted as if he'd just taken a not guilty verdict, "but Earnie Libido's still a free man on bail, and we've got twenty-four hours to think of how to keep him that way. And now the issue for Judge Knott isn't how to deny him a new trial or how many years to put him in the slammer; it's whether Blugeot should sit on the case. We've been given a reprieve; now let's get to work."

SHORT INTERMISSION

We worked in the next hours on the motion for new trial and sentence of Earnie Libido. We knew the odds of having Judge Knott disqualify Judge Blugeot were about as good as Knott declaring a general amnesty for all prisoners in the Tombs. So we knew we were going to face Blugeot the next day. We used the time to expand our legal papers.

The only event worthy of note during this brief interregnum occurred while I was preparing the sentencing memorandum and exploring the idea of victim restitution with Earnie Libido. One of Wilkes's favorite attempts at offering specious options to sentencing judges was the familiar refrain, "This case belongs in the civil courts. Let the alleged victims seek their reparations there. This is not a criminal case despite what the prosecution and the jury may have thought."

Thinking that I might paint Earnie as a possible civil defendant in a giant class-action suit brought by his victims and that this might give the judge an idea that justice would be eventually carried out in another forum after he inflicted his terrible criminal punishment on Libido—and most important, that if Earnie were a free man, capable of earning a living, he might also be a man capable of paying out lots of moola to the successful civil suitors—I asked our convicted telephone solicitation swindler if any of his victims had filed civil suits against him. He replied in terms that quickly ended this line of defense. Earnie Libido said:

"They can't sue me; I took all their money."

KNOTT AGAIN

The next morning as we walked Earnie Libido to court, I had the feeling it would be a one-way trip. Earnie Libido's life as a free scam-man was drawing to a close. Or so I feared. Wilkes, on the other hand, seemed strangely tranquil. I wondered about the source of this serenity. Usually, at times like this, Wilkes was like a racehorse at the starting gate, full of tension and hellfire, barking out orders and ready to explode with energy once the gun went off. This morning he was calm to the point of appearing lethargic. Maybe he was satisfied with the minor miracle he pulled in getting another judge to look at our bias challenge against Judge Blugeot. Maybe it was another day of freedom for our client. Maybe he was on drugs. I couldn't figure it.

Judge Knott was not the kind of judge you looked forward to seeing. He was every bit the defendant hater Blugeot was, except he could not have cared less about keeping it a secret. Knott fancied himself the ideal judge—capable of quickly handling enormous workloads—but fortunately, not given the chance. The trains ran on time in his court. Each morning he would stand in the doorway to his chambers that led to the court and watch the courtroom clock second hand move toward the twelve, and at the instant the clock read 9:00 A.M., he would charge the bench to bring the proceedings to a start precisely at the appointed hour, and woe be to the poor unfortunate who walked in a few seconds late. Fortunately, thanks to the law we made on a few of my friend's successful contempt appeals, lawyers cannot be contempted anymore just because

they are a second or so late to court—as long as they make up
a plausible excuse for the record.

Once a trial started, Knott presided as if ending the lawsuit
as quickly as possible were the only goal of the proceeding.
Trials in his court were done in record speed. This often was
accomplished by excluding huge portions of the defense testimony based on reasons no sane lawyer could possibly anticipate. But no sane lawyer would ever willingly appear in front
of Judge Yulburton Knott. After his reputation was established, only the ignorant and the unlucky were assigned to his
court: the ignorant because they were too stupid to know
enough to challenge him; the unlucky because they had cast
their challenge against some other black-robed monster only to
find that casting out one devil brought on a bigger one.

It was all by plan, of course. The judges knew that if
Y. Knott were the known alternative, few lawyers would cast
a challenge against their assigned judge. And they were right.
Not many challenges were launched except when Knott was
the primary assignment. Then challenges flew like cannonballs.
This is how Knott had the spare time to devote to the writing
of his nightmarish vision of perfect justice.

But this time we had no choice. Whether it was Blugeot or
Knott made little difference. Either would be an efficient con-
ductor of the judicial railroad to Sing Sing for Earnie Libido.
With the ever efficient Knott at the wheel, however, it would
be more like a bullet train to oblivion.

ALL RISE

At exactly 9:00 A.M., Knott charged the bench like a new king
taking his throne. We were all in place as the judge surveyed
the scene of battle before him. He smiled his smile of toxic
sweetness and said, "Now, Mr. Wilkes, I have read your vo-
luminous pleading against Judge Blugeot despite the fact that
it violates my five-page limitation. I read it because I have
seldom seen such libelous, scandalous calumny in my entire

career as a lawyer and judge. This is, in my judgment, contemptuous in the extreme."

We were off to a bad start, it seemed. Wilkes had not uttered
a word, and he was on the verge of contempt. As expected, it
got worse.

"I of course deny the frivolous motion to challenge Judge
Blugeot for bias and immediately reassign the case to his court
for sentencing and, what else, oh yes, the motion for new trial.
In reverse order, of course. Now, if you think you have goaded
me into jailing you as a means of continuing Mr. Libido's case,
you are quite mistaken. I note your penchant for such tactics.
They are notorious. Therefore, I will avoid the trap by putting
in the record my comments and merely send you to the courtroom of Judge Joseph Blugeot."

"Gosh," said Wilkes, "what a surprise."

"I shall not be goaded, Mr. Wilkes."

"I must say, Your Honor, that I am shocked and saddened
by your comments. Your not even allowing me to argue my
motion is most regrettable. I might have then heard just what
is so allegedly slanderous in my papers, or had the ear of the
court for just a few seconds prior to Your Honor's ruling. This
is the tradition of practice at the bar, I believe."

My friend was making his record of being judicially screwed.
He was doing it in his usual fashion—without it reading anywhere near as nasty as he said it. This preserved a dandy appeal and also infuriated the trial judge. What could be better?

Wilkes continued to pour it on. "I anticipated this action.
It saddens me to say this, but I feared there might be such
summary treatment, and that is why I prepared this challenge
to Your Honor's sitting in judgment of this motion based upon
your clearly established record of animus toward me and my
clients. I would like to file this motion now." Wilkes plopped
an inch-thick sheaf of papers on the clerk's desk.

Knott looked at the new motion to disqualify as if it were a
bundle of live cancer cells. That Wilkes would even dare challenge the judge selected to rule on the challenge to Blugeot
made him angry. But as he had prepared himself to do, he

maintained his composure so as not to be baited into any slips of the tongue and so reveal what he was actually thinking. He did not pick up the new motion, and instead said, "I shall hear no more motions or argument. You are wasting precious tax-payer seconds by your palaver."

"How about thirty seconds in the name of Due Process?"

"Mr. Wilkes, I am about to give you thirty days in the name of common sense."

"*People* v. *Common Sense*, Judge? Could I have the cite to that case? And may I not have my motion to disqualify you even heard?"

"This is a game. You will just challenge every judge in the building to avoid the day of judgment for your client. Just where would you like this matter heard, Mr. Wilkes?"

"I was thinking about Lourdes as my first choice. But really, any other department will do."

That was it for Knott. His self-restraint had limits. He was far too rigid and intolerant to allow these remarks to go un-punished. In that way, like most hate-filled people, he was capable of being manipulated toward a desired end—if your desired end was to get thirty days in the slammer just to con-tinue a case.

"That'll be thirty days, Mr. Wilkes." Judge Knott paused, looked directly at my friend—as if to say, "Now, hear this, Smart-ass"—and said: "But it is to begin after, repeat af-ter, the hearing in *State* v. *Earnie Libido*."

With that, he dismissed us with an imperial wave of the hand. Wilkes yelled back at him as he was disappearing into chambers, "You have the power to do this, but not the juris-diction. My affidavit disqualifies you! You heard it here first! Remember!"

So we were off to Judge Blugeot's courtroom. Knott's bailiff followed Wilkes with handcuffs noisily and openly at the ready. On the way to Blugeot's court, I was amazed, as I never ceased being amazed, at the fact that Wilkes was unperturbed by the morning's events. Me, I would have been numb with fear for my client, my practice, and my rear end. Getting thirty days in the Tombs is like getting drop-kicked into the asshole of the universe. I know. I've been there.

But that is why Wilkes was unique—few if any persons I ever met in this life have been so uncaring about what the others, particularly those seated in the pantheons of power, thought or said about him. He cared mostly about what he thought about himself. My friend resided in a different world from most.

As we approached Blugeot's court, Wilkes gave me an order to go and punch out an appellate writ to stay his custody until his contempt appeal could be heard. "Argue the jurisdictional point big," he said. "If we win it, it'll nullify everything that happens today. It'll be worth going to jail for. If I have to."

As I left him, I saw him pull from his briefcase several thousand pages of legal materials, a *Blacks's Law Dictionary*, and a penal code. He explained, "I'll try and make this hearing in Blugeot's last as long as it takes you to get the stay." With that, he disappeared behind the swinging doors of Blugeot's courtroom, books in hand, and a puzzled but still free Earnie Libido in tow.

20

Back to Blugeot

It is not good to have respect of persons in judgment.
PROVERBS, 24:23

This is not Russia. This is the courtroom of the Honorable Joseph Blugeot.
JOHN WILKES

"Yes, I did relay the words conveying that you were a racist honky motherfucker, Your Honor. Of course, I meant no disrespect."

These were the first words I heard Wilkes say to Judge Blugeot as I entered the courtroom. It had taken all morning and part of the afternoon for me to file the bail motion, so I guessed that Wilkes had been talking nonstop for about four hours. The judge looked about as angry as I had ever seen him. Prosecutor Miles Landish was on his feet protesting Wilkes's last comment as contemptuous and asking the judge to shut Wilkes up by jailing him. As I sat down amid this activity, I thought that the morning's filibuster must have been entertaining.

Wilkes looked at me for a sign as I plopped down in a chair beside his standing figure. I whispered that the appeal was filed and that we'd just have to await word from the court whether he was to be freed on bail. Either that, or as soon as the filibuster ended and Earnie Libido was sentenced by Blugeot to a few hundred years, my friend would join his client in jail for the first thirty days.

WORKING THE CROWD

The courtroom had been nearly empty when I left Wilkes earlier that morning to begin my work filing the bail petition, but on my return, it was packed with people. They were chattering and snickering and giggling guilty little laughs at my friend's remarks and at the judge's retorts. It was a rare engagement, titillating, in fact, for a Wilkes filibuster was a spectacle, although usually a brief one as my friend was often bucketed in the early going. How he managed this morning in front of this judge to keep his lips moving and stay out of irons was a mystery, but he was closing in on his personal best for longevity. Usually when a judge lets a lawyer talk too much, it is because he's about to lower the boom and doesn't want it said that the defendant did not get his fair say.

Wilkes continued his monologue to the impatient, frustrated, and purpling Judge Blugeot. "And by those vulgar words which were the primal essence of my beleaguered young client's terrified thoughts at the time of his sentencing, I knew I could no longer have the great privilege of appearing in front of this learned court. I knew no matter what my true and innocent feelings, no matter how well intended I might be, that you, Judge, could never understand or forget or forgive my conduct but would always harbor the foulest ill will against me and my future clients. And I have long rued the day of that most unfortunate interchange of words between us, and I have hoped for a small sign that perhaps someday you could let bygones be bygones and that I might once again appear in this hallowed tribunal in the unhampered pursuit of justice."

PURSUIT

Wilkes leaned over to me and whispered, "Of course, in this court you're always in the pursuit and never reach the target." I smiled to myself. This was too volatile a situation for the participants to betray a hint of the mocking that was going on. Wilkes, too, kept his serious mask on.

These were the rare moments with Wilkes. There he was telling the most outrageous lies right in the face of the judge, falsehoods so obvious and in language so perfumed with sickening flattery that I knew my friend was having the time of his life. We knew—hell, everyone knew—that the judge knew what was going on. One look at his coloring face told you that. The growing audience, swollen such that people were now standing shoulder-to-shoulder in the back of the court, knew what was going on. That knowledge put the tension in the air. We knew that this could not go on.

MESSAGE TO THE DELIVERER

But the tension also made the experience all the more satisfying. How often was there a chance to talk to a self-righteous, intolerant son of a bitch in such a way? How often could one lie so fabulously in a judge's face, and by it let him know exactly what you thought of him? What a way to let loose the accumulated anger at the outrages of so many years against the one who so often was the architect and dark deliverer of such pain! And all in words so contrary to the real message being given! God! This was lawyer heaven!

Wilkes continued: "It appears that the hoped-for day of our rapprochement is to be delayed, Judge Blugeot. Still we must do the People's business as two professionals, perhaps coolly and at arm's length for the moment, perhaps not as frequently as I would desire, and perhaps without that gift of fraternal trust and brotherly love that always lubricates life's frictions, but at least with civility and honor as in the great tradition of eight hundred years of common law."

Wilkes was so melodramatic, so falsely sincere, so full of baloney, he was sounding like the keynote speaker at an undertaker's convention. He continued.

"Now, as I was saying an hour or so ago, I believe my being here at this time is legally improper. I told you what happened in Judge Knott's court earlier. He has contempted me and ordered me to defend Earnie Libido in this courtroom and then promptly go into custody. His bailiff is sitting right here.''

Blugeot relaxed at this thought: soon Wilkes would be where he belonged, in the Tombs.

Wilkes pointed to Judge Knott's bailiff and said, ''The bailiff is prepared, no doubt, to dutifully execute his master's order. There, Judge: he's the uniformed man sitting right here in the front row with the big grin; the man who has been rattling the handcuffs with which he intends to manacle my wrists and escort me into custody as if I'm some vicious criminal. Stand up and take a bow, sir. Don't be bashful. You're only following orders.''

The bailiff, reddening with embarrassment, remained seated.

''Well, Judge, I've got to tell you in all candor that I'm hardly in a mood to defend Mr. Libido, emotionally upset as I am by the action of Judge Knott and his executioner here. I am still reeling from the *ultra vires* manner in which I was treated in Judge Knott's court, which was in vindictive retaliation for challenging his legal standing to sit and rule on the legality of my earlier challenge to Your Honor's jurisdiction in hearing this case. And if I might digress a moment . . .''

DIGRESSION

Judge Blugeot fidgeted on the bench. He was past comprehending Wilkes. He could not stand more delay, aching as he was to sentence Earnie Libido to all those years in custody. But he could not shut my friend up, much as he tried. Malevolently, he interjected: ''Wilkes, your time is up. Your entire irrelevant presentation this morning has been one transparent and tiresome digression in which you continue your campaign to flout the authority of two tolerant trial judges. I will not hear any more of your petty, sneering, reprehensible attack on Judge Knott. Vent your spleen elsewhere. Now, either we get on with the sentencing of the defendant Earnest Libido or we'll just let Judge Knott's bailiff take you away right now.''

Miles Landish offered a brief suggestion to end the discussion: "Judge, put this man in cuffs! By God, contempt him!"

"Sit down?" asked Wilkes, ignoring Landish's remarks altogether. "Why, I have not yet addressed Your Honor on Mr. Libido's motion for new trial. I have not discussed the matter of striking the many defamatory comments from the probation report. I have not argued the question of the appropriate sentence for Mr. Libido. Then there will be the issue of bail pending his appeal. I have not called the witnesses in support of each of these important matters because they should follow a ruling on my challenge to Judge Knott's ruling on the propriety of my earlier challenge to your sitting and ruling on the above issues. Will I not even have a chance to allocute on these issues?"

Wilkes did not give the judge a chance to answer. "Of course I have that constitutionally guaranteed opportunity. This is not Russia. This is the courtroom of the Honorable Joseph Blugeot, where it is never said that a man may not be allowed to present his case."

Well, not quite. It is never said out loud in court in the judge's face. Except for today. Wilkes continued: "This is not a court where a judge gives the tiniest taste of fairness to the participants and then does whatever he pleases. No, this is an American courtroom, where a man may have his day in court and where no man, not even one wearing a robe as black as his heart, can tip the scales of justice to deny a man his say."

DUEL

Friendly members of the gallery, mostly fellow sufferers of the defense bar, were moved to murmur to each other. Wilkes's words struck a familiar chord—that which Wilkes said could not be true was the absolute truth: no defendant got a fair shake in Blugeot's court. The gallery grew somber, as if prescient that it was the moment for the bullfighter to sink his sword. The comedic aspect of the event ebbed from the courtroom. This was now a deadly duel.

Blugeot, feeling the power of his exalted position and prompted by more whining objections from the prosecutor, Miles Landish, had had it. He was going to end his frustration by use of the full measure of his terrible power and end Wilkes's mocking monologue. He yelled at Wilkes, threatening him in Latin and Italian and even English with more contempt; he reminded him what a "stay in the Tombs" could be like. He ordered his bailiff and Judge Knott's bailiff to prepare themselves for action. Wilkes ignored the threats and continued the filibuster.

DARK FORCES

"You speak in many tongues, Your Honor, which has always been a testament of your vast talents, but the things you say, I regret hearing. What you say does not deter me from doing the job the Constitution of this great country charges me with doing. In courthouses throughout the land I and my friends in the defense bar have moved us all toward that ideal of making the reality of daily American life approach the promise of our Constitution."

"Will you just shut up, Mr. Wilkes?" commanded the judge.

"Judge, please, please contempt him and stop this nonsense," pleaded Miles Landish. "I'm sick of this drivel."

Wilkes continued as if not hearing either of his adversaries, knowing full well that embracing himself in country, the flag, and the Constitution would not save him from the likes of Judge Joseph Blugeot. "Sure there have been times when we backslid, but we have always recovered the lost ground and moved forward as a people. And I and my friends of the defense bar have helped move the reality of our existence toward that ideal, as hard as the job may be at times. It is hard because—"

"I said shut up!"

"—there are so many obstacles, so many dark forces in the

way of equality and simple fairness. For even in the house of
the law, there is still blindness, hatred, dishonesty—"

"Damn you! Bailiff, if he says another word—"

"—favoritism, stupidity, and intolerance. How many times
will police perjury be accepted as gospel in these courts?"

"I'll not hear another word!"

"How many times will outrageous rousts of black kids on
the streets of Harlem be upheld in the courts as lawful deten-
tions?"

"Wilkes, I cannot tell you how much pleasure it gives me
to say—"

"How many times will prosecutors withhold evidence of a
defendant's innocence and get away with it?"

"You have had it!"

"This is not the promise of the Constitution; this is the de-
basement of the Constitution. Every time it happens we move
miles from its promise, the promise of individual freedom and
equal justice we all took an oath to enforce."

"Seize that man! NOW!" The bailiffs, given ample warning
by Blugeot, quickly moved to Wilkes's sides and grabbed his
arms—obviously the wrong place to grab. My friend's mouth
kept moving without pause.

"But we of the defense bar have a dream—a dream of a day
when everyone can walk into a courtroom where equality
means something; where honesty is respected and lies are de-
nounced; where official brutality—"

"Christ, will you just shut up?" asked the judge.

"—is punished and compassion is doled out not only to the
highly placed, but to the lowly placed as well—"

"Contempt! Contempt! Contempt!" yelled the judge.

"—and where a man can expect to be treated like a man
instead of a number, an enemy alien, or a piece of garbage."

TALK DIRTY

God, I loved it when Wilkes talked dirty to a judge. And what
Wilkes was saying was absolutely obscene to Blugeot, whose

face was now puffed to the point of exploding. Holding Wilkes
in contempt would not discharge the rage the judge felt for
Wilkes, who himself had ably demonstrated his profound contempt for the judge.

Blugeot tried to respond to Wilkes's latest insult. His mouth
began uttering words in Latin and Italian to the bailiffs. Landish kept begging for a jailing. The bailiffs didn't understand
what to do because they were, at best, monolingual. They just
stood there holding my friend's arms while he kept speaking.

"After so many years fighting in the trenches, I now feel
like old Ulysses felt, tired and worn, but still able to call to
mind the good days—and there have been good days—when I
and others joined in memorable battles against *dark forces* which
obstruct progress toward the promise of the Constitution. We
have done justice in the past. We will do it again."

The bailiffs, now looking at each other and then to the judge
for direction, were befuddled as the judge kept up his incoher-
ent Mediterranean mumblings while my friend continued his
own part of the weird duet.

"Times have changed, and it is now more difficult to defend
the citizen-accused. But when I get to feeling burned-out by
this work, by the pressure and omnipresent pain inflicted by
the *dark forces* in this system, which try and too often succeed
in keeping me and my brothers and sisters of the bar from
pushing the law's reality forward, I recall the words of Ulysses.
These are the words which keep me going despite the difficul-
ties heaped upon me. Ulysses said:

> 'We are not now that strength which in old days
> Moved earth and heaven, that which we are, we are—
> One equal temper of heroic hearts,
> Made weak by time and fate, but strong in will
> To strive, to seek, to find, and not to yield.' "

"Jesus Christ, Judge!" yelled Miles Landish. "Do something! Speak English! Stop this man!"

At this, a few lawyers in the audience, perhaps moved by

Wilkes's words or the Tennyson poem, jumped out of their seats and came to me to ask what they could do to help. What a wonderful surprise this was! They knew they were volunteering for kamikaze duty.

JUDGING JUDGE KNOTT

Wilkes quickly saw this as an opportunity to move from filibuster to the attack. "I see that my witnesses are here, ready to attest to the fact that Judge Yulburton Abraham Knott is biased against me and my clients, and indeed, any criminal defense attorney and citizen-accused. This will prove what I was not even allowed to say in his courtroom—that he should never have heard the motion I made to recuse you from this case. Having no jurisdiction to rule on my motion to recuse you, Your Honor, Judge Knott's ruling is a nullity. In doing so, I will prove that he is unfit by temperament, disposition, and intellect to hear any criminal case, and for that matter, any civil case as well. These witnesses will prove what is known to everyone but never admitted. They will establish the truth about just one corner of darkness in this courthouse. As my first witness, I call my esteemed friend and honest lawyer, the Honorable Jacob Witzer."

As Jacob Witzer, one of the surprise volunteers, approached the witness stand, prosecutor Landish was on his feet screaming, "This is outrageous; he can't do this! Come on, Judge, wake up! There is no issue before this court concerning Judge Knott. Judge Knott cannot be judged in this court. This is misconduct! This is misconduct! Don't let him do this!"

FACE-OFF

Judge Blugeot was now the darkest burgundy in color. He stood up trembling and pointing his finger at Wilkes as Witzer took the stand. He tried to speak, but nothing came out. Soon we could hear a barely audible Italian phrase, *"Rassettarsi la testa,"* which Wilkes told me later was Sicilian slang for "Shut the fuck up." He kept repeating it over and over; the repetition gave his voice strength, and it began to rise in volume. *"Rassettarsi la testa! Rassettarsi la testa! Rassettarsi la testa!"*

As he repeated the mantra, he did the most amazing thing. He ran down from the bench, went over to Wilkes, grabbed him by the lapels, and yelled in my friends's face: *"Rassettarsi la testa! Rassettarsi la testa!"*

Wilkes was surprised by the judge's behavior, but he did not move; he stood his ground so that the two men were eyeball-to-eyeball. The judge kept repeating his order to shut the fuck up: *"Rassettarsi la testa! Rassettarsi la testa!"*

Wilkes yelled back at the judge in Italian, *"Che disgrazia! C'e molta gente qui! Non ho nulla da dire!"* ("What a disgrace! In front of all these people! I've nothing more to say!")

"Rassettarsi la testa!" yelled back the judge in Sicilian.

"Fidatu executur!" ("Trusted executioner!") yelled back Wilkes in Latin.

Seeing at last an opportunity to finish Wilkes, prosecutor Landish got up close to the two men and yelled at Judge Blugeot, "Outrageous misconduct! Contempt the bum, Judge! Bucket the bastard!"

But the judge wasn't paying attention to the English-speaking peoples of the world at the time. He was in Wilkes's face, mad as hell, screaming his favorite Sicilian phrase over and over and over.

It was an uproarious scene: the mad judge and Wilkes yelling at each other in Italian and Latin; Miles Landish right next to them screaming his plea for Wilkes to be held in contempt and jailed; the bailiffs both standing with their hands locked on Wilkes's arms and not quite sure what to do; and the court reporter sitting in awe of the whole event, having given up taking any of it down since the judge and Wilkes squared off in dialect.

LIGHTS OUT

After a few moments of this, Blugeot finally did something more than spray Mafia slang in my friend's face. The judge reared back and launched a vicious swing at Wilkes. My friend, still yelling Italian at Blugeot, ducked his head in time so that the wildly thrown right cross swept cleanly over his head and landed flush on the nose of Miles Landish, abruptly cutting short his latest request for Wilkes's internment.

Landish went down as if the bones in his legs had emulsified; he fell onto his well-padded backside, out like an unplugged light. Wilkes, still crouched, kept his eye on the wild-eyed, delirious Blugeot. *"Come sei maleducato!"* he said to the judge in the vernacular of the moment ("What bad manners you have!")

Blugeot responded with a left hook to my friend's midsection. The blow seemed pathetically weak as left hooks go, one Wilkes could have blocked easily had he wanted to, but my friend had other ideas. He accepted the blow like a batter who takes a slow curve on the back to gain a cheap base on balls. On impact, Wilkes gave a loud "Oooooofff!" and crumpled to the floor, landing right on top of the unconscious Miles Landish.

Wilkes immediately began moaning loudly. To everyone in particular he shouted a pained: "The lousy bastard cracked my goddamn ribs! Is there a doctor in the house?"

The two bailiffs had by now let go of Wilkes and in self-defense grabbed the wildly swinging judge, who was still screaming in Latin and Italian at my prostrate friend. They lifted Blugeot bodily and hauled him into his chambers.

With the judge taken away in the arms of the law, it was time to get Wilkes the hell out of there before the arms came back for him. I called on members of the defense bar to assist me in rushing my stricken friend to a hospital to attend to his injuries. Six came forward, and we carefully lifted—after all, it was at least possible that he was actually injured—the wailing

Wilkes off the dozing Landish, carried him to a car, and from there whisked him to the hospital.

DIAGNOSIS

At the hospital, Wilkes was placed on a gurney and wheeled into the emergency room complaining of chest pains and demanding to be attended to by his personal physician, Dr. Feelgood, Dr. Simon Comfort. Fortunately, the doctor was on duty and soon came to attend to his longtime patient.

Dr. Feelgood knew Wilkes well enough by now to realize when a long stay in the hospital was a legal necessity. The circumstances of this hospital admission were such as to allow an immediate diagnosis. He took a quick look at my friend's bare chest and said, "Wilkes, you've come down with another bad case of litigious meticulosis, severely bruised if not fractured ribs, a clearly indicated subdural hematoma with possible nerve and lumbar vertebrae implications."

At this news, Wilkes smiled faintly. The good doctor continued.

"We'll have to start a series of tests to determine the exact scope of these injuries, so I must insist that you remain here for at least . . ."

He paused to look in my friend's eyes to see just how long a stay would be needed. This form of communication was a familiar routine between the two. Wilkes's eyes must have screamed for a millennium, because Dr. Feelgood said: ". . . for an indefinite period of time—at a minimum. Put him in the ICU, boys."

As they wheeled my friend away, his head turned toward me and he grinned a pain-free *"Vini, vidi, vici,"* which, if you ever studied Caesar or smoked Pall Malls, you would know means, "I came, I saw, I got a continuance."

The orderlies began pushing the gurney, and I watched it bang into and open two swinging doors marked INTENSIVE CARE UNIT: QUIET AT ALL TIMES. As Wilkes disappeared down the hallway behind the doors, he began chattering with the orderlies about his food, visitation, telephone, and entertainment demands for this stay, which promised to be a long one.

Standing there, listening to Wilkes's fading chatter, the still-swinging doors fanning a small, cool breeze, I thought with satisfaction that John Wilkes had indeed won another continuance for his client, a rest in his favorite hotel, and the day.

21

The Hospital Visitor

When men are pure, laws are useless.
When men are corrupt, laws are broken.

DISRAELI

I got visitors wid some paper lookin' for apples and oranges
and dey gots motor oil instead, and now dey wants ta play
fuck around in da courts.

MOE VILGRIN

The morning following the debacle in Blugeot's court, Earnie Libido—at large and ever grateful—and I were making our way to the hospital to check on Wilkes and give him the latest news in the off chance he had not heard. The news was really news, the kind that makes it big not only in the newspaper, but in the courthouse hallways, bathrooms, and chambers. Here's the Adell Loomis story as it appeared in the *Times*:

JUDGE PUMMELS DA AND DEFENSE ATTORNEY

The usual tranquil setting of the Supreme Court was transformed yesterday afternoon into violence as a one-sided slugging match erupted between a judge and two lawyers. In a bizarre courtroom session, Judge Joseph Blugeot is said to have jumped off the bench during a hearing and savagely attacked both defense attorney John Wilkes and prosecutor Miles Landish. Ironi-cally, Wilkes had been urging that the judge had a preexisting bias against defense lawyers and particularly himself just prior to the attack. While denying the accusation, the angry judge ordered him restrained by two bailiffs and then bolted from the bench and began wildly punching the defenseless attorney.

In the process, the judge decked

prosecutor Miles Landish, who may have been attempting to restrain him. Landish was carried from the courtroom unconscious, but was fully alert later when this reporter spoke with him. In an exclusive interview, the somewhat baffled Landish said late last night, "I saw the judge come down. I asked him to throw the guy [Wilkes] in jail for contempt, and whadyaknow, he throws a punch and I'm waking up in the jury room with some ant-head doc shovin' smelling salts up my snoz."

Landish, sporting two very black eyes and a possible broken nose, added that he did not believe the judge was swinging at him. "Hizoner was aiming at Wilkes. Had to be. He had no beef with me. Christ, we're on the same team."

Judge Joseph Blugeot was unavailable for comment, but did release through his clerk the following statement: "Yesterday during court, I took the unusual step of alighting from the bench to intercede on behalf of my two bailiffs, who were attempting to restrain an unruly lawyer who refused to obey a court order to be quiet. When the lawyer attempted to attack me, I defended myself. I understand that in the fracas the prosecutor was hurt, and I believe the defense lawyer must have hit him while attempting to strike me. For the moment, I have no plans to bring charges as there are more expeditious means of sanctioning obstreperous lawyers. Tomorrow I will be on the bench as usual to commence trial in another criminal case."

The defense lawyer in the center of this controversy is John Wilkes, the controversial well-known lawyer and former candidate for judicial office. Wilkes, although disliked by many in judicial and prosecutorial offices, has been called on many times to represent such luminaries as former senator Hyman Taurus Fabricant, former judge Milton Purver, local basketball coach Joe Guts, famed TV evangelist Reverend Bob Smite, and a host of lesser-known celebrities.

Wilkes is currently in Bellevue Hospital under the care of Dr. Simon Comfort. The doctor, in a telephone interview yesterday evening, said that Wilkes's condition is stable. "He is conscious and in good spirits, but I'm keeping him here until I run a full battery of tests. Internal bleeding, broken bones, or even spinal damage have not been excluded at this point." Wilkes was too ill to be made available by the doctor for an interview.

Because a packed courtroom watched the action yesterday, there will be no shortage of witnesses. I have interviewed at least half a dozen, and all echo the views of the one eyewitness closest to the melee. The witness, who requested anonymity, said that the judge's attack was unprovoked and astonished everyone in the court. "He lost it," he said. "He went crazy. The judge was swearing at Wilkes in Italian or Latin and swinging at him. He made his bailiffs hold Wilkes. It was a cold-blooded act of Nazi brutality. I am surprised the judge has not been arrested."

WALKING TO BELLEVUE

Earnie Libido and I chatted merrily on our trip to see my friend and Libido's savior. Adell Loomis's piece was terrific, and why not? She had been in love with Wilkes ever since she wrote about his campaign for the Supreme Court and always gave him great coverage.

Libido was ecstatic. He was free and for the moment had no future court date. Wilkes had successfully eliminated Blugeot from the case. Another judge would have to be appointed and familiarize himself with the case. This would take weeks—an eternity for us, given the mere two days time we had been in the case thus far. God! So much had happened in the last forty-eight hours! That was what living in Wilkes's world was like: you were always superalert to experience some new excitement, action, change, challenge, or conflict. It was like being in war.

As we approached the hospital, I thought of the many times Wilkes had visited the place. Once he came to get his stomach pumped after swilling a melted cube of butter—this to prepare himself for a drunk driving trial in which he bet the jury he could try the case without difficulty after drinking as much as his client was accused of drinking. He did. The client was acquitted, and Wilkes came to Bellevue to get his innards turned inside out.

AUDITIONS

Then there were the times he came because of the urgent need for a continuance on a case. When all else failed there was the ready diagnosis of exhaustion by Dr. Simon Comfort—always good for a week or more delay. These hospitalizations were vacations to my friend, a time to catch up on his reading, to relax and watch the tube, flirt with the nurses, and talk to friends on the phone and in person. It was also a time to audition new clients, but only if they passed the initial screening—"Can you afford my outrageous fees? Well then, come on up!"

Libido and I reached Wilkes's room just before noon. He was in fine spirits and greeted us warmly. Reclining on the top of the bed wearing a bathrobe and slippers that were definitely not hospital issue, he seemed the picture of good health.

I saw a pile of books on his bed stand, the top one being the recently published *Andromeda Strain*. On the bed were two yellow pads with a lot of scribbling on them. Wilkes noticed my eyes on the pads and said, "I have been deluged with calls from prospective clients eager to hire the battling barrister despite his current disabled condition. I've had to fight them off. I've seen three in this room already this morning. It's great to be loved!"

I asked him, "Seriously, how are you?"

"Never felt better in my life!"

"Did you read the news yet?" I was sure he had.

"Sure. Adell called and told me we'd made page one. She wouldn't tell me who her anonymous informant-eyewitness was—she claimed privilege of the press, but I knew it was you, eh?"

I nodded, and he grinned an ear-to-ear, check-out-the-enamel smile.

"Blugeot's a goner and he knows it. He's disgraced, no matter what happens next. He'll be challenged now in every criminal case. He'll be known as the forked-tongued judge of uncontrollable rages. He'll never get elevated. And he's given me what every defense lawyer in New York would give up a year's orgasms for—a lifetime pass from the cases of the necrophilic-tongued Joe Blugeot!"

As we talked of the tremendous victory, I wondered how Blugeot would react. Exceedingly proud and arrogant, a man whose identity was totally drawn from his work and the constant flattery from the toadies he bossed, this episode had to be devastating for him. No matter what happened in terms of prosecution—which was highly unlikely given his status as a member of the prosecution team—he would now be looked on as an eccentric, a curiosity if not a madman. Blugeot was smart enough to know all this and mean enough to . . .

DR. FEELGOOD

My thoughts were interrupted by the entry of the good Dr. Simon Comfort. Dr. Feelgood had on the hospital green uniform of his profession, wore a custom-made gold and ivory stethoscope on his chest which looked like a voodoo necklace, and had a surgical mask lowered around his neck. Without saying a word, he put the business end of the scope on Wilkes's toe, which was still covered by a fine leather slipper, and said to all, "Just as I expected, a weak pulse. I must insist that you take it easier until this gets stronger. I shall enter on the charts that your condition is unchanged."

"That part is damned accurate," laughed Wilkes. He looked to me and said, "You know why this guy wears a mask, don't ya? Just wait till we get his bill. You'll find out!"

Wilkes threw his head back and laughed at his own joke. He said to Earnie Libido, "Earn, this is the doctor who first perfected the operation called the walletectomy. He makes my fees look reasonable."

The doc smiled at all this. He and Wilkes loved joking with each other about their beloved professions. "You know what a tragic waste is?" asked the doctor.

"Sure," said Wilkes, "a busload of doctors going off a cliff with three empty seats."

"Ridiculous!" replied the doc. "Doctors would never ride in a bus. I'm afraid the bus was almost filled with members of your learned profession. You're doing pretty well with this battery of tests, Wilkes. Now answer this one. Why does this hospital no longer use rats in lab tests and now uses lawyers? There are three rather obvious reasons."

Wilkes hummed for a moment while he reached into his memory bank. "First," he said, "lawyers are almost human and thus good for experimentation with an eye toward human extrapolation. Second, they are far more plentiful than rats. Third, hum, you got me again, Doc.''

"Third and most important," stated the doc in a stern voice, "there is far less chance of the technicians growing attached to them prior to vivisection. This was a tremendous problem with the little, furry creatures. No one wanted to destroy Mickey Mouse.''

The phone rang, and Wilkes looked to me to answer it. He explained in a merry voice: "My pulse! My heart! My ribs!''

I answered. It was another citizen-accused looking for New York's man of the hour to defend him. The man's voice was queer. It had a low, raspy tone which sounded like a growl, and he spoke in a dialect of Mob-English. He said, "Er, look, buddy, I'm callin' to talk to yer man Wilkes. I druther go box-to-box on this and not open channel 'cause yer man and the assholes don't see eye-to-eye, which is good 'cause neither do I, see? Anyways, some visitors with paper came into my place lookin' for apples and oranges and found motor oil instead, and now they wanna play fuck around in the court for the hardware, see? Well, I ain't gonna take no fall for them four-teens and sixteens. I need a mouth to put that paper up their asses. So is your guy off premises, er what?''

I did not understand all of what this fellow was saying, but it made no difference for the moment. I asked Wilkes if he wanted another audition, and he said sure if the fellow passed the screen test. I asked the voice if he was prepared to part with a fortune, and he answered, "You got your brains in the drain, bud? I know who I'm hirin', and I'm good for what you got in mind. When's a good time?''

I nodded to Wilkes that the voice was apparently ready to divest himself of his money, and Wilkes said loudly, "Well then, send this gentleman in distress up to see us at once!''

MOE VILGRIN

While we waited for Maurice Vilgrin, the name I extracted from the voice before he said he'd be up to see us in ten minutes, I repeated what he said to me and confessed I did not know exactly what the hell he was talking about. Earnie Libido's expression grew somber. Normally a motor-mouth, Earnie said slowly, "I used to hang around guys who talked like that. He's low-level Mob, no question about it."

Earnie gave a worried look to Wilkes and said, "Look, you gotta get better and then be prepared to defend me. I have a huge financial investment in your health and time, and for both reasons I ask that you not take more new cases, especially a little search warrant case for army rifles. That's just my wish. Now, I'm not telling you what to do. Not me. No sirree. Just thinking of self-preservation, you know."

Wilkes laughed. "Don't worry, Earnie. We have more cases than we know what to do with. But I enjoy the auditions. It keeps me on top of what's happening on the streets, and better yet, I get to refer all these lost souls to good attorneys and keep them from the V-6s which infest the city. It makes the lost souls happy; it makes my friends happy; and it makes me happy!"

Earnie smiled in relief and appreciation and said he had just come up to say hello to his favorite attorney and now would be moving along. As soon as he left, Wilkes said to me, "But if this new guy has an interesting six-figure case, you'd be surprised how much work I can squeeze into our busy schedule." He laughed again loudly. Then he called on the phone to the nurses' station. "Room service?" he asked. "Send up a few bottles of my favorite wine. I'm about to have more company."

"I just love the nurses here," said my friend. "Of course, I love all women, but these ladies are mature in years, tough as nails, and goddamned if the one on duty now doesn't have blue hair!"

INTERPRETER

He was ebullient. Irrepressible. Outrageous. Fun. I asked him what exactly this Maurice Vilgrin was talking about. "I understood a little," I said. "He's got a problem with guns. He wants to hire you. But that's about it. What's box-to-box mean?"

"Phone booth to phone booth. It's what the crooks say to use when they suspect a wiretap on their home lines, which is always. I can't tell you how many cases I've had where the crook says, 'I don't care if they are listening. Fuck you!' Then they go on to spill the beans right on the phone. Dumb. The pros always go box-to-box to talk business."

I asked, "And he said he had visitors with paper looking for apples and oranges. I guess that means the cops came with a search warrant looking for . . ." I paused without an answer.

"Dope probably. You know, like fruit of the poisonous tree. But they found motor oil instead, which means they found heavy artillery, M-14s and M-16s, and Mr. Vilgrin wants us to challenge the warrant and get all his weapons back."

"I'd say we've decoded the message," says me. "I will venture that he's not charged yet and wants the guns back quick because maybe he fears that if the appropriate ballistics are run on some of them, a homicide or two might get solved real quick."

Wilkes looked at me promptly. "Why, Schoon, you're a great detective. You've got this guy figured out. So who shall we refer him to? This is no six-figure case at the moment, that's for sure."

Before I could answer, the room grew dark with the shadow of the most frightening man I'd ever seen. Moe Vilgrin introduced himself.

MOE SHOWS

From his weather-beaten, scuffed, and soiled shoes to his short, flat top hair, he was six feet tall. He weighed at least 270 pounds, and given his pear shape, not much of it was muscle. The skin on his block head was swarthy, bore a full day's beard, and had a dark blue tint to it. His eyes were big, dark, too far apart, and separated by the bridge of a wide nose that looked like it had been flattened by an anvil and pushed over his face by a cement spreader. He had lips as thin as two slivers, and a chin—if you could call it that—that dropped quickly from the bottom lip like a ski jump to his stump of a neck.

To Wilkes, still reclining on the bed, Vilgrin rasped out his greeting, "Eh, you Wilkes?" His mouth was full of chipped yellow and tan teeth.

My friend nodded. Moe looked to me. "And you da guy I just talked to on the box?" I nodded. "And we can now talk, what chew call it, confidently, conferdentally, confiden-charly?" We nodded.

Moe Vilgrin sat down in a chair next to Wilkes and explained his problem to us pretty much as we had it figured. He said he needed his guns back but did not necessarily want to claim they were his possessions. "Like maybe I got 'em to hold for someone. But maybe some are dirty socks."

"I understand perfectly," said Wilkes. "You didn't buy them. You didn't use them. You never got them dirty. But maybe the owner did, and you don't desire to claim in court that they are your possessions. I don't suppose the true owner would care to come forward?"

"Nope. Could get embarrassing," said Moe. He reached for Wilkes's water jug and asked ever so politely, "Hey, mind?" Before Wilkes said "go ahead," Moe downed his first glass and was pouring his second.

Wilkes said, "If you have a few dirty socks in the hamper which are best left unseen, then there's not much point in advertising that they're yours."

"Yeah," replied Moe.

THE ARSENAL

"So there's the rub," I said. I understood that anyone idiot enough to claim some of the guns would be giving a message to the cops that the others should get detailed inspections. And if you claimed them all and ballistics had been run, you might be signing your own indictment. I asked Moe how many socks there were altogether.

"Four hundred seventy-eight."

Wilkes and I looked at each other, stunned at the size of Moe's arsenal. I could see Wilkes was now intrigued. Moe was clearly in with big, bad company, and they were in a tight legal jam. Just the challenge for a clever lawyer: to maneuver his client to safety.

"Of course," said Wilkes, "you could just forget about them. I mean, you are not charged. It's not a crime to possess rifles. Many a good huntsman in New York has rifles in his closet. Others keep them for self-protection."

But usually not enough to start a revolution, I thought.

"Yeah, Wilkes. Maybe yer right." Moe paused to down his third glass of water. He smacked his thin lips and rubbed them with the cuff of his long-sleeved shirt. He motioned to Wilkes for a glass of water while he poured himself another, and my friend took the offering and sipped it.

"But I figure that it ain't gonna rest. The assholes are gonna be coming for me when they can't find a few serial numbers, 'cause maybe from all the movement, some got rubbed out. So I need to put someone on retainer to throw my bail and get me out quick and file legal crap to knock out the bad paper."

"Well," said Wilkes. "Perhaps I will be able to help you. Let me give you some instructions. First, send me the warrant they left behind. I need the number on it so I can go downtown and get the affidavit. Also send to my office this amount of money to retain me, and then keep in touch."

Wilkes handed Moe the paper with his fee written on it. Usually when prospective clients looked at the fee, they fainted, wept, or screamed. Moe Vilgrin just looked at the numbers and nonchalantly put them away in his shirt pocket.

THE REFERRAL

Wilkes then asked Moe who had referred him to us. I knew that Wilkes was not interested in sending a thank-you note to the generous and wise referrer; he was curious. He had never been a lawyer for the Mob. It had its stable of house *consiglieri* to take care of low-level bums like this. And Wilkes had once run against one of their men for the Supreme Court, which displeased the capo very much. So it was odd that they would send us this meat-head soldier on such a sensitive case.

But maybe all was forgiven. Maybe they saw that it was time to hire an Erle Stanley Gardner–type defender like Wilkes— "a fighting lawyer who is willing to go to hell to save a client even when the client isn't worth saving." As I thought about this, the phone rang. I grabbed it and told the party to hold on a second.

Moe stood as the phone rang. He looked to Wilkes and said, "No one referred me. I'm wildcatting. I don't want nobody to know dat I mighta lost da artillery. Might be dangerous. Certain people get mad, and then I might get lead poisoning. Ha! Ha! Anyways, I read about you in da paper, and I says, dis is da guy for me. Maybe you can get my stuff back. So I'll check out da money thing and get back to yous. Tanks for seeing me today considerin' yer present circumstance."

WIRED FOR SOUND

No sooner was he out the door than Wilkes was on the phone interviewing another prospective client, a paranoid who wanted Wilkes to sue every authority figure in the country. Wilkes handled the call quickly, and then the phone rang again. I could see Wilkes was going to have a wonderful time in audition all day, and I told him I would go back to the office and get some work done. I left him as he said into the phone,

"Now, what's this about an arrest for armed robbery? Of course you didn't do it. . . ."

BACK AT THE RANCH

I worked in the office all that afternoon on a million minor tasks that had to be done. The law, it is said, is like a jealous mistress, but I always thought it more accurate to say that the law is like Rommel of the Desert, ever ready to roll over you, to bury you, to make your life miserable at the slightest break in your defenses. And even if there is no weakness in your line, the law can still destroy you, because for all your strength and preparedness, you can't stand up to all its pressure.

The law is like that. It tests you every day. Probing for a chink in the armor, which when found is exploited, expanded, and entered. It never takes a rest. It makes many demands. Ignore them at your peril.

Like for instance: Don't answer a phone message from a client quickly enough and get hell or get fired. Don't file a motion in time and just watch the preening court clerk read you the rules and send you packing from the courthouse ("Local rule number twelve-oh-three, as amended yesterday by general order fifty-seven, subparagraph J-six, has revised the rule to require filing all motion papers seventeen days in advance of a hearing instead of ten. I'm afraid you will have to prepare a special motion for leave to file this tardy document and have the chief judge of the district approve it before I can accept this. And by the way, you'll have to type the entire motion over, because you have single-spaced your block quotes, which is also in violation of Local rule . . .").

Don't tell the prosecutor that you accept his magnanimous settlement offer within the ridiculously short time limit he gives, and reel with rage as he tells you that you are an hour late and the deal is off and that on reflection he has decided to double the number of counts to plead to and the years he will recommend for a sentence. And when you tell your client the deal he accepted is no more and that the new offer is doubly worse, you get fired and sued.

So the law is no jealous mistress. It's a tank division ready to do you in at the first opportunity. Because Wilkes taught me to understand this, I knew the details of the business had to be minded. I was the guy who handled this important minutiae. It was essential work, often tedious, but it was part of the bulwark.

FEELGOOD FEELS BAD

At four in the afternoon I got a call from Dr. Feelgood. He sounded very upset. "You better get down here right now. Something is wrong with Wilkes."

"What!" I said. "What could be wrong? I left him at lunch, and he was in perfect health. It can't be his ribs. He get indigestion from your food?"

"I haven't got time to explain, Schoon. I don't know if I can right now. Please get down here fast. We're doing everything we can."

The last words hit me like an ax in the gut. A nauseating numbness spread over me. I had never ever heard the doc speak to me or Wilkes in such somber terms. Wilkes really was in trouble. I hung up and dashed to Bellevue.

I got to Wilkes's room within fifteen minutes. He was not there. I sprinted to the nurses' station and demanded to know his location. She told me he was in superintensive care. "That's room 7117, but you can't go there. No visitors allowed for this patient. Doctor's orders."

"Like hell," I said. I ran down the hall, pushed open the door, and to my horror, there was my friend on the bed with an oxygen mask on his sunken, lifeless face. All the life spirit was gone. He was unconscious.

I noticed a guy in the corner. But it was not just a guy—it was a goddamned priest whispering last rites. No! No! Noooooooooooooooooooooooooooooooo!

This was a nightmare! It could not possibly be happening.

I was there with Wilkes just four hours ago and he was in top form, laughing and kidding, auditioning the masses who loved and wanted him, and feeling great.

I wheeled around and yelled down the hallway toward the nurses' station, "Get Dr. Comfort down here, now!" I ran to the station yelling again and again, "GET ME THE GOD-DAMNED DOCTOR!" The rattled nurse didn't argue; she made the announcement, "Dr. Comfort, to the nurses' station, stat!"

NO CLUE

The doc appeared in a minute, and I was on him immediately. "What happened? I bring a man in perfect health to a god-damned so-called hospital, and in less than twenty-four hours you've killed him! What is this place? Dachau? What's he got?"

Comfort looked devastated and bewildered. Wilkes was his friend, too. He didn't have the serene isolation from this tragedy that doctors usually have when they are about to lose another patient.

"I dunno what happened. Nothing to do with his ribs," he said. "He was fine at noon and seemed fine at two. He was still working the phones and having a good time, but then he started complaining about shortness of breath and feeling weak. He began drinking water from the faucet in his bathroom sink. And then he starts convulsing and becomes delirious. He starts sticking his finger down his throat and vomiting. Within the hour he was semiconscious, feverish, with labored breathing. Now, an hour later, well, you've seen him. Unconscious. Losing vitals. I've run his blood downstairs for testing. We're hooking him up on intravenous feeding to pump nutrients in him. Got him on oxygen. Right now I don't have a clue."

"What the fuck is that priest doing in there? Are you telling me he's gonna die?"

"His heart is barely beating." The doc looked down. "I can't explain. Let's go down to the lab and get some answers."

Doing something other than watch Wilkes die seemed like a good idea. We speed-walked to an elevator and descended to the lab where the blood work was being done. When we got there, a technician handed Dr. Comfort a sheet.

The doc examined the computer run and said, "We've run a test for just about everything, Schoon, and—What! Jesus H. Christ!" He stopped and looked to the technician. "Is this the workup on the blood sample I gave you?"

CICUTOXIN

The technician assured him it was: "Every poison known to man." The doc turned to me and said, "Wilkes has been poisoned with cicutoxin, *cicuta maculata L.*, better known to admirers of the philosopher Socrates as hemlock."

"Hemlock?" I shouted. "What?"

"It's an herb, part of the carrot family, but it won't cure your vision. It's correctly known as water hemlock. Looks harmless, like parsley. One bite of it, and after convulsions, paralysis, and respiratory failure, you are dead meat."

"What can we do? What's the antidote?"

"There is none. What we can do is keep him breathing and hope to God the dose he got doesn't finish him."

DEATH WATCH

We went back to the room. Comfort ordered a search of the floor, all rooms, wastebaskets, sinks, closets, drawers, clothes, and laundry for anything looking unusual. He ordered a check of the kitchen to see if the food supply had been tampered with. He ordered that no food or water be given the patient until further notice.

I told him he wouldn't come up with anything. I knew one thing—this was no lapse in hospital hygiene; it was an attempt on Wilkes's life.

We ran to Wilkes's old room and looked for the evidence that would confirm my suspicions. But when we got there, there was a new patient in the room. Everything'd been replaced or changed. Damn!

I rushed to the public phone in the hallway and called our investigator, Uriah Condo. I filled him in on Wilkes's condition and my suspicions. I asked him to go to the court and do some checking there. Then I went back to Wilkes's room to watch and wait.

ROOM 7117

Room 7117 was a grim scene. Wilkes still had the oxygen mask on and the look of death. He was attached to so many tubes and wires that he looked like he was donating all of his bodily fluids and electricity to the hospital.

Simon Comfort was over him, with a couple of blue-haired nurses at his side. He looked to a scope that measures the nutrient drip into the intravenous line; he checked the cardio monitor, which registered a slow, weak, and arrhythmic heartbeat; then he looked to another scope to check tracings I couldn't figure.

"What's that?" I pointed to the scope the doc was still checking.

"Brain wave. There's still activity there, thank God." I'll never forget those words, because as he said them, all hell broke loose. Alarm bells went off. Red lights began to flash.

The cardio monitor was showing a flat line!

Doc ripped Wilkes's pajama top apart. "Code blue! Code blue!" screamed one of the blue-hairs.

"Defib! Now!" yelled the doc. Immediately one of the blue-hairs slapped Wilkes's chest with a conductive material while the other reached behind her, flipped switches, and pulled out two electrodes the size of hand massagers. Comfort grabbed them and yelled, "Max power! Hold him!"

The zaps from the electrodes shook Wilkes's body. His chest heaved upward, his knees bent, and his head arched. The doc hit him again. The *zzzappp* sound was chilling, and it was backed by the low bass of the generator, which vibrated an octave below hair clippers and ten times as loud. The air had the smell of burned flesh. The craziest thought passed through me—I had witnessed an electrocution!

The doc, the nurses, and I fixed on the cardio monitor, which, at the moment of the electrocution, filled with a helter-skelter pattern of lines. We watched as they cleared.

"There's a beat," said the doc. "There, look! There's a beat!"

I saw the blips, faint, slow, and irregular.

22

A Death in Chambers

Justice is like poison: whether it kills or heals depends on the dosage.

WILKES AND PARACELSUS

If they had any morals, they'd be demoralized.

JOHN WILKES

The terrible news of Wilkes's death was carried on page one of every New York morning newspaper. Adell Loomis's coverage in the *Times* was typical:

The legal community was shocked yesterday afternoon upon learning of the sudden death of controversial and flamboyant criminal defense attorney John Wilkes. Hospitalized two days ago for observation following a scuffle in the courtroom of Judge Joseph Blugeot, Wilkes succumbed late yesterday evening at Bellevue from what his physician, Dr. Simon Comfort, described as a "toxic reaction to an ingested nonmedicinal foreign substance. We'll know more after the autopsy." Foul play has not been ruled out.

Wilkes's law partner, Winston Schoonover, was too grief-stricken by the loss of his longtime friend to comment. He was at the hospital last night when the sudden end came for his friend.

District Attorney Frank Hogan issued a statement late last night stating, "The death of John Wilkes is regrettable. He was a formidable adversary, although we did not agree with his behavior, tactics, or ethics. Other than that, we have and shall make no further comment."

Judge Blugeot, whose alleged punch sent Wilkes to the hospital, stated: "I was surprised to hear of his death. His personal style of conducting himself brought on his demise. What ye sow ye shall reap."

Wilkes will be cremated and his ashes will be dropped from a plane over the Tombs. No funeral services are planned.

WHO DONE IT?

The news was a shock to everyone. It was like the morning after a huge election upset. Everyone is surprised, but the losers are devastated and the winners are gleeful. There were many happy DAs and judges and probation officers after the news of Wilkes's departure.

I knew who poisoned Wilkes. It was the guy who visited him in the hospital. The guy who called himself Moe Vilgrin. The guy who wanted Wilkes to try to challenge a search warrant and get his guns back. The story was baloney—a ruse to get into the hospital room, spike Wilkes's water with poison, and make sure he drank it. It had worked beautifully.

I had our investigator, Uriah Condo, check out the warrants at the clerk's office at the court. None had been issued resembling the one executed according to Vilgrin's story. We already had figured the guy as Mob just by the way he talked. But why would the Mob want to take out Wilkes? He had taken a dive to lose an election to one of their bought-and-paid-for candidates, Lester Throckton, Jr. Wilkes hadn't represented them and so hadn't disappointed or crossed them. Why the hit?

The answer to that question came when Condo told me who was going on trial in the courtroom of the Honorable Joseph Blugeot. The defendant was Carmine "The Hitter" Bachizzio, a man whose nickname was not earned on the baseball diamonds of New York. Carmine was chairman of the board, sole stockholder, and chief executive officer of Murder Incorporated. He was Mob all the way. He was on trial for murder.

The clincher as to the fix was the news that Carmine's attorneys did the most amazing thing—they waived jury trial before Blugeot. How obvious can you get! Only two types of lawyers waived jury in front of Blugeot: idiots and fixers. Mob lawyers were not idiots, so it was clear that this case was wired by Carmine's attorneys and the forked-tongued judge.

The only explanation, given the timing, was that Blugeot had got word to Carmine's attorneys and made a Godfather offer which was not refused—one precious reasonable doubt acquittal was offered in return for one home run hit on Wilkes.

VENGEANCE

So there it was. Plain as a newspaper headline. Overwhelming evidence of Blugeot's guilt. Absolutely. But this mountain of incrimination wouldn't be enough to raise an eyebrow of suspicion over at the DA's office. There was no evidence in the courtroom sense, just a correct hook of a theory in search of someone to hang the evidence on it. The DA wasn't about to go looking for that kind of evidence. Not on our word.

If this score was to be settled, it would not be by the usual channels of prosecution. What did they care anyway? Wilkes was a pain in the ass to most of them, and they weren't about to believe a story as wild as the one I knew was true—that the multitongued Judge Joseph Blugeot issued an ex parte order for the murder of one John Wilkes with all deliberate speed.

If justice was to be done, it would be done in the old-fashioned way—privately. This did not bother me. Taking my personal vengeance against the man who murdered John Wilkes would be a great joy.

But how to do it? How to expose Blugeot, his mobster cohorts, and their murderous scheme? How do you do this lawfully, or at least quasilawfully, without tipping your hand and getting killed early on for your trouble?

This was no easy matter. If Blugeot was in this scheme, he had the entire organization of Mob Families at his disposal to take care of any threats of exposure. And there could be no doubt he would use it. He already had.

What we needed was a master plan, a brilliantly clever Machiavellian scheme to take our vengeance without using conventional methods of law enforcement. How to destroy Blugeot and Carmine without getting killed or ending up doing life at Sing Sing? That was the question.

ONLY ONE MAN

I knew of only one man who could conceive and pull off such a plan. Only one man could match wits with these devils and have a hope of not only living through it, but triumphing. And enjoy it, too! That man was the recently departed John Wilkes.

Who lives! Yes! Lives! Wilkes had figured out what had happened the first moment he began to feel the poison attack his body that afternoon in the hospital. That was why he self-helped himself to a stomach pump by sticking his fingers down his mouth and disgorging what he could. It was why he drank gallons of good faucet water from the tap—in New York, faucet water is "good" on the days it isn't orange-brown in color and doesn't make you puke your insides out. Compared to the poison, it was nectar of the gods.

It had been close, though. Wilkes came about as close to joining hands with the Grim Reaper as you can get and still come back. On that ICU room bed, his vital signs disappeared. His heart stopped. He was clinically dead.

Then Doc Comfort electrocuted him back to life with his handy defibrillator. But it was still nip and tuck for hours after that. Wilkes's heart beat faintly and irregularly. We feared that if he made it, there might be permanent brain damage from the ordeal.

FIRST WORDS

"Blugeot. Bastard. Did it." These were the first words he whispered to me that evening when he regained a semblance of consciousness. He turned in his bed and grabbed me by my shirt and tried to pull me close. I leaned in to hear the second thing he said before he lapsed back into unconsciousness: "Make me a dead man."

I knew what he meant. Wilkes had a lust for life and a wonderful instinct—which he always followed—for survival. He knew that if someone in the Mob had the job of killing him, any miracle recovery would bring on another attack. The Mob's rule in such cases was as simple as it was brutal: "If at first you don't succumb, we'll try, try again."

To surface alive would have been like competing with Rasputin for the Mob version of "How can I kill thee, let me count the ways." The ugly, bearded monk took poisoning, a dozen shots in the back, and a drowning before they got him. Wilkes would settle for ending the competition on the first leg of the murder-method triathlon.

SEALED FATE

Dr. Simon Comfort was our friend. He had almost lost Wilkes and was plenty pissed when I told him who tried to kill Wilkes. He made it possible to smuggle Wilkes out of the hospital after announcing his death. As soon as Wilkes was movable, we threw a sheet over him and wheeled him out of his room and down to the morgue.

All the way down the hall and into the elevator, the doc kept declaring Wilkes dead in such a way as to make sure no one would ever come near the body. He said at the nurses' station, "Make way. This body's contaminated with a virulently contagious unknown killing agent."

To the morgue attendant he said, "Dead man coming through. Give me an icebox quick and get out. I'm gonna seal it. This body has something deadly in it, and it still may be alive.'' Exit the morgue man.

Then the doc slapped a notice on one of the little refrigerator units they put stiffs in. It said: DANGER! DEADLY COMMUNICABLE DISEASE ACTIVE IN THIS BODY! SEALED BY ORDER OF DR. SIMON COMFORT.''

We then carried the weak and weary Wilkes to a car and took off to a hiding place in the Bronx. Then I called Adell Loomis, swore her to secrecy, and told her why, for the time being, Wilkes was better dead than alive. And the rest, as they say, was history.

HISTORY

History, of course, in the Napoleonic sense—a fable agreed upon. Our fable was essential to Wilkes's recovery. He was still a very sick man when I took him to a small room in a nowhere hotel in the Bronx. Here he would stay incognito until our job was done. Word of his survival would put a hundred hit men on the pavement looking to finish the job.

From his sickbed, Wilkes dictated the plan. It was simple in design. Blugeot made a deal: a hit for an acquittal of a murderer. The murderer had delivered by murdering Wilkes, and now it was time for the judge to make good on his end of the bargain. There could be no welshing now or Blugeot would find himself sucking polluted East River water.

My job was simple as the plan: make sure that the trial of Carmine the Hitter ended in a guilty verdict force-delivered from the lips of Judge Joseph Blugeot. Those words, "Guilty as charged," would not come easy.

CONFESSION SUPPRESSION

I entered the courtroom of Blugeot the next morning. It was nearly empty. The lawyers were arguing a pretrial motion about whether Carmine's confession should be suppressed. I stepped into the court just as the judge ruled.

He said: "This is a difficult call. The evidence is that the police told the defendant that his desire to speak with his chauffeur prior to talking to them would not be honored. True, the defendant only wanted to talk to him about getting a cigar. Nevertheless, this was an invocation of the right to remain silent. Therefore, I have no choice but to suppress the confession. Additionally, since the police exploited the confession by getting the murder weapon with the defendant's prints on it pursuant to a search warrant based upon the tainted statements, that, too, must be suppressed. Fruit of the poisonous tree and all that. Anything more today, gentlemen?"

Fortunately, there was no more that day. Blugeot's colors were flying bright. He had all but made the acquittal of Carmine the Hitter a certainty by knocking out two-thirds of the evidence. With no gun and no confession, the prosecution was left with little more than a bloody hankie and one terrified survivor of the would-be double homicide.

I watched as Carmine waltzed out of the court with his battery of lawyers. The wide grin of a man who knows he is winning stretched across his skeletal, oily face. I saw a remorseless killer on trial for murder act like he didn't have a care in the world.

Maybe he didn't. The good judge was taking care of all his worries quite well, thank you.

Only the surviving eyewitness remained as live evidence of Carmine's crime, and it was obvious that Carmine and the judge had plans for him. We had to act, and fast.

The first thing I did after the motion hearing was to speak with the amazed and angry prosecutor, Jayford Finley. I told him the case was fixed—that there had been a payoff of the judge (I didn't say with what)—and that I wanted to help.

He believed me instantly. No unwired judge in the world would have suppressed evidence on the ground that the defendant asked for a stogie. Blugeot did, and Blugeot never

suppressed evidence on *any* grounds, much less the baloney
he relied upon that day. We huddled that night in Wilkes's
dingy hotel room and put into action Wilkes's plan for the next
day.

MAMMI

Stop Mob Murder!
  Convict the Guilty!
  Tag the Hit Man!
  Carmine's a Killer!

These were a few of the inscriptions on the huge signs held
up by members of the newly formed civic action group Moth-
ers Against Mob Murder, Inc. (MAMMI). Wilkes, Uriah
Condo, and I had worked the phones all night to bring together
this unique group of friendly hookers, ex–satisfied clients, and
any female willing to hold a placard, look belligerent, and take
in twenty bucks for screaming at dangerous-looking Italians.

The ladies handed out the fliers we typed which detailed the
overwhelming evidence that previously existed against Carmine: the confession, which had been suppressed because the
police violated the Hitter's right to get a cigar before he talked
to the police; and the handgun suppressed by the judge under
the new fruit-of-the-poisonous-cigar doctrine. The handbill also
detailed the eyewitness account of the survivor of the attack,
who saw Carmine holding a smoking gun over the deceased
while shouting, "Here's one from the Hitter" as he pumped
in another round. We also put in the flier a color picture of
Carmine's bloody monogrammed handkerchief, which had
been found near the murder scene. Carmine had used it to
wipe off the victim's blood from the handgun. In the picture,
you could see "THE HITTER" embroidered in large letters
on the edge of the hankie.

SUPPRESSING, NOT DEPRESSING

Suppression didn't bother us. We could publish all of the evidence with impunity, rouse a sleeping public—or at least appear to—and let the judge know that *everyone* knew that Carmine was as provably guilty as a man could be.

We wanted the judge to know that the whole world was watching. We wanted noise; we wanted anger; we wanted the courtroom air heavy with the emotion of a violent mob verging on hostile action, but holding back for the moment to see if intimidation got the job done.

To make perfectly clear to the judge that he was being well watched, Wilkes asked Adell Loomis of the *Times* to gather up a horde of reporters and come to the hearing. I also told every other reporter I could reach to show up, so that by the time of the next morning's activities, the court was crowded with curious reporters, insincerely belligerent MAMMI members, and the inevitable coterie of brain-numbed groupies and faceless hangers-on who called themselves veteran court watchers.

The more the merrier.

Judge Blugeot entered the courtroom amid the buzzing of the gallery, obviously uncomfortable at playing out the planned acquittal in front of such a dubious audience. Before he sat down in the throne, a member of MAMMI shouted, "Judges who let crooks get away with murder should be hung by the neck." A bailiff went over and escorted the still-shouting woman out. She earned a twenty-buck bonus for her act of heroism.

Blugeot called the session to order; he had to use the gavel a number of times to get the room quiet. He announced that he would clear the court if order wasn't restored.

A member of MAMMI shouted, "You'd like to kick out the public and the press so's you can suppress more evidence." Another twenty-buck bonus was promptly escorted out.

Then the prosecutor rose, and the crowd quieted.

CANARIES SING

"Your honor," said Finley, "I must tell you of a most remarkable development. Two inmates of the Tombs were in a cell with Carmine during his all-too-brief stay there prior to his release on extraordinarily low bail. They have just this morning come forward to offer evidence of his confession made to them while in jail. Since Your Honor has seen fit to suppress the incriminating statements the defendant made to the police, I am happy to report that such evidence is still available."

A loud cheer went up in the audience. I myself contributed a very audible "Yeah! Damn right!" Others were louder and more profane. More twenty-buck bonuses were earned as more of our angry MAMMI ladies were ejected from the court.

Carmine's hand slapped the wooden table. He leaned over to one of his mouthpieces and said loudly, "Hey, this crap ain't supposed to be happenin'." The mouthpiece said, "No shit," and got up to shout, "Objection! Outrageous withholding of evidence! Sandbagging! Where's the discovery on this? They paid off some stool pigeon creeps to say this stuff. Frame! Frame!"

This was an ironic objection considering the fix Carmine's boys had orchestrated. The prosecutor added to the excitement, "And Mr. Carmine Bachizzio did not ask for a cigar prior to boasting to the inmates about wasting the deceased victim."

Judge Blugeot was nonplussed at the unexpected developments. Here was a routine Mob murder case being followed like it was the impeachment of the president. And now the DA was coming up with this new evidence! The judge looked at Carmine worriedly and said to the DA, "Yes, Mr. Finley; how do you explain this late development?"

Finley replied, "Judge, this case is very important to a lot of people in this city, as you can see. The publicity about this case and about the unique ruling yesterday suppressing the statements and the murder weapon has caused several public-spirited attorneys to contact me with evidence from their clients about Carmine's statements in the Tombs.''

Of course, Wilkes and I knew better. We knew all you had to do to get jail house confession evidence was advertise the prosecution's desire for such evidence and wait for the stampede of crooks coming out of the woodwork ready to sell their story for a very reasonable price. This time, however, it was us doing the asking and selling. Uriah Condo got the list of prisoners in the holding tank the day Carmine was brought in. Then, a few interviews and sales pitches later, we had two birds ready to sing on Carmine.

THE TIDE

Blugeot could not keep the two jailbirds from chirping without being so obvious as to admit he was going to acquit Carmine. If he did that, he'd be investigated, maybe prosecuted or censured or impeached. He would be ruined as a judge. Not that these pressures prevented bad judges from fixing cases, mind you. The crime, like all crime, was in getting caught at it.

On the other hand, if he welshed on the deal, he'd be a dead man. He was now feeling the competing pressures of either being disgraced or dispatched. Given his unstable mental situation, anything could happen.

After a lengthy legal squabble, he had to let the two prisoners get up and testify, noting to Carmine's lawyers that ''Of course, I shall take into account the curiously late appearance of these witnesses, their present circumstance, and the consideration they have undoubtedly received from the prosecution for their testimony.''

Any satisfaction the judge got out of this discounting statement disappeared as soon as the two birds testified that Carmine bragged about wasting two guys—he didn't know at the time that one would survive—and laughed that he'd be out of custody as soon as his lawyers contacted their judge.

It was common knowledge to us in the trenches that the Mob

had a few judges in their pocket, but it was chilling to hear it said from the witness stand. It made Blugeot even more uneasy.

Over the next two days, Blugeot let Carmine's attorneys take every shot they could at the two canaries, but the two birds were never flustered and did pretty well in sticking to the story.

The next witness for the prosecution was the survivor who, but for our intervention, would have been vacationing in the Alps courtesy of Carmine. Uriah Condo tackled him as he was about to board a flight at La Guardia. A few hours later he was arrested as a material witness and taken downtown.

Then the prosecution got to work on him: with promises of protection to quash his fears for his future; with appeals to his desire for vengeance; and with threats of a shortened life span. In other words, the usual promises of a change of identity, a move to the West Coast, a new job, new home, new car, excellent life, health, and medical insurance, a guaranteed annual income, three round-trip airfares anywhere in the United States each year for the whole family, and a pass on any crime he had committed during his life.

On the other hand, if he refused to testify for the prosecution, he'd be held in jail without protection, contempted for refusing to testify, prosecuted for obstruction of justice, and sent to a prison dedicated to housing mobster friends of Carmine.

Given these choices, the witness decided he'd play ball with the DA and go to bat against Carmine the Hitter.

IF THEY HAD MORALS

The survivor testified—perhaps even truthfully—that he saw Carmine with a gun as he was pumping bullets into his deceased friend and himself. He said, "I saw Carmine shoot my buddy in the head and wipe the blood off his gun barrel with his hankie." He identified the bloody hankie found at the scene—the one with Carmine's monogram.

By the end of the third day of trial, Carmine and the *consiglieri* left the courtroom very subdued, understandably worried and angry. When I reported this to my friend that night, Wilkes observed, "Why, if those bastards had any morals, they'd be demoralized."

Carmine's defense team knew they were in a pickle. If Carmine testified in his defense, Blugeot would have to let in his suppressed confession to impeach his newfound words of innocence. If he didn't say anything, the evidence of guilt was now so overwhelming and unrefuted that an acquittal would be preposterous.

Everyone knew what Blugeot knew—that if Carmine was acquitted now, all hell would break loose.

It was an absolutely delightful dilemma.

JUDGMENT DAY

The news coverage of the case brought in more people to crowd the courtroom. MAMMI placards still bobbed atop the heads of the crowd in the corridor; chants of "Convict Carmine" could be heard throughout the courthouse; media cameras were everywhere, capturing the event for news at eleven.

The DA began the fourth day with a new bombshell for Blugeot. We had suggested, and Finley readily agreed, that if there was any chance of victory, maximum pressure had to be brought to bear on Blugeot.

The prosecutor asked leave to approach the bench. He asked that Carmine and his mouthpieces join him and his guest at sidebar. There he informed Hizoner that the distinguished United States Attorney for the Southern District of New York was at his side to observe the balance of the proceedings because of disturbing reports that pressure had been put on the judge to acquit Carmine.

Blugeot almost fell over as his fearful eyes met those of the U.S. Attorney. Carmine's lawyers screamed that this was intimidation of the judge, to which Finley responded privately in

Carmine's ear, "Well, at least we won't kill the judge if he goes your way."

It was a comment made in the best Wilkesian tradition. Outrageous. Provocative. Off the record. The result was that Carmine slugged Finley and had to be restrained by his mouthpieces and carried back to his seat. It was a fitting foundation for the DA's announcement that "The People of the State of New York rest their case."

Carmine's side had no choice but to rest. The lead attorney tried to sneak in an unsubtle reminder of contract law to Blugeot in doing so: "The defendant, a man who has always kept his word and who protests his innocence to the end, rests in light of the pathetically weak evidence presented by the State."

WAITING FOR BLUGEOT

All eyes turned to Blugeot. The courtroom was completely silent for the first time in four days. The judge squirmed, his face colored, and his hands trembled. He cleared his throat for fifteen seconds while his mind searched for a way out of the options of certain death or dishonor.

Carmine's eyes fixed on Blugeot. His right hand grasped a pencil as if it were a dagger which he repeatedly plunged into a yellow notepad.

We all waited to see which road of self-destruction the judge would choose. Blugeot continued to squirm. Finally, after a long, hand-wringing period of silence, he spoke: "The evidence in this case is overwhelmingly demonstrative of the defendant's guilt, and I would have no choice but to find him guilty as charged and remand him immediately into custody but for the reasons I shall now announce. As has been reported to me at sidebar this morning, rumors are afloat that attempts have been made by the defendant to influence this court.

"In my years on the bench, I have simply disregarded similar attempts and gone on about my work. I did so in this case, but it now appears I erred. I should have reported the attempt to obstruct justice and recused myself. I shall do so now. The appearance of justice demands it. I have lived my entire life for justice to be done. I won't stop now. I now declare a mistrial. Jury dismissed.''

By this, Blugeot tried to turn his cyanide pill into a placebo. He did give Carmine a temporary free pass on the murder, but only by making it certain that other charges would be pressed against him in state and federal court. Carmine and his gang were not fools. They knew exactly what had happened. They stormed out of the courtroom, angrily plowing through the mass of reporters and cameras in the corridor, to plot their remedy for the judge's breach of contract.

BREACH OF CONTRACT

It took exactly four days for Carmine to figure what sanction Blugeot's breach of promise was worth. He had bargained for full and permanent exoneration on a murder one, and had only received a temporary incriminating dismissal and, at most, a momentary reprieve.

We knew that Carmine the Hitter would take strong action, especially when the news broke of his arrest and incarceration by the U.S. Attorney for bribery, obstruction of justice, and civil rights offenses for the homicide. In America, it is a violation of a citizen's federal civil rights if you murder him. Other countries are less fastidious. They call it murder.

The day following the federal prosecutor's indictment came the recharge on the state murder case, which was assigned to a judge other than the self-recused Honorable Blugeot. And the day following this came the expected private sanction for the judge's breach of faith with Carmine the Hitter. The deal had been one ''hit'' for one ''walk.'' Since Blugeot didn't serve up the intentional base on balls to let Carmine walk out of court a free man, Carmine's team replied quickly to Blugeot's grievous error.

The week following Carmine's arrest, Judge Joseph Blugeot of the Supreme Court of New York was found dead in his chambers, a victim of foul play. Witnesses claimed he had last been seen talking to a rather large, pear-shaped man with a block head and frightening countenance. The Mob's designated hitter, Maurice Vilgrin, had been passing hemlock again.

With the contract executed, it was time for Wilkes to resurface from the dead. He did it in his usual way—outrageously. Even though our manipulations had saved Wilkes from further Mob action and evened the score with Blugeot, my friend—against my best advice—decided to reappear in a most scandalous manner, one guaranteed to let everyone know he was back.

HE'S BACK

As the news accounts reported it, "The formerly deceased John Wilkes arose from the dead and appeared at the funeral home of Judge Joseph Blugeot."

A service for the dearly departed was about to begin, and the place was packed with loads of judges and attorneys from the courthouse. The bigger part of the crowd was there to be seen, or there out of a misguided sense that anyone who wore a robe, even a thoroughly corrupt man like Blugeot, deserved a final good-bye. Of course, most were there because it was a great way to escape work and get paid for it.

When they saw Wilkes, they broke their respectful silence for the black-robed monster in the coffin. As many gasped, the new Lazarus walked like a proud groom down the center aisle of the mortuary, waving at friends and acquaintances and grinning widely at enemies.

Wilkes reached the open coffin and looked at the stiff judge beneath him. With his back to the huge and now fervently whispering assemblage, Wilkes said loudly to the unhearing— as usual—Blugeot, "I have come to pay my respects to you, *fidatu executor.*"

He turned to address the gathering and said, "I have the eulogy. It is in Latin, which is appropriate to the occasion since it is a dead language." Wilkes got off a few sentences in the extinct tongue before the family of His Horizontal sprung into action. Ugly words were shouted, fists were shaken, and a few burly males came over to grab the still-sermonizing Wilkes and throw him out of the building.

I was able to get Wilkes into my car before the small bunch of burlies could pummel him. As we sped out of there, I asked a panting and excited Wilkes what he had said in his abbreviated Latin speech.

He said he had prepared the sermon from the words of the sixteenth-century Swiss philosopher Paracelsus, who had written: "Poison is in everything, and nothing is without poison. The dosage makes it either a poison or a remedy."

Wilkes paused as we swerved around a corner, and I checked the rearview mirror to look for angry mourners in chase. He continued, "I told them that justice is like that. Judge Blugeot overdosed on the same concoction of justice he dispensed. What ye sow, so shall ye reap. Good-bye, *fidatu executor*."

23

Tale of the Tape

I don't like to tell tales about dead judges behind their back.
                                                    EARNIE LIBIDO

Digression is the better part of valor.

                                                    W. SCHOONOVER

The judge looked at Wilkes and Earnie Libido as if they were hideous insects. It was time to rule on the motions that had been pending for so long. So much had happened since we entered Libido's case: the legal battles with Judges Knott and Blugeot; the courtroom fisticuffs between Wilkes and Hizoner Blugeot; the attempt on Wilkes's life at the hospital; his well-publicized phony death; the fixed mistrial of Carmine "The Hitter" Bachizzio; the timely death of Blugeot; and the re-emergence of Wilkes back to robust life, to the joy of some and the shock of many. All this in just over a week!

Now here we were, before the Honorable Phinneas Thackery, the erratic, white-haired, homophobic judge whose fierce independence from the norms to which most judges slavishly adhered made him occasionally fair. The Law of Averages (Rule 42) states: While those judges who are pathologically incapable of being fair to the defendant never are, those who are wildly unpredictable will occasionally, although never intentionally, favor a defendant.

Thackery had just heard our motion for new trial predicated upon the incompetency of Libido's former attorney, the arrogant Charles Alvin Seneca Hardson. "I'm ready to rule," he glowered. His eyes peered at us between the top of his fashion-able reading glasses and his bushy John L. Lewis eyebrows.

Before the judge could say, "Motion denied," a hysterical voice shouted from the gallery: "All those with more than thirty seconds to live, step forward!" We all instinctively turned to see the grotesque interrupter as he yelled: "Not so fast, John Wilkes!"

MANIAC

It was a maniac we saw standing there in the front row. He looked prehistoric: His head was big, his hair wild; the fore-head sloped so that his eyebrows protruded like an ape-man's; the nose was short and flat, and the nostrils flared; a beet-red face was twisted in rage. Out of the cavernous mouth came an inhuman cry to Wilkes: "You are dead meat!"

For God's sake! It was—it could not be!—Blugeot! Back from the dead! And he really had been dead! Wilkes gave the eulogy at his funeral! I saw him do it! But now the bastard was standing right in front of us looking like a werewolf and hold-ing a gun the size of a cannon!

As soon as Blugeot displayed his gun, everyone in the court hit the deck or, like the bailiffs, ran for the doors. All except Thackery, who stuck around to preside.

Wilkes shouted to Blugeot, "As always, *fidatu executor*! I thought the world had seen the last of your cowardly Nazi sleazebag countenance, you son of a bitch! Get the hell out of this courtroom, you filthy, pathetic, slimy excuse for a human being! You defile this room with your nauseatingly repulsive presence, you piece of shit! You're lower than a one-legged, syphilitic pig! Oink! Oink! Oink!"

Wilkes's vicious taunting of Blugeot was unbelievable! Here was this armed madman who had already tried to kill him and nearly succeeded, whom Wilkes in turn disgraced and dis-patched, now returned for bloody revenge. He looked ready to shoot! It was really not the time to tell the fellow exactly what you thought of him. Digression is the better part of valor, I thought. It was time for me to intervene.

TO DIGRESS

"Now, now, Judge. Take it easy," I said. "Are you here as a witness or something? Really great to see you."

Blugeot paid me no attention. He howled back at Wilkes, *"Rassettarsi la testa!"* Wilkes barely paused to let Blugeot squeeze in these few words. It was as if Blugeot's appearance applied a moral enema to my friend's pent-up outrage. The verbal hemorrhage coming from Wilkes convinced me that my young life was in its final, brief chapter.

Wilkes thundered: "You may be alive, although I always doubted that when I was in your courtroom, but you shall live forever stained in eternal memory as the Mob's bought-and-paid-for man. No one will forget that, dung-lips! Unending disgrace! Suck on that!"

Adrenaline saturated my brain. The monster before me was sure to blow us away within seconds, and yet Wilkes would not be stopped! It was as if he took this most inopportune moment to unleash twenty years of frustration. John, I thought, sure we all have our little peeves about judges, but Jesus Christ! There's a time and place!

The frenzied Wilkes returned to snorting pig sounds at the deranged judge, who, standing less than ten feet away with a howitzer pointed at us, looked totally berserk and anxious to kill.

I had to get the gun. Scared out of my wits, I moved toward Blugeot with a waltz step—not too quick, but smoothly, and with grace that would have made Fred Astaire proud. I knew the probabilities of success were low, but a slight chance of living was better than none at all. As I moved, I kept my eyes on the aimed gun and trembling trigger finger which indicated impending disaster. As I closed on Blugeot, my left arm rose slowly in order to reach around Blugeot's waist to begin our deadly dance. Too late! My right hand never got close to the gun before . . . The first shot came in slow motion. The red-yellow flash of sparks flew out of the barrel like a volcano blast; trailing smoke oozed from the barrel, then lingered and formed a doughnut ring around the muzzle. The speeding bullet blasted toward its target.

I saw the sudden horrible impact of the projectile slamming into Wilkes's chest. His white shirt crimsoned and exploded. His body flew backward through the air and landed heavily on counsel table, scattering the pleadings like leaves in a high wind. Then over he went to the floor. Deadweight. His last words had been "Oink! Oink! Oink!"

I looked to Blugeot in horror. His wild eyes shifted to mine, and his gun locked like radar onto my chest. The monster gave a sick smile and again misstated my name, "Good-bye, Schoonblower." I saw another ghastly flash from the muzzle! Instantly I felt a crushing hatchet blow to my chest! I clutched my gushing bosom as if to hold in the precious contents! But the warm blood rushed out as I screamed as loud as I ever yelled in my tragically shortened life, "Ouch!"

OUCH!

This was my nightmare every night for a solid month following Blugeot's death. His demise stalked me into my sleep. His ghost came to taunt me, to worry me, and to tell me I was as bad as he. I had hated him in life. He was a rotten, evil judge and had tried and nearly succeeded in killing my best friend and partner. I knew what I almost lost. Blugeot was every bit the no-good son of a bitch that Wilkes described in my dream. I was happy the Mob did him in.

Nevertheless, the nightmares were evidence of my discomfort with our manipulation of the Mob and the murder of the judge. Wilkes, on the other hand, could not have cared less about the loss of Hizoner Blugeot. There were no pangs of conscience. He was happy to be alive, to have succeeded in maneuvering the Mob to do in the evil louse, and to be back in the courtroom defending our esteemed fee-paying client, Earnest Libido, former con man, now recently self-rehabilitated, liberty-loving citizen. Wilkes lost not a wink of sleep over the world's loss of the Honorable Judge Joseph Blugeot.

I admired that in my friend. He did his thing and moved on without looking back. He had no regrets. What was done was done. He had long periods of joyous, spirited life— punctuated by a few brief depressions, which were impossible to predict and often of no known cause.

Me, I relive all my decisions, right and wrong, and kick myself for not doing better on all of them. Wilkes would say to me about Blugeot's death, "Come on, Schoon, his loss is the world's gain. Would you grieve over Hitler's death? Christ, think of how many more people he'd have screwed."

Anyway, we were now before the Honorable Phinneas Thackery and thankful that Libido's case had no homosexual attributes. The judge was something of a social Darwinist who believed that the weak should be swept under the rug. Getting them out from underfoot of a healthy society made life prettier and less complicated. As a typical WASP judge (white Anglo-Saxon prosecutor), his list of "weaklings" suitable for rug interment included the unemployed, people of color, independent women, criminal defendants, and most of all, homosexuals.

Knowing the judge's hatreds in the latter area, we made sure that Libido entered the courtroom each day on the arm of a voluptuous female paid to "Oooh" and "Ahhhh" at every favorable bit of evidence entered on behalf of her escort. Although this bit of courtroom choreography was blatantly sexist, we were merely following the defense lawyer's "warm zeal" mandate: If it helps the client and is arguably legal, it must be done with all the warm zeal you can muster for the occasion.

Or, as Wilkes would say, "If I can get an acquittal, I'll get naked, or act stupid or humble or gullible or as obsequious as the biggest bootlicking brownnose in town. Why, I'd wear a dress, or act like I was trying to be fair, or even—as much as it'd kill me!—be nice to the judge!"

Such are the demands on the modern-day criminal lawyer.

Today's motion involved the ineffective-assistance-of-counsel claim by which we were trying to get a new trial for our esteemed client, Earnie Libido, over the uncooperative carcass of Charles Alvin Seneca Hardson, the attorney who unsuccessfully defended him on the telephone solicitation fraud charges.

C.A.S.H.

Hardson was a peculiar fellow. He fancied himself a dandy. Built like a bowling ball and just as bald, he could not possibly look good in anything, much as he tried. And the more elegantly he dressed, the more ridiculous he looked. Whatever he wore was always ornamented with a distinctive gold silk hankie sticking up from the breast pocket of his thousand-dollar suits. It was his flag—his initials sewn in fluorescent green thread at the top told the looker all he needed to know: that CASH Hardson had no sense of color, a body that could not hold clothes, and an acronym-moniker that thoroughly described his very being.

If you needed more evidence, you could look to his fingers, every one of which was adorned with a gold ring with some oversized, ostentatious precious stone stuck on it. On the left wrist was a top-of-the-line gold Rolex, the kind that told time and the world that this was a money-making machine of a lawyer.

Or you could go see his office. It could have passed for a bordello designed by William de Kooning during a psychotic break. The ceilings were mirrored; small but ugly chandeliers hung in each office; the walls were all covered with red velvet wallpaper; the thick rugs were a maroon soft-pile; the chairs were covered in heavy, black leather; and the desks perfectly matched the office ambience as each was enormous—far too big for each room—made out of black walnut, and shined like patent leather.

On CASH's desk and nearby walls were pictures of himself

draped around every luminary he ever came within a photo shot of—and behind his thronelike, overstuffed swivel chair was a sign that read: "I don't save souls. I save asses."

When Earnie Libido testified to seeing this sign, Wilkes commented to the court, "So, Your Honor, it appears that Mr. Hardson falsely advertised as a proctologist as well as a competent lawyer!"

CASHING IN

Hardson was a ruthless predator of the citizen-accused. Clients didn't retain him as much as they were entrapped by him with boasts of his incredible string of courtroom victories, disparaging comments about every other defense lawyer in the city, and promises of having cases dismissed—or that he would surely bring in a miraculous victory if a jury trial was required. In either case, the client would never do a lick of time. Since few lawyers would make such outrageous claims and because clients wanted to believe him very much, CASH got a lot of clients.

Hardson also postured as a lawyer who would never represent a cooperator, that is, someone who would bargain with the prosecution in return for favor. He would say, "If you want a lay-down lawyer, go see—who was it you've seen already?—yeah, those guys. I'm a trial lawyer, not a dump truck."

While these Wilkesian sentiments sounded, if not noble, at least principled, it was pure bull. CASH postured in such a fashion only because he believed it would attract big-fee clients looking for some hired gun to represent the underlings of a crime organization and keep their mouths shut tight.

Wilkes didn't represent cooperators because he thought it outrageous for someone to sell out and escape the lash only by creating misery for another soul. CASH said he wouldn't do it for the monetary reason—you couldn't get Code of Silence big-fee cases if you represented talkers. But CASH wasn't even true to this. He did maneuver his clients to plead and cooperate when it could be done quietly and without publicity.

It was understandable how our client, Earnie Libido, would be attracted to the likes of CASH. They were peas from the same pod. Earnie had liked the idea of a fighter in the courtroom, a tiger who would rip the lungs out of any witness who dared breathe a word against him.

But hell has no fury like an ex-client convicted, and the closest target for the client's wrath is his former attorney. In this case, the wrath was deserved.

Earnie needed to portray CASH as an incompetent attorney in order to save himself from a long stretch in the pen, and Wilkes, who didn't much care for Hardson, was eager to be of service. CASH had already made noises about suing for libel anyone who would dare call him incompetent, but Wilkes was not worried about defaming him: "I can't possibly libel Hardson. Truth is an absolute defense."

It also helped that anything anyone says in the courtroom is completely safe from lawsuits. It is called immunity and saved Wilkes millions and millions of dollars in libel and slander awards.

EARNIE SINGS

On the stand to tell us how he was cruelly ensnared by CASH, Earnie—ever garrulous—was eager to oblige: "My first visit with the man, and CASH, that's what he wants to be called, he tells me I'm innocent even before I could assure him of that recently contradicted truth. But he says I can't lose the case with him as my trial lawyer. And then he says something I still don't understand—he tells me not to compromise his ability to defend me by explaining my side of the story. I thought that was real peculiar. Maybe CASH will tell us what he meant. I mean, is the guy a clairvoyant er what?

"He then says he knows the judge, that is, the recently departed and lamented Judge Blugeot—terrible loss to the world; his family has my very deepest sympathies—and that for an extra bundle of my money, he can make sure the judge sees everything goes my way, and I gave CASH my hard-earned money in small bills and in a brown paper bag like he told me—an IRS requirement he says. I dunno. Why, maybe CASH can explain that, too.

"Of course, I had no belief he would actually try to bribe the judge; he just sort of indicated that the money might go in that direction and, see, like maybe the judge had a favorite charity that needed a couple of thousand bucks or like maybe he wanted some tickets to see the Yankees. Course, with the money I gave him, he could have filled the stadium.

"But look, I don't like to tell tales about dead judges behind their back, but I been thinkin' that see, maybe this judge did take the money. I guess we'll have to hear from CASH on that, because the judge ain't talkin' and CASH didn't give me no receipt for the bribe.

"Well now, as you can see, Mr. Hardson didn't do a damn thing for me. He just sat there at the trial and watched as all the lies were told about me and didn't put none on, er, I mean he didn't put my evidence on. How could he? He never asked me what the truth was. The son of a gun even told me not to testify because he thought we'd win without my contribution. But he never talked to me. I thought I had a lot to add. But he assures me that he's got all the bases covered. Don't worry. The judge is on our side. Well, the judge may have been, but the jury sure as hell wasn't.

"It's in the bag, he'd say. From the odor of liquor on his breath every morning, I'd say he was in the bag most of the time. I used to call him on it during the trial, and he'd just say it was his mouthwash I smelled. Probably was. I think the guy gargled with Jack Daniels.

"Yessirree, I get my innocent butt convicted with an inebriated, unprepared alleged lawyer falling over himself to do nothing to defend me. He guaranteed an acquittal. I'm suing for breach of contract.

"And you know what he said after the verdicts? He's barely got two seconds to spend with me. Just enough time to say,

'Too bad, but you were convicted by a jury of your peers,' and run off to net another client in search of a mouthpiece. *Caveat emptor!*

"As far as the jury of my alleged peers which he picked goes, I didn't see any self-made businessmen there. That group looked like the reunion of the Spanish Inquisition. But I don't blame them. If they would have heard my side, they would never have convicted.

"CASH took almost all my money, and, Mr. Wilkes, you got the rest, so I'm a pauper who paid the piper, yes, sir. Like the lemmings, I followed CASH over the cliff."

Earnie Libido went on like this for two days. There were the inevitable objections about his run-on narrative, but he got to say what he wanted without too much difficulty. He said a lot of powerful bad things about Charles Alvin Seneca Hardson. Incompetence was the mildest of his criticisms.

ROCK AND HARD SPOT

For Judge Thackery, this was a tough case. Like all judges, the thought of reversing a criminal conviction was an anathema, and to do it based upon the malfeasance of the defense attorney an abomination. As much as judges like Thackery disliked criminal defense attorneys, they would rather kiss them on the ass than give their client a new trial.

We knew this going in. We knew that the only way to win was to overcome Thackery's obsession for upholding verdicts by playing to his abhorrence for attorneys. Given the likes of Charles Alvin Seneca Hardson, we had a chance. And Judge Thackery was erratic; therefore, he might be fair.

CASH REPLIES

CASH charged the stand like a bandit chasing a stagecoach. He was boiling mad as he proceeded to regale the court with his splendid preparation, his brilliant tactics, and the misfortune of having an overwhelmingly guilty client.

Wilkes's cross of CASH was quite short considering the length of CASH's self-serving rationalization for his defense of Earnie. It was decided by this brief exchange:

Q. Do you have your files here in compliance with my subpoena?

A. Regrettably, sir, I lost that huge file and all its contents, including all of my valuable work product.

Q. If you had the file, that would have had your retainer agreement in it? It would have given written proof that there was no bribe of Judge Blugeot?

A. The charge is an insult to a dead man's memory.

Q. But not to you?

A. Me, too.

Q. How much did you charge Earnie?

A. Fifty thousand dollars.

Q. How much for the bribe?

A. There was no bribe, sir. He gave me fifty thousand dollars in a single cashier's check. It all went into my general account.

Q. What if Earnie tape-recorded your retainer conversation and had the tape here? Do you think that might refresh your recollection?

After CASH recovered from a brief faint, he asked for a recess. Then he cornered Wilkes and begged to confess his incompetence in representing Earnie—if the tape wasn't played. CASH feared Wilkes's reputation for turning up such miraculous pieces of evidence too much to dare see if my friend was bluffing—thus proving the wisdom of the old saying: Have your miracles well publicized.

Wilkes, ever magnanimous after the recess, quietly set the tape down and skipped further discussion about it. He returned to again cover the territory about the trial. This time CASH had a totally different version. He apologized to Earnie for being under too much stress to do a good job for him; he admitted that during the trial he did hit the bottle too often; he apologized to the court for being totally unprepared in representing Earnie; and he even apologized to Wilkes for letting his pride get the better of his memory on direct examination.

He confessed that his pathetic representation, as he put it, "was inexcusable and the cause of my client's wrongful conviction."

Talk about a friendly witness!

CASH clearly preferred disgrace over disbarment and prosecution. He heaved a great sigh of relief when Wilkes said, "Nothing further."

His salvation, however, was short-lived. The prosecutor, recognizing he had lost this case, eagerly pressed the judge for an order to force Wilkes to turn over the tape, which still rested—like a turd in the salad—on the exhibit table.

The judge was also eager to hear the tape. If he had to overturn one criminal conviction, it would only be fitting that it happen during the birth of a new prosecution. CASH and Libido might be good for a conspiracy-to-bribe charge. Wilkes protested that the tape was privileged, that it was his work product, and that it could not be seized as it was his personal property and had never been introduced as evidence.

CASH was in torment during the argument. He prayed for Wilkes's magic to convince the judge of the correctness of his ludicrous legal position. But his fear escalated to absolute horror when Wilkes's protests were overruled.

A tape recorder was summoned and placed on the judge's bench. The tape was slipped in and the court's microphone positioned near the speaker of the small recorder. Judge Thackery pressed the play button, and we heard the loud hiss of the blank beginning of the tape. Then a voice came on, a singing voice which was unmistakably none other than my friend's. He was singing loud and off-key a song befitting the moment: "My country 'tis of thee, sweet land of liberty . . ."

24

A Rare Judge Doth Appear

The prosecution, may it always be right, but the prosecution, right or wrong.

JUDGES' CREDO

"Libido's a cheap crook, and we're gonna get him."
"That's a lie," said Wilkes. "He's not cheap!"

Earnie Libido got a new trial. He got it because John Wilkes made Earnie's former lawyer, Charles Alvin Seneca Hardson—"CASH" to his enemies and acquaintances—look like the sleazy, money-grubbing slimeball-incompetent he was.

Truth will out. Even in a court of law. Sometimes.

ADVANTAGE LIBIDO

So now Earnie was back in the hunt. Unfortunately for him, he was the object of the chase—a better fate than being captured certainly. He did have three advantages going for him now. He had a long and boring white-collar case that would take weeks to try; and no one likes to try cases a second time, especially long, wearisome ones.

Second, the judge who tried Earnie's first case, the very late and unlamented Joseph Blugeot (he of the Latin forked tongue and Mafia disconnection), was now lifeless, horizontal and pushing daisies in a lush green field with other stiffs. Earnie would not have that monster to deal with the second time around.

Third, Earnie now had the Honorable John Wilkes on his side. By this time in my friend's career, the mere knowledge that Wilkes would be defending could send a prosecutor on sick leave, a long vacation, or even into voluntary early retirement—anything to avoid the experience of dueling with "that devil Wilkes."

Of the three advantages Earnie Libido had going into his second trial, having Wilkes for his defense was by far the biggest. In combination with the others, though, the advantages were considerable—especially compared to the usual case, in which the defense measures its advantages by the number of continuances it gets before inevitable disaster.

By comparison, this case was now very different from the run-of-the-mill conviction case. In keeping with its oddball nature, Earnie got another big break when a new trial judge was selected to try his case.

BUCHANAN-PIERCE

There are, as there must be in any big-city judicial system, a number of judges who would rather spend their weekday afternoons playing an imitation of Arnold Palmer on the fairway than Roy Bean in the courtroom. These are the rare men and women with sufficient common sense to know that for the majority of the human wreckage passing through their courtroom each year, justice is best served by quick pleas and short sentences. They take no joy in killing people, or sentencing them to cages for life, or life-plus-twenty.

New York has had a few such judges. John Wilkes rarely got to practice before them, but when Earnie Libido's case got reassigned following the grant of the new trial, the gods were smiling, and we were sent out to the courtroom of Arthur Fillmore Buchanan-Pierce. Named after four of the most mediocre presidents of the United States, Judge Buchanan-Pierce had spent most of his sheltered early life trying to overcome the hex of his lackluster namesakes, a cosmic-sized inferiority complex, and a nose the size and shape of a pistol grip.

With a proboscis maximus and minimalist psyche, it was inevitable that he would study the law—the law was the closest man could come to acquiring the awesome powers of God. With God-like power would come stature and respect. With that, maybe Arthur Fillmore Buchanan-Pierce might not feel like a dumb, ugly duckling.

So like many before him, Buchanan-Pierce—B-P to his friends—launched himself on the well-sailed course to the land of the cloak and gavel. He studied hard at law school and earned himself a place at a good downtown firm. He spent years in a predictably boring civil practice, pleasing the partners enough to be made one, putting in time chairing as many time-wasting bar committees as possible (his most important one reported on the critical issue: "Should all legal pleadings have numbers on the left margin? The Bar Says Yes") and doing well-publicized *"pro bono"* work on company time for such noble activities as the annual "Gladstone Ball," a gala black tie dinner-dance for bar Brahmins, the judicial aristocracy, and hundreds of lawyers seeking the opportunity to kiss their asses.

The volunteer work was something B-P enjoyed. As an inadequate personality, helping others and fixing things gave B-P a feeling of worth. And B-P was building one helluva resume—the perfect passport to the Order of the Black Robe.

To realize his dream, B-P had to dress, look, and act the role of the judge-to-be. He kept his hair short and his face clean-shaven; he wore the darkest conservative suits, the whitest shirts, and plainest ties; he consorted only with the most appropriate, relevant people; most important, he talked, even in the most casual of conversations to his closest friends, with the cool reserve of a judge. A typical conversation would be:

"Good to see you this morning, miss. Please be seated. Splendid day, what? Might I do something for you?"

"Yes, you can. How about passing the cornflakes, Daddy?"

B-P acted and looked like judicial timber, a mighty oak ready to cast a huge shadow over the lives of thousands of saplings for the next twenty years until comfortable retirement. Only B-P knew the truth—monumental inadequacy lurked under his mask of stability, rectitude, and reason; he desperately needed the status and power that would come under the cover of the black silk. And the sooner the better.

THE FATAL FLAW

Each year, thousands of lawyers like B-P follow the correct, well-plodded life-style of the aspiring judge-to-be; most, however, lack the one other essential ingredient required to make it to the bench—the fatal flaw in so many judicial aspirants. It was not B-P's flaw, however.

One month prior to his nomination to the bench, B-P contributed fifty thousand dollars to the Democratic machine which ran the city and doled out the judgeships like auctioneers at Sotheby's. It was the best job money could buy—better than even mayor. After all, you got to wear a robe, to sit high above the commoners who daily came to grovel before you and say "Your Honor," and to rule. It was like being a god.

And so, like many others before him, B-P took the bench thinking his struggle was behind him: no more late nights at the office, no more bootlicking at the feet of the senior partners, no more fawning to please some son of a bitch plundering corporate client, and no more dehumanized acting, like a robot programmed by Emily Post. Now he had power and respect. Now he was somebody. Now he could be himself.

Whoever that was.

B-P's first assignment was domestic court. Every day for one year he saw bitter, angry men and women use the courtroom to tear themselves to pieces for hold on a child, a dog, the family silver, or for nothing at all except the sheer delight in inflicting as much damage as possible on the other. B-P was shocked at the ferocious level of hostility in this court.

At first B-P tried to fix all the busted marriages, thinking that levelheaded counseling and time would heal the wounds, but all he got for his trouble was the snickering contempt of the lawyers, and the epithets and threats of the angry spouses. They were there to make war, not peace. Unconditional surrender of the enemy was the sole objective.

In domestic court, B-P was reduced to witnessing tribal wars of emotional cannibalism. He learned the best thing to do was stay out of the way as the warriors slaughtered each other. He felt as useless as a one-legged man in a butt-kicking contest. He asked for and got a transfer.

He was assigned to landlord-tenant court. There, he met slumlords who collected high rents for unheated hovels worse than the Tombs. These sultans never visited, much less lived in, the dumps; they never paid a dime to keep the places fit for any form of life except germs, rodents, and insects.

B-P tried to protect the tenants by holding up evictions, ordering building improvements, and even (and this was at first very difficult for B-P) sentencing many of the worst lords to jail for contempt of his improvement orders. During the year B-P was in landlord-tenant, not one slumlord went to jail for telling him to shove his contempt orders; they were well represented, appealed, and got stays and reversals. Meanwhile, the tenants stayed cold and miserable. B-P felt like he was a bad joke. He asked for and got a transfer.

B-P was sent to juvenile court. There he met kids he saw in divorce court and landlord-tenant; then they were silent, sullen, uncontrollable. By the time he got to juvy court, they were different; now they were crazy, drugged, or vicious. Many were killers. They scared the bejesus out of Judge Arthur Fillmore Buchanan-Pierce.

After a year in juvenile court, a shell-shocked B-P thought of the ancient Chinese saying: "The worst thing that can ever happen to you is to get what you really want." After three years on the bench, B-P felt more inadequate than ever. He had been a paper-pushing priest for the holy institution of divorce, an unwilling enforcer of the right of slumlords to put people in toilets and charge for the privilege, and the man who opened wide the turnstiles to prison for the sociopathic black and brown youth of the city. He felt like a piece of shit. He asked for and got a transfer.

ADULT COURT

B-P was transferred to the judicial big leagues—adult criminal court. By this time his attitude toward being a judge was changed in every respect. He saw that his dream of power and glory was ludicrous. He had sought the bench out of his obsession to be more of a man than he thought he was. His strengths (work, stability, and calm reason) were not strengths at all—they were weaknesses: manifestations of his fears of being inadequate, rejected, and most of all, of being found out.

In other words, B-P was like any other judge except that now he knew he was not God. Such humility, unknown to his brethren on the bench, made him as different from them as murder is to justifiable homicide.

B-P felt being a judge was as meaningless as the sound of one hand slapping the air, that he had no real power or respect, and that he was a fool. As it turns out, this is the essential existential philosophy to be a good judge in the twentieth century.

Not only did B-P's attitude change; so did his appearance. His hair was now long. He had a full beard and mustache. He wore a leather jacket and blue jeans under his robe. He talked like a human being and spoke his mind. He began to feel better about himself.

In adult court, he saw the utter waste of time devoted to jury trials. The vast majority of people were guilty of something, so why get exercised about the situation? With the courts backed up like bad toilets, not many cases could go to trial. They needed to be settled. In plea bargaining sessions, his refrain to the lawyers would be: ''Make a deal. Find a crime your client really did and confess. It's good for the soul, and that's the only good you'll find in a criminal court. You won't get hurt too bad in the court of Arthur Fillmore Buchanan-Pierce."

B-P told the truth. He was the best deal in town. Lawyers did everything they could to maneuver their cases to his court, and Wiggins, his ancient clerk who had been a servant of the criminal courts for forty years, was very accommodating to calendar a case for a plea before the judge. For a small gratuity.

HAPPY LANDING

It was a joyous day for us when we were assigned to the courtroom of Arthur Fillmore Buchanan-Pierce for the trial of *State* v. *Earnest Libido*. And the first chambers conference with the judge justified our optimism.

Old Wiggins escorted us into chambers. Wilkes began the session with his usual hard-line negotiating posture: "Judge, the State has charged my client with a few dozen counts of fraud, which essentially means he puffed when he was trying to sell his personalized luggage tags, ink pens, and key tags. That's no lie. We, of course, deny all liability, but this case could be settled if they'd just make a reasonable offer. I'll take a misdemeanor plea, deferred sentencing, and dismissal in one year."

B-P looked to Miles Landish, the prosecutor in the DA's office who always volunteered to take a case after it became known Wilkes was defending. Landish made a career out of going against Wilkes, always trying for revenge for his last embarrassment. He addressed the judge coolly. "Our offer is that he plead to the sheet, and no deals for sentence. We will recommend state prison."

"How magnanimous both of you are," commented B-P. "I know a little about this case. The DA already has had one shot at the defendant when Hardson was defending; the conviction was undone."

"Right," said Landish. "Not our fault that Hardson was incompetent. We're ready to go again at the earliest date."

"Judge," said Wilkes, "you can see they are being unreasonable, and I'll tell you why. Landish has this thing about trying and losing cases against me; it's part of his sick need for public humiliation. The facts of the case are irrelevant to him. This is personal between me and him. Of course, I harbor no grudges, but his attitude is a real problem. If we try this thing, it'll last weeks, and for what? To determine if a fifty-year-old businessman with no criminal record puffed on his sales pitch to customers? With that as precedent, we could prosecute every merchant in America. Hell, Landish himself puffs every time he talks about the strength of his case. He should be indicted as a fraud, too."

Landish interjected, "Wilkes, you're a pinhead jerk. No deals. Let's rack twelve. Libido's a cheap crook, and we're gonna get him."

"That's a lie," said Wilkes. "He's not cheap!"

The judge looked at the two angry lawyers. He knew Landish was a bully and Wilkes was, well, Wilkes. This case was not that big a deal even if the combatants wanted to make it World War III. B-P looked to Wilkes and asked, "Just what is it you're really looking for, Mr. Wilkes?"

"Probation."

"Done."

"What!" screamed Landish. "You don't know anything about this case, Judge. Libido's a menace to society. This is an act of judicial irresponsibility."

B-P looked at Landish. He was not intimidated by harsh words and threats. "First, Mr. Landish, I am aware of my responsibility. I, of course, reserve the right to change my mind if there's something significant about this case which hasn't been mentioned. If the situation is markedly different from what I think it is and I can't live with putting the defendant on probation, I'll allow him to withdraw his plea and go to trial. Second, no attorney, especially one with a reputation for over-the-borderline ethics such as yourself, will tell me what is responsible. I suspect that if we do go to trial, I shall have many opportunities to measure the ethical caliber of your performance. I would look forward to it, because if you violate one discovery order, sandbag, or in any way act unprofessionally, I would not hesitate to administer an appropriate sanction. Now, let's get out there and settle this case.''

As we marched out of chambers and into the courtroom, Landish was angry, Wilkes was pleased, and I was in shock. The experience of having a judge stand up to a prosecutor and tell him to drop dead was so foreign to me, I could hardly believe it. Most judges wouldn't cross a DA for fear of getting the reputation as a softheaded, bleeding-heart, liberal-pinko crook-lover. And if you're a judge who wants to advance up the black-robe ladder, you'd rather hang ten innocent men than have that reputation. A judge on the come wants to be known as one who will play ball on the team coached, managed, and owned by the district attorney.

DA's are like that. They like absolute power. If a judge won't be controlled, well then, he'll have to be destroyed. Judges know and live by this unspoken rule of power: ''The prosecution, may it always be right, but the prosecution, right or wrong.''

B-P was unique. He didn't play ball, or give a damn about sucking up to the DA, or lust after personal advancement and power. In fact, he didn't even give much of a damn about the job he had, and so did what he wanted as opposed to what he expected others wanted him to do. He was a dangerous man.

I was still tingling with ecstasy as I went to fetch Earnie, who was in the corridor catnapping on a bench. As I nudged him to consciousness, I said, ''Earnie, we've got a deal! Such a deal I should tell you!''

Earnie quickly came alert. ''I'll take it! I'll take it! What is it?''

I told him about the deal: guaranteed probation; he walks if he pleads guilty to all counts. Earnie readily agreed to plead, and after I reviewed with him the solemn legal litany for entering a plea, we half trotted back into the courtroom. B-P took the bench and the session began. All was well.

THE PLEA

"Wiggins, call the case," said B-P, still showing his irritation at Landish by staring at his bulbous body as he spoke to his grizzled clerk. Wiggins was at least seventy years old, skinny, hunch-backed, and looked as if he was on death's doorstep. His hands trembled from the ravages of old age and hard living as he picked up the telephone-book-sized indictment and pulled it close to his thick, rimless glasses. He called out the case of *State* v. *Libido* and then looked up to see that everyone was in his appropriate place. He looked for the longest time at our client, Earnie Libido.

B-P then addressed the defendant. "Mr. Libido, your attorney has argued long and hard to convince me to give you a break despite your multiple offenses. He has done a fine job." B-P winked at Wilkes and continued, "Over the objection of the DA, I am inclined to grant probation if the facts are as I now know them. What say you to the charges, guilty or not guilty?"

I had prepped Earnie on how to play the role of a defendant pleading guilty: just answer all the leading questions in such a way as to give up every precious right you have. We all looked at Earnie. I knew he knew what to say.

Earnie's white cheeks crimsoned; his balding head broke out in sweat; his normal loquacity turned to halting mumbling. He whispered to the judge, "Not, er, not, uh, not guilty."

B-P was puzzled. "Not, not guilty? Is this some double negative play on words? A joke perhaps? What's up, Mr. Wilkes? He's got to say the magic 'G word,' you know."

Having led more than a few clients to the river of pleading guilty only to have them recoil at drinking the noxious water, Wilkes asked for time out: "All this is happening too quickly perhaps. Just give me a moment."

We escorted a trembling Earnie Libido out into the corridor to see what the hell was going on. One moment he was eager to plead guilty, the next he was recalcitrant. I was irritated, and so was Wilkes. We had lucked out in getting this judge.

We had obtained a great deal. We had primed Earnie on how to plead guilty gracefully. And now the ungrateful bastard was balking!

STATUE OF LIBERATION

Wilkes grabbed Earnie's coat lapel and said, "What the hell's going on, Earnie?"

Our client was silent. Sweat continued to pour out of his bald head like a gusher in the middle of a pink marble floor. He nervously grabbed his hankie and soaked up the moisture. "I can't go back in there. I gotta get outta here," he said.

"That's the idea," said my friend. "You plead and I'll walk you out."

"You don't understand," said Earnie. "There's one little thing I forget to tell you."

"Evidently. What's the problem?"

"First tell me, what is the, how do you say, the statue of liberation on armed robberies? Say the last one happened about four years, eleven months ago?"

I chimed in. "It is five years, and it's called the statute of limitations."

"Well, look, see, I gotta problem here, see? Remember the Ralph Goldman Gang? Remember the string of dazzling robberies they pulled five years ago all over Manhattan? Remember? Remember? Spectacularly planned, expertly executed, and exceptionally profitable. Remember?"

Wilkes and I said in unison, "Yeah." We did not want to hear what we knew was about to be said, but Earnie would not be denied.

He continued. "Remember how they thought they figured out who the leader was and published his picture all over the place in the papers and on TV? Remember? Good-looking guy, that Ralph Goldman. Full head of hair. Very photogenic. But none of the Goldman Gang got caught. They just stopped the robberies after the publicity and were never heard from again. Remember?''

We said we remembered. Earnie stuck out his hand and with an embarrassed grin said, ''Well, guys, meet Ralph Goldman.''

SURPRISE, SURPRISE

Wilkes was stunned. Then furious. He grabbed both of Earnie's lapels and shook him. ''You ugly little bastard! What the hell are you telling us this for? You little shit! Why not keep up the charade for another month until the statute runs? What's the point! Haven't I got enough problems? You asshole! Do you delight in torturing your attorneys? Idiot!''

''Good questions!'' said Earnie as he backpedaled into the wall. ''Very good questions. Believe me, I wanted to keep it all to myself forever. But I can't go back in that courtroom because I think that goddamn old fart clerk recognizes me. Maybe from the papers or the TV, or maybe he's one of my victims or, heck, I don't know. But I can tell from the way he's looking at me, he's on to something, and if I go back in there and he keeps looking at me, he'll figure it out. If he does, not only ain't there gonna be no probation for poor little old Earnie Libido, but mean old Ralph Goldman's gonna get life plus sixty.''

''Mr. Wilkes, judge wants to go back on the bench.'' Who should appear in the hallway but old Wiggins peering out the swinging doors to the courtroom. Fortunately, Earnie's back was to him. The old geezer was squinting through his spectacles and sizing up Earnie as if he were a suspect at a lineup.

''We'll be right in,'' said Wilkes calmly. As old Wiggins disappeared, Wilkes said to Earnie, ''You're right, the old man smells something about you. But we've got to go back inside. Come on.''

THE COVER-UP

B-P looked at Wilkes and Earnie as if they were from outer space. "Mr. Wilkes, is this another joke?"

"Not at all, sir."

"Then why is Mr. Libido wearing a paper bag over his head?"

"Because from this day forward, this is the manner in which I wish him to appear in this court. We have decided to go to trial. Mr. Libido cannot plead guilty to something he has not done. I am sure the court understands. And because this will be an identification case, we want to eliminate the possibility of prejudice by witness contamination as much as possible. Of course, the bag comes off when the court wants it off, but we ask that this procedure be permitted to preserve the opportunity of a fair trial. I ask for a six-week setoff for trial."

The bag, of course, was to hide Earnie from Wiggins. The requested delay was to safely get over the statute of limitations problem.

"He wants to go to trial? He doesn't want the deal?" This from a disbelieving Miles Landish.

"He wants to go to trial?" repeated a disbelieving B-P.

"Next open date is in two weeks, Judge," said Wiggins, who looked at the bag covering Earnie's head as if he had X-ray vision.

B-P laughed. "Okay. Two weeks it is. And your client can wear his Halloween costume, but only for as long as I want."

25

The Goldman– Libido Trial

The right to speedy trial is Orwellian doublespeak for the right to a speedy conviction.

JOHN WILKES

If ugly were smarts, Myrtle Kernel would have been the female Einstein.

W. SCHOONOVER

"On Friday, June 16, two years ago, Earnie Libido got up as usual at five in the morning, kissed his wife and four small children good-bye, and drove to the office to try and earn a living for his family. It is at that office where Earnie made the calls which are the subject of the false charges brought by the prosecutor, Miles Landish. It is those false charges which bring us here today."

So began Wilkes's opening argument to the jury in the case of *State* v. *Libido*. It had been a wild time getting to this point. In fact, we were in trial now only because Earnie was afraid that if he took the great deal we worked out for him, his true identity would be discovered. For Earnie was not Earnie. Earnie was the erstwhile Ralph Goldman, celebrated bandit, robber extraordinaire, gang leader, consummate cheat, well-known crook, and stickup artist turned nonviolent telephone solicitation swindler.

We were in trial for one reason—to keep Earnie's head in

a paper bag for one month of trial so no one, and especially not the shriveled court clerk, Wiggins, would recognize him and get him indicted prior to the statute of limitations running on the numerous Ralph Goldman crimes. We had to keep this damn case going for a month. Then the statute would toll for Ralph Goldman. With that hurdle behind us, we'd then have to figure out what the hell to do about the rest of the trial of Earnie Libido. For now, it was a game of beat the clock.

Of course, Wilkes had to explain his client's curious appearance to the jury: "Yes, ladies and gentlemen, Earnie Libido is a man I'm proud to represent. Come up here, Earnie. Mind your step. Fine, now face the jury and remove the bag. You see before you, ladies and gentlemen, an innocent man. Innocent, I say! Why, you couldn't miss it with a missing machine. Put the bag on, Earnie, and return to your seat. Now, ladies and gentlemen, as I said during our week of voir dire, Earnie has to wear the bag so as not to risk the horror of witness misidentification in this trial. How many innocent men are doing time right now because of that tragic mistake of misidentification? Too many! I swore my client would not risk conviction in this case because of it. Thus, the bag. If you don't like it, please blame me. I just won't have another poor, innocent man convicted—"

"Stop it!" The inevitable harsh, thundering objections poured from the swollen lips of His Corpulence, Miles Landish. "Misconduct! Contempt! Calls for sanctions, Judge!"

"RISE when you address the court!" shouted Judge Buchanan-Pierce. He was not fond of the plodding, humorless Landish. B-P thought trials were a waste of time and felt that if he had to endure one, at least it should be entertaining. Therefore, he came to love Wilkes. And B-P did not really care if attorneys spoke to him while seated, but it was an impoliteness not to, and he was not about to miss a chance to nail the prosecutor.

B-P asked both parties to approach the bench.

"First," he said, "I'll have no outbursts like that from you, Landish. I still haven't even heard a proper objection from you to Mr. Wilkes's comments. But I did hear you say words like contempt and misconduct and sanctions. All of these will be very relevant to what I will do to you the next time I hear an outburst like that. Do you understand me, sir?"

Landish understood. He understood that the judge was humiliating him and wanted to hear him grovel and cringe in response. Such is a judge's right. But Landish seemed not to hear the judge. From his bloated face came the words:

"Let the record reflect that on our way up to the bench, Mr. Wilkes called me a fucking jackass."

"That's untrue!" said Wilkes. "I only called him a jackass. I stand by that. He is a jackass."

B-P, of course, agreed with that, but had to say something to protect the record. "I shall ignore these vulgarities. I instruct both of you to calm down. Now, get out there and try this case."

And so it was that the trial of Earnie Libido began.

THE LAW'S DELAY

As faithful readers of these exploits know, the Old Wine Defense is something my friend perfected like no other lawyer before him. To Wilkes, the right to speedy trial was Orwellian doublespeak for the right to a speedy conviction. Cases had to be aged like fine wine to understand them, to wear down the opposition's will to resist, or better yet, to make them forget about the whole thing. Wilkes could take a matter that should have been resolved in an hour and make it neverending.

Earnie's case was nowhere near the longest-delayed case in Wilkes's career, but it was vintage representation nevertheless. By getting a trial on the issue of Earnie's incompetent first lawyer's representation, he created enough delay to cause a number of the elderly victims of Earnie's telephone solicitation swindles to either die of old age, move to unknown parts, or lose their memories in the murky pit of senility.

This led to an interesting first phase of the trial. Landish tried to introduce the transcripts of these missing-in-action victims, but Wilkes objected. He made the prosecutor put on evidence—outside the presence of the jury—to show that these witnesses, some seventeen in number from the first trial, were now nowhere to be found, or if located, that their memories were nowhere to be found. This was required by the law to show that the witnesses were truly unavailable. If so, Landish could ask that their previous testimony in the first trial be introduced because of their absence.

Wilkes fought Landish on every point. He challenged the authenticity of the death certificates; he wanted open-casket identifications; he challenged the conservators of the senile witnesses by claiming, somewhat ironically, that the experts were not competent to render their opinions that the witnesses were incompetent; he demanded that the allegedly senile witnesses be brought before the court and examined by neutral experts. And when the investigators testified that they had diligently looked all over earth for the presumably alive but missing witnesses, Wilkes challenged them on that, too. He made the investigators name every place they looked and then asked why they didn't check elsewhere.

This was only the first line of defense. We knew we'd lose on many of the arguments, but they were godsends because they ate time, lots of time. The clock on the statute of limitations was still ticking, and few knew for whom it actually tolled. It tolled for Ralph Goldman.

POPPING THE BIG ONE

After two weeks of arguing and cross-examining DA investigators, conservators, pathologists, and civil servants—all this watched by Earnie out of two small holes in the brown shopping bag—we lost on eight of the witnesses who had either died or turned senile. The judge ruled they were legitimately unavailable. He was prepared to let the DA read the transcripts of these witnesses as their testimony. Then Wilkes popped the big one.

"Oh," said my friend nonchalantly, "there is one other objection to these transcripts being read. We all seem to have forgotten that Earnie Libido got a new trial because his first trial lawyer was incompetent."

The others may have forgotten. Wilkes hadn't. He had saved this two-week-delayed devastating objection for just this occasion. He continued:

"Earnie's first attorney, the ever-learned Charles Alvin Seneca Hardson, admitted at the previous hearing that he was totally unprepared for Earnie's first trial; that he was drunk during it; and that he was ashamed of himself after it. He was confessedly incompetent. Thus, no competent lawyer cross-examined these witnesses at the first trial. This denial of confrontation during the first trial unfortunately means that there can be no use of the transcripts at this or any other time."

Had Wilkes made this objection two weeks earlier, there would have been no further hearing on the issue, because he was right, and no matter how dead or missing or senile the witnesses were, their words from the transcript would not be heard by this jury. Anticipating the judge's annoyance at wasting two weeks of court time with the jury outside twiddling their collective thumbs while Wilkes litigated every marginal, petty little legal and factual point, Wilkes said with consummate insincerity:

"Sorry I didn't think of this earlier, but it is a major point."

B-P seemed to take it well, or perhaps the point of what Wilkes had just said had not sunk in. He looked at the surprised Miles Landish. "What say you to this?"

"I say, I, er, I, uh, I have, hell, we had nothing to do with Hardson's incompetence." Landish was slow to catch on to the slam-dunk nature of Wilkes's objection. When he did, he whined: "Hey, now! It is not our fault Libido picked out an incompetent lawyer to represent him. Come on now, Judge, make him live with the consequences. Don't penalize the People."

THE WOUNDED DUCK

Landish's desperation made me think of the beautiful Chinese phrase "The wounded duck flutters." Landish was in a panic as he saw the case of Earnie Libido slipping from his grasp. Landish could not know that Wilkes was trying two cases simultaneously (Libido's and Goldman's), and it was the latter that concerned my friend most at the moment; it is why my friend said to B-P: "Perhaps we should take a few days to brief the issue further."

In his briefcase was a none-too-brief fifty-page brief I had already written on the issue; however, we were after delay at this point to beat Goldman's cases, and not to establish our scholarship in Libido's. My brief would not see daylight this day.

"No," said B-P to Wilkes, "I think your point is a good one."

Landish grew even more distressed. If he lost this point, a big part of his case was gone. "I say Libido did it intentionally. He got an incompetent attorney to throw the case so he could later claim his right for a new trial and make the poor victims come back, knowing they would not want to go through this again."

"Perhaps we should have an evidentiary hearing on that allegation," offered the ever-cooperative Wilkes.

B-P looked at the flustered Landish. The prosecutor continued ranting, "I believe Wilkes was behind the whole thing."

"I would be happy to testify to the contrary," said Wilkes. "But only after hiring separate counsel to advise me. Perhaps we could set all these matters down for briefing and an evidentiary hearing. Say maybe five days from now?"

B-P was going to cut through all of this. He knew Wilkes's point about the denial of confrontation was irrefutable. Only his happiness at seeing Landish flounder overcame his ire at having wasted so much time with the jury out. B-P said, "Mr. Wilkes's belated objection to the introduction of any testimony by transcript is well-taken. The transcripts will not be admitted since there was no cross-examination in the constitutional sense at the first trial.''

Landish fell into his seat. As usual, the wooden arms caught the flab of his hips, allowing him to slowly ooze into his chair. Once seated, his head bowed down to look to his chest as if to see the giant cavity where the heart of his case used to be.

It was a tremendous win. The clock on the statute had but two weeks to run. Wilkes had chewed up two weeks of time without one witness being called upon to identify Earnie (and thus not pulling the bag from his head and revealing to Wiggins the much-wanted Ralph Goldman). The only downside of the strategy was that by excluding all those witnesses, Landish was down to only one remaining victim. The problem now was that by beating so much of the Libido case, there was no way Wilkes could stretch the case so that we beat the Goldman clock.

TO BE CONTINUED

Suddenly Wilkes began sneezing uncontrollably. First, he sneezed a few gentlemanly phony sneezes into his pepper-laden handkerchief, which triggered real sneezes of such startling force and energy that it caused Wilkes to stagger back several steps with each *AAAHHHHHCHOOOO!* Keeping his nose in his hankie kept the thunderous sneezes going. Wilkes kept moving backward toward the door of the court. Between blasts of ''AAAHHHHHCHOOOO!'' Wilkes managed to squeeze out these words:

''I need a recess.''

Which was granted. B-P had no choice. The authenticity of the sneeze attack could not be denied. Wilkes got his recess— which lasted two and one-half days—and our statute of limitations goal was that much closer.

MYRTLE KERNEL

When we returned to court, Landish was prepared to call his first, last, and only victim to the stand, Myrtle Kernel, a five-foot-eight, mustachioed lumberjack of a lady who, if ugly were smarts, would have been the female Einstein. We first saw her in the hallway briskly walking past us toward the women's rest room.

Wilkes then did the damnedest thing. He told me to keep Earnie going in the direction of the court while he turned in her direction. At the end of the hall he caught up to her, and they were alone, matching strides. Then—this is embarrassing to recount—he gave her a vicious elbow to the gut, which almost doubled her over. She made no noise I could hear; she just looked up at Wilkes like he was a madman. Then Wilkes sped past her and disappeared into the men's room and came out as soon as she went into the women's.

When Wilkes got back into the courtroom, he quickly took his seat and kept his head down. This was quite understandable. Having embarrassed and demeaned himself with that display in the hallway—imagine, hitting a lady!—who wouldn't hide his face in shame? Wilkes was so into his shame, he kept his hand over his face during all of Myrtle Kernel's direct examination. I figured that the stress of playing beat the clock for Ralph Goldman while defending Earnie Libido was too much.

Landish quickly got to Myrtle's several counts of fraud attributed to Earnie. His questions were in the eloquent style of the veteran prosecutor. He asked. "And then what happened?"

"Well," she said, "a man calls me up out of the blue and says I've just won a wonderful prize. He says, 'This is your lucky day, because my company, National Specialty Marketing, has selected you at random to be a big prizewinner in our special nationwide promotion campaign, and you get your pick between a new car, a superexpensive, top-of-the-line gold and diamond watch, or five thousand dollars in cash.' And at first he says all he wants me to do is agree to have my picture taken holding his product line—personalized novelty items like either ink pens, luggage tags, or key tags. All with my name and address on them. Then they're going to use the photo for their campaign along with the news of the big prize I won and my endorsement of their product. And then he has me choose the prize, and I got all excited and I picked the money, 'cause I'm kinda short on that, and he says fine. Then, just as I think that's it, he says, 'And one more thing.' I gotta pay two hundred fifty bucks for the personalized novelty items. But this sounds okay since I'm getting the big money, but he says I get my prize and photo taken after they create the luggage tags for the photo, and he wants my check right now, and so I must send it that day, not tomorrow, but right then and there, express mail to a P.O. box. Only if they receive it in twenty-four hours will I be guaranteed the prize. So I send my check, and that's the last I hear of National Specialty Marketing. I never got no money, no photo, no luggage tags. All I got was fleeced for two hundred fifty dollars.''

KERNEL OF TRUTH

In the flesh, Myrtle Kernel might have looked like one of God's mistakes of creation, but she was pure honeyed truth on direct examination, probably because what she said was true. Earnie had fleeced enough people in his life to warmly clothe a full Yankee Stadium. Myrtle was just another easy mark whose gullibility was exceeded only by her greed. But now it was time for another brilliant question from Landish.

''And then what happened?''

Myrtle replied: ''After I sent the check, I felt funny about the whole scene. I mean, here's this fella giving money away randomly. Why me? Why am I so lucky all of a sudden? And why would he be so concerned about my two hundred fifty bucks getting sent to him? In a few days I went to the post

office and asked a postal inspector about it, and he traced the
P.O. box, and they staked it out and took a picture of the man
who picked up the mail, and they interviewed him, and I identified his photo and his voice on the tape recording they made.
It's that man right there, the one with his head in the paper
bag.''

"No further questions," said Landish. He sat down and
started smiling after noticing Wilkes and thinking (as I did)
that Wilkes's head was hung in defeat.

Wilkes pulled his hands from his face and sneered back at
Landish. He rose and stepped toward the witness until he was
only an arm's length away from her. When Myrtle Kernel first
recognized who it was that would be examining her, she instantly stood up, pointed her long, leathery index finger, and
began yelling at my friend, "You lousy bastard! You prick!
You shithead!"

Now, this was a great way to start cross-examination! The
woman's Milquetoast countenance was gone. Way gone. Wilkes
had started well without even asking a question. "Madam,"
says Wilkes ever so politely, "have I offended thee? I just want
to ask a few questions. It's my job, ma'am."

"You son of a bitch! You hit me in the hallway not ten
minutes ago! You lousy bastard!" Myrtle got uglier, a seeming
impossibility upon first viewing, as she got madder. "You ain't
gonna ask me anything, buster."

To the jury, Wilkes turned and smiled. "My friends, I must
deny the allegations of the allegator." The jury smiled back.
A few giggled. Turning to Myrtle: "I never saw you before in
my life. Did I brush against you, perhaps, as we entered the
courtroom or something? If I did, well then, of course, I didn't
know of it, but I extend a thousand apologies."

"You are a lying sack of shit!" says Myrtle. "You're worse
than the bag-headed asshole you represent. You did it to me
as I was going to the bathroom." Myrtle would make a good
resource for a cussing thesaurus.

Wilkes looked genuinely puzzled. Great actors make you

believe. He said, "My heavens, ma'am, I of course have never been in a women's rest room in my life. The story grows more perverse with each moment. Your Honor, I think I have a delicate motion to bring regarding, how shall I say it, the mental stability of the witness. May we approach the bench?"

SKINNY McDERMITT PLOY

B-P looked at the witness as if she were mad. And she was mad, very mad, but not *that* kind of mad. I now saw the brilliance of Wilkes's maneuver. He had just put into operation the only repetition in recorded history of the famous Skinny McDermitt Ploy, made notorious by a celebrated ancient lawyer from Chicago who won a case by infuriating a witness into such belligerence toward him that she was declared incompetent right on the spot by the judge. I had forgotten all about it. Now Wilkes had pulled it off.

B-P said to Wilkes, "Let me see if I can take care of this." Turning toward Myrtle, he warned her, "Mrs. Kernel, I ask you to calm down. I shall not ask again. If you do not act civilly, if you cannot control your tongue, if you cannot answer questions, I shall strike your testimony and have you removed from the stand. Do you understand me?"

"But this prick, er, this guy assaulted me. He tried to fuckin' kill me!"

Wilkes generously offered the following analysis for the jury and the court: "Gracious me! Now it's attempted murder. Why, next it will be genocide! Interesting that she tells us about this now. Where's the police report? My goodness, there are a thousand of our city's finest in this building, and no one saw this imaginary bid at homicide. She did not even report it. I suspect we have a woman with either an overactive imagination or a very poor ability at identification. Probably both. I renew the motion, Your Honor."

The prosecutor at last squeezed out of his chair to add something other than "What happened next?" But B-P warned him that he would hear no further "ridiculous accusations against Mr. Wilkes." The judge called us up to the bench and said, "Mr. Landish, I find this woman out of control. I find her accusations damaging to the defense."

"Well, she isn't helping my case much neither," said a subdued Landish.

"Either control her or I'm declaring a mistrial. You have five minutes. We are in recess."

CALM RESTORED

When Myrtle got back on the stand, she refrained from the epithets against Wilkes, but her hatred of Wilkes shined through the cross-examination like a white phosphorous flare in a cave. Every word she uttered was tinged with gnashing, guttural bitterness. As counterpoint, Wilkes was the model of decorum. While her words were filled with loathing and malice, Wilkes was gentle and kind and even caring in that phony sincere way he had. Everyone was so caught up in the saintly way Wilkes examined and the enraged way Myrtle responded that what she said became lost in her spite.

Except the final area of cross-examination; it would be recalled. Wilkes asked Mrs. Kernel, "Now, ma'am, one more question. The last thing you said to my esteemed friend over here, Mr. Landish, was that you identified my client as the man you saw in a photo shown you by the postal inspectors?"

"Yeah. That's right," said Myrtle.

"Well, since you never saw my client in the flesh, and since his head has been bagged for the whole trial, how do you know the man they showed you in the photo was the man who called you or even that he is the same as the man whose head now is covered by the bag?"

"Just compare the photo with your client, Mr. Capone, and you'll see quite a match."

"So you admit you've never seen my client in the flesh? You were perhaps given a helpful hint at identification by someone from the prosecution side?"

Myrtle caught on that she was exposed in a bit of overstatement, but she hated Wilkes too much to admit it. "No one coached me to say nothin', Mr. Shyster Lawyer."

When Wilkes had someone caught in a lie, he didn't let go. "So you are merely assuming that the defendant is the man in the photo?" Wilkes went over to Earnie and pulled the bag from his head. He said, "Look at this face, ma'am. Do you have X-ray vision or something?"

"Do I have to logic it out for you, Mr. Shyster Lawyer?"

"Ma'am, your job isn't to reason why; your role is to testify. Who told you to identify the man in the bag as the defendant?"

"Just call it a good assumption. I picked the man in the bag as the bagman."

Wilkes knew that he had a point here even if it wasn't quite as profound as he was making it. I mean, it didn't negate the paper evidence—the incriminating telephone bills and notes in Earnie's office. But when you're on a roll in cross, the smallest point can look as big as a softball-sized olive in a martini glass. Even though Myrtle was right about the photo matching the likeness of Earnie Libido, Wilkes still looked at the jury as he said sanctimoniously, "Yes, madam, an assumption, AN AS-SUMPTION—the mother of all screwed-up identifications and false convictions. No further questions."

Before Wilkes sat down, Myrtle got in one more lick, "Here's somethin' that ain't no assumption. You ARE an ass-hole!"

You could hear an audible clicking of tongues from several jurors. They hated Myrtle.

Landish should have scored heavily on redirect when he pulled the photo out and put it next to Earnie's exposed puss. The photo looked a lot like Earnie, all right. And Ralph Goldman, too. Old Wiggins gave the photo exhibit extra attention when he got hold of it. But it was too late. The jury wouldn't believe Myrtle if she said she was ugly.

FINAL ARGUMENT

We had a week to go to beat the statute when Wilkes rose to give his final argument. He had persuaded the judge to let Earnie continue wearing the bag because Wilkes said he wanted to use it in final argument. In his illustrious career as a defense attorney, John Wilkes had argued cases for a long time, but arguing for a week in a one-witness case was too much to hope for. But he tried, and here are a few choice excerpts.

On reasonable doubt (Day One, A.M.): "I picked you people because you struck me as reasonable. But now you may be confused. You don't understand the instructions; you can't quite figure the charges; and the testimony leaves you baffled. That's reasonable doubt."

Attacking Myrtle (Day One, P.M.): "Here's a woman who spends her life inoculating herself against reality. She stands alone here: uncorroborated; unsupported; unbelievable. She reminds me of the woman I examined once who said she was forgetful. I asked her if she had committed perjury in the case. She said she forgot."

Pimping the DA (Day Two, A.M.): "Myrtle should have paid attention to the commandment 'Thou shalt not bear false witness.' But she broke it with Earnie, and I guess just for the heck of it, she broke it with me. Remember what the Good Book says, 'He who keepeth not his commandments is a liar, and the truth is not in him.' "

"I object to such quotations," said Miles Landish. My friend immediately retorted, "Your Honor, can't God's word be quoted in this courtroom?'

"Yes, the Lord may be heard in this chamber." (What else could he say?)

Bagging the jury (Day Two, P.M.): "If you think you have been fair in this trial, then when Mr. Wiggins reads your verdicts to us and the bag is removed from my client's head, it should not make any difference to you if it is my friend Earnie Libido who is revealed, or your friend, your son, or your spouse. For God's sake, don't strike this man down on the word of Myrtle Kernel! The world needs men like Earnie. An active Libido is a good thing."

And that was pretty much it. Wilkes could only bamboozle the jury for two days of argument. I mean, how many ways can you attack a single witness? Landish's rebuttal was only a few minutes. He said simply, "The photos don't lie. The boxes of records seized at the defendant's office don't lie. And Myrtle Kernel, although she didn't much like defense counsel, didn't lie. I can look the defendant in the eye and with a clean conscience ask you to find Earnest Libido what he is: guilty."

After the judge finished with instructions, it was time for the jury to deliberate. We prayed for at least three days of deliberation to beat the Goldman clock, but we didn't even get to say "Amen" before the jury came back and said they had a verdict. A verdict in four minutes!

We sat nervously as the verdict was passed from the foreman to the bailiff, to B-P, and to old Wiggins. The clerk stood and said the magic words, "Not guilty."

We were stunned. Not by the verdict, but by its speed. Then our worst fears were realized. "I know that man!" said old Wiggins excitedly while looking directly at the unbagged Libido. "I finally figured it out. I recognize him!"

Wiggins ran around his little desk next to the judge's throne and hot-stepped over to where Earnie Libido sat sweating and cringing. Wiggins positioned himself in front of the now-whimpering Earnie and said, "You're the guy who used to clean up out there, right? Remember the robberies?"

Earnie just looked at Wiggins. He was being terrorized by the old man's ambiguity, but Wiggins cleared it up quickly. "Sure, man, you're the kid who used to be the janitor on this floor. The guy who caught the four punks who tried to rob me one night after hours. God Almighty, that was thirty years ago, but I never forget a face. Let me shake your hand, son.''

A dumfounded Earnie stuck out his hand while looking at Wilkes. ''Oh yeah,'' lied Earnie. ''Great to see you again. I thought that was you. Even thought I might call you as a character witness for me. Fortunately, we didn't need to call any witnesses. This was a clear case of mistaken identification.''

ABOUT THE AUTHOR

As Boswell was to Dr. Johnson, as Dr. Watson was to Holmes, as Burns was to Allen, Winston Schoonover was to his longtime law partner John Wilkes. Friend. Biographer. Straightman.

Born and raised in Fairport, New York, near Rochester, Schoonover took to public writing as a teenager. In high school, he authored and published a scandalous, short-lived underground newspaper, *The Baywipe Gazette*. In college, he wrote a series of self-published plays about an Argentinean dermatologist whose skin business led him into affairs with high-society women (including Eva Peron) and political intrigue.

After college, the need to make a living and a 1948 De Soto drove Schoonover to New York University Law School from which he emerged with a law degree and a job in the New York City law offices of John Wilkes. A quiet and studious lawyer, Schoonover was the opposite of Wilkes in character, although they complemented each other perfectly as partners. For over a quarter century, Schoonover aided his scandalous partner in defending their oddball assortment of clients against every sort of criminal charge, many of which are recounted in this book.

Schoonover now lives in Southern California with his wife, Donna, and their two dogs. He is at work on a new book about Wilkes's exploits at the Nuremberg Trials.